D1104760

SIX MINUTES
TO FREEDOM

Also by John Gilstrap

Nathan's Run

At All Costs

Even Steven

Scott Free

SIX MINUTES TO FREEDOM

KURT MUSE
and
JOHN GILSTRAP

CITADEL PRESS
Kensington Publishing Corp.
www.kensingtonbooks.com

CITADEL PRESS BOOKS are published by

Kensington Publishing Corp.
850 Third Avenue
New York, NY 10022

Copyright © Kurt Muse and Associates LLC and John Gilstrap, Inc.

All Kensington titles, imprints, and distributed lines are available at special quantity discounts for bulk purchases for sales promotions, premiums, fund-raising, educational, or institutional use. Special book excerpts or customized printings can also be created to fit specific needs. For details, write or phone the office of the Kensington special sales manager: Kensington Publishing Corp., 850 Third Avenue, New York, NY 10022, attn: Special Sales Department; phone 1-800-221-2647.

CITADEL PRESS and the Citadel logo are Reg. U.S. Pat. & TM Off.

First printing: July 2006

10 9 8 7 6 5 4 3 2 1

Printed in the United States of America

Library of Congress Control Number: 2005938604

ISBN 0-8065-2723-4

To Anne, my beautiful bride, my sweetheart, my best friend, and simply the most extraordinary woman I've ever met.

And to Joey Skinner, whose smile is sorely missed.

—KM

To Joy and Chris, who make every day exciting, every voyage worthwhile.

—JG

Acknowlegments

So many people believed in this project. Through their support, a bit of history that would otherwise have gone unnoticed has found a voice. Our agent, Anne Hawkins, played a big role in that, as did our friends at Citadel Press. Special thanks to Steve Zacharius, who's been in John's corner for a long time, and to Michaela Hamilton, whose excitement and enthusiasm are contagious to everyone.

President George H. W. Bush kept others waiting in the anteroom while he continued talking with us for nearly an hour longer than we'd scheduled. As we were discussing the military heroics that are so much a part of *Six Minutes to Freedom*, there came a moment when his eyes filled with tears and he rhetorically asked, "My God, where do we find these men?" There's no answer, of course, but we traded theories, and the moment was as special as moments get.

The meeting with President Bush never would have happened without the assistance of General Brent Scowcroft, and for that and for his valuable time, we offer thanks. Similarly, Senator Connie Mack of Florida gave generously of a morning over breakfast.

But for the intervention of Pat Barney and "Sam" Shockley, neither author would likely have ever met the other. Thanks to them, Kurt and Annie met John and Joy, and we all realized that we'd stumbled onto something special.

Thanks also to everyone whose special cooperation helped us get this story straight: Carol and David Skinner, Charlie and Peggy Muse, Kimberly Muse, Eric Muse, Robert Perry, Marcos Ostrander, Jim Ruffer, General Fred F. Woerner, Richard Dotson, Fulo Morales, Bosco Vallarino, Rita and Alex Sosa, Roderick Esquivel, J, K, L, T, P, S, and, of course, Father Frank.

Prologue

The first thing Urrutia noticed was her body. It's the first thing every man noticed when encountering Betty Fernandez, and for years she'd played it to her advantage. It didn't matter to her that she was married, and it apparently didn't matter to her husband that she flaunted her shapely breasts, narrow waist, and perfect hips. She liked the attention, and maybe her husband enjoyed it, too. Perhaps there was a vicarious thrill in having a woman that other men wanted.

Until they saw her face.

Urrutia allowed the possibility that she might be naturally attractive, but if so, the beauty lay perfectly camouflaged behind thick layers of makeup. It was as if she'd learned cosmetology in the circus, or perhaps in a mortician's office. The cosmetics were trowled on so thickly that they had a texture of their own. Now that she was crying, the mask had started to melt, and it had become too hideous for Urrutia to look at.

He decided to speak to her breasts.

"You can't do this to me," Betty sobbed. "What will people think? What will they say?" They both spoke in their native Spanish language.

Urrutia tossed a quick shrug and allowed himself a smile. They sat in the opulent casino manager's office on the fifth floor of a downtown hotel. "God only knows what they'll *think*," he said. "But I imagine they'll *say* that you have a gambling problem that is out of control.

They'll say that you owe this establishment many thousands of dollars and that you steadfastly refuse to pay your debt."

"I don't have this kind of money," she sobbed. "You know that. I've told you that."

"But your husband does," Urrutia said. "For him and his family, your debt is pocket change, a few boxes of cigars."

"I can't!" she shouted.

It was their third go-round on the same conversation, and as he'd hoped, her frustration was morphing to desperation. "Then you shouldn't have made the bets," he said. "The casino extended credit on the good faith that you would repay it. It is a business, Betty, not your personal amusement park."

Urrutia allowed himself another look at her face to witness the meltdown. It was important that the next part be *her* idea, not his. When he saw the realization dawn in her muddy eyes, he looked away again.

Betty straightened her posture and rocked her shoulders back. "There has to be some way to make the debt go away," she cooed, folding her arms to emphasize her cleavage.

The sexual advance disgusted him. He was an officer in the Panamanian Defense Forces, not some john on the street, willing to forgive real debt for services from someone who looked like a clown-painted whore. "It's not my money," he said, working hard to filter the disdain from his voice. "It's not even the casino's money. You know that."

Of course she knew that. The casinos were indeed a business, purportedly run by the gambling commission, but the managers of record were in fact minority shareholders in their lucrative offerings. The lion's share of profits flowed through circuitous routes into the pockets of the man who could make or break anyone in Panama: General Manuel Antonio Noriega.

"Tell me, then," Betty begged. "There has to be something. Some way that I can please you and General Noriega without disgracing my husband."

Urrutia gave it some thought. It was almost time for him to spring his trap. "Is it true that your husband, Simon, is active in the National Civic Crusade?"

The despair in her eyes turned to panic. "Please don't harm him," she said.

Urrutia laughed derisively. "Do not worry," he said. "No one fears the revolutionary fantasies of men like your husband. His words mean nothing to us." Sedition was nothing more than navel gazing when the dissent remained confined within the Union Club. Rich and powerful men like Simon Fernandez were too comfortable in their wealth to risk it all by putting their words into action. The hearts and minds of peasants were the real key to power, and General Noriega kept the rabble well contained.

Urrutia leaned closer to his prey, folding his arms on the polished cherry desk. "But he knows many like-minded people, does he not?"

The realization registered as horror. "I cannot spy on my husband," she gasped.

Urrutia considered that for a moment, then sighed. "Very well, then," he said. He stood. "You leave me no choice but to call him to collect your debt."

"No, please." Betty jumped to her feet and reached across the desk to stop him. "Don't call him. I can do it. I know I can. I was wrong before."

"No," Urrutia said, recoiling from her reach. "You've made your position known. I cannot take the risk of having you—"

"He'll never know," Betty sobbed. The running mascara had turned her eyes black. "Please, I swear to you, I can do this. He'll never know."

"I cannot ask you to do something you find to be objectionable."

Betty leaned closer still. "I know I can help you," she said. "I hear things all the time. I can pass them along to you."

Urrutia held her gaze for a long moment, then eased himself back into his chair. "We're interested in *important* information, Betty. You understand that, right? The money we're talking about here—the money that we're willing just to wipe off the books in return for your cooperation—runs to the thousands. You can't repay a debt like that with information that I could find later in the newspaper."

"I understand."

"The type of information I want is first and foremost factual. And I want it to be unique. Do you think that you can supply that to me?"

Betty nodded frantically, launching a tear onto the polished surface of the desk. "Yes, I'm sure I can. Simon talks all the time about his conversations. What sort of information are you looking for?"

Urrutia thought for a moment then shrugged. "I think we both know the kind of information that we would find useful. Do I really need to go into the details?"

Betty sat there for a long moment, clearly searching her brain for something—anything—she might know that would prove her worth as an informant. Urrutia had seen the look countless times in countless other faces, victims hoping to stave off the dislocation of another bone or to silence the screams of their loved ones. His was not a pleasant business, but it was necessary to maintain order in today's chaotic world. It was rare in his experience to see such total capitulation after threatening to destroy something as inconsequential as dignity.

It was only a matter of time. He would wait silently, allowing her to scour her brain for some tidbit of information that would prove her value as an informant. Everyone knew something that was useful, after all, and the first bit was always the most difficult to extract. Information was like water in a siphon. Once the flow started, it was merely a matter of opening the spigot.

It took less than five minutes for Betty's lightning bolt of inspiration to strike. "I do know something," she said, her voice trembling with excitement. "But first you must swear again that my husband will not be harmed."

Urrutia renewed his promise, and as he listened, it occurred to him that this was perhaps the best $15,000 he had ever spent.

PART 1

April 1989: "Shopette"

1

The American Airlines jet banked hard to the left, revealing the lush jungle landscape below. Still too high to make out individual people on the ground, Kurt Muse could nonetheless make out the major landmarks of the Panamanian countryside. Over there, the island of Taboga rose out of the murky waters of the Pacific. If he squinted and used a little imagination, he thought he could see the ranch his father had cut by hand from the dense tangle of undergrowth. That body of water he could see in the far distance—actually, it looked more like an extension of the overcast sky, but Kurt knew it was there—was the Atlantic Ocean. It was the rare visitor to his adopted home who didn't find it thrilling to swim in two oceans on a single afternoon.

The floorboards rumbled as the pilot lowered flaps and slats, marking the beginning of their final approach to Panama City's Omar Torrijos International Airport. Kurt looked away from the window and scanned the faces around him. He'd made this trip dozens of times, and over the past couple of years, it seemed that each approach brought a deepening sense of dread among the passengers. What little conversation existed on the flight—one never knew the true identity of one's seat mate—all but ceased.

The flight had originated in Miami, the home of shopping malls and the kind of freedom once known in Panama. Ahead lay a regime of daily oppression and humiliation. Yet, here they all were, drawn back to misery by the simple pull of home.

Kurt had lived in Panama since he was five, the son of Charlie and Peggy Muse, whose pioneer spirit had brought Kurt and his brother and sister to Central America in pursuit of a simpler lifestyle and warmer climate. They'd found all of that, plus remarkable success in business. It helped, Kurt supposed, that the country teemed with Americans, thanks to the Canal Zone, but Charlie Muse had wanted more for his kids than a little slice of the United States relocated a thousand miles to the south. Whereas the Canal Zone kids kept mostly with other Americans and attended American schools staffed by American teachers, the Muses had always lived on the local economy. Kurt and his siblings spent their childhoods in Panamanian classrooms, learning and playing Panamanian games with Panamanian children, easily identified in any crowd as the only fair-haired gringos in a sea of brunettes. Now, at age thirty-eight, Kurt's towering frame made him easily identifiable from a hundred yards away.

Kurt so wished that he could spin the clock back to those simpler times, back to the days before Noriega's rise to power, when you could say what was on your mind without fear of arrest and torture, when people who killed others were few, and those who dared to do so were punished for their crimes. Panamanians were by nature so nonaggressive and polite that they made easy pickings for a brutal dictator's rise to power.

Here on his return flight, with feet dry on Panamanian soil, the PDF sapos—Panamanian Defence Force snitches—no longer needed to keep their profiles low. Even without the uniform, you could tell who they were the instant they stood from their seats, strutting like thugs, pushing their way down the aisles while the other passengers hurried to get out of the way. The passengers' fearful deference reminded Kurt of little kids on the playground. Bullies versus victims, with no referees.

In a month, Kurt thought, it would all be over. In just over thirty days, the people of Panama would go to the polls, and when that time came, Kurt and his La Voz de la Libertad—Voice of Liberty—would be ready for them. The transmitters were in place—cold ones, tuned to frequencies they'd never used—and poised to override the commercial stations with messages from Guillermo Ford, Roderick Esquivel, and Bosco Vallarino, reassuring the people that their leaders were ready to lead again. Caught flat-footed, there was no way that the regime would be able to stop the broadcast in time. With that kind of encouragement, maybe the population would flood to the polls. If they did, there could be no stopping the results. The PDF could intimidate a hundred people, or maybe a thousand, but if ten thousand, fifty thousand citizens stormed each polling place, the military and the police would be neutered.

And once the people had spoken, the United States would have no choice but to protect the voters from Noriega's retribution.

Kurt's dreams harbored fantasies of La Piña—the Pineapple, so named for his acne-cratered complexion—being strung up by his heels and ravaged in the manner of Il Duce in the waning days of World War II. If the citizens could cut his flesh just one time for every murder he'd committed and every life he'd ruined, even the bones would be gone by the time it was all done.

Kurt waited for the aisle to clear before he stood. Ten rows ahead, he saw his friend, Tomás Muñoz, self-consciously avoiding his gaze. They were too close to the finish line to blow the race through some stupid security breach. In a perfect world, they would have taken different flights; but a perfect world would have provided more flights from Miami to Panama City.

It was nearly eight o'clock, and Kurt was anxious to get home. He'd left his wife, Annie, back in West Palm, caring for her cancer-riddled grandmother, which meant that their fifteen-year-old daughter, Kimberly, was home in Panama City by herself, no doubt celebrating the absence of little brother Erik, who was spending the week with his best friend. Kurt made a mental note to give her a call as soon as he got through Immigration, before he headed for the car.

If he ever cleared Immigration. With three flights arriving at the same time, the three customs booths were completely swamped. The lines looked more like a crowd, a group of strangers awaiting their turn under the not-so-watchful eyes of a dozen machine-gun-toting PDF guards in olive-drab fatigues. Most kept their M-16s slung on their shoulders, but a few held them locked and loaded at a loose port arms. Be it ever so humble.

Kurt tried to spot Tomás again, but the crowd had swallowed him.

Something jumped in his gut. It was the proximity of their final goal, he was sure. After being so clandestine for such a long period, it was hard not to worry about anything that seemed even slightly out of the ordinary. Noriega *had* to know that the elections were their final prize, and now was the time when he would sell his soul to stop them.

Tomás was fine, Kurt told himself. Even if something went terribly wrong, he'd be fine. Tomás was nothing if not a survivor.

Kurt's mind drifted back to the ominous conversation he'd had the night before with Richard Dotson. A lifer with the State Department, Richard had been carrying Kurt's flag through every corridor in Foggy Bottom, and now that they were getting down to the wire, Richard was getting jumpy, too.

Last night, in the safety of Richard's Silver Spring, Maryland, home, the two men had tipped a few drinks and settled into the ritual of self-congratulation. They were so close to winning. Everything was in place. The old interagency rivalries had dried up in the face of a clear directive from the Oval Office that Noriega was no longer a friend to the United States, and it looked for all the world that a home-grown coup was about to topple one of the world's most brutal dictators.

As the two old friends stood outside in the April chill last night, sipping scotch and smoking an early victory cigar, Kurt had asked, a propos of nothing, "So what happens if things go badly and we're discovered?" He'd meant the question as a throw-away, a rhetorical musing fueled by a swelled head and a loosened tongue. He'd expected to hear Richard scoff and say that it was nothing to worry about, that things were too far advanced for that to be even a remote concern.

What he got instead was an unsettling downshift in mood. "If that happens," Richard said, "you're on your own."

It was all about politics. The Voice of Liberty had originated in Kurt's head, not in the halls of any U.S. agency, and no one in power wanted any confusion on that point. The money and equipment Kurt had received from Uncle Sam was all off the books, and they'd accomplished more with it as amateurs than anyone had a right to expect. Uncle was pleased, but he was not responsible. That's what "on your own" meant, and Kurt was sorry he asked the question. They'd always been on their own, for God's sake. Why would it be any different now?

Kurt shook the fearful thoughts away. Of all the complications inherent to a conspirator's life, paranoia could be the most crippling if it wasn't kept under control. Kurt longed for the day when he could stop living the charade and return to a normal life. He was tired of driving circuitous routes to make sure that he wasn't being followed—lessons in tradecraft learned by watching James Bond films. He was tired of fearing the day when the PDF would crash his front door and brutalize his family.

More than that, he longed to be released from the burden of living so many lies simultaneously, constantly second-guessing every comment to make sure it was consistent with last week's cover story. It was the stuff of ulcers.

Most hurtful were the lies he'd told to his family. He told himself that the lies were for their benefit—to keep them out of harm's way if things went wrong—but even he knew that it was empty rationalization. Truth was, his father (who was also his boss and the old-school family patriarch) never would have approved of La Voz de la Libertad, and by keeping him out of the loop, Kurt simply made his own difficult life a little easier. In his father's mind, the Muses were guests in a foreign land; internal Panamanian politics was none of their concern. What *was* their concern, he believed, were the livelihoods of the forty-two employees who depended on the Muses for their income. For Kurt to risk any of that on a naive patriotic whim would have been unconscionable.

Annie knew the truth, of course, and Kimberly probably suspected something (you don't come home from school to find the exiled vice president of Panama hiding in your living room and not suspect *something*), but they were fine with it. Kimberly knew not to ask, and Annie knew how to help.

At last, Kurt found himself at the head of the Immigration line. He cast his gaze down, avoiding eye contact like a good Panamanian, and prepared himself to answer the questions he'd been asked a thousand times. The trip was personal in nature, to visit his wife's sick grandmother. No, he had nothing to declare.

Two men occupied the cramped Immigration booth. The first man, from the Immigration Bureau, took care of the basic paperwork, which he then handed to the second, a soldier who matched the passport against a thick dot matrix printout of undesirables.

Kurt craned his neck in one last futile search for Tomás, and the instant he looked back, he knew that something had gone terribly wrong. It was the way the Immigration guy was holding the passport. Rather than the cursory glance followed by the whack of the entry stamp, he held the little book in both hands, vertically, as if it were a *Playboy* centerfold. He seemed to be studying it. And then he smiled.

As he handed the tiny book back to the soldier, Kurt followed the clerk's gaze to a piece of paper someone had taped to the reinforced glass of his partition. At first, Kurt was confused.

Then his guts dissolved. The sign was hand written in Spanish. He had to read it backward:

> *Kurt Muse*
> *American Citizen*
> *Arrest Him*

His life was over.

They came at him slowly—calmly, even. With a glance from the two men in the booth, two more soldiers sauntered over from their positions near the wall to close off any escape route. "Excuse me, Mr. Muse," said the Immigration man, "but there seems to be a slight problem. Would you mind coming with us, please?"

Kurt's mind raced. This was the nightmare. This was the impossible scenario. After all the fumbling and close calls at the beginning of their adventure, he'd talked himself into believing that he was invincible. This simply could not be happening.

For an insane moment, he considered making a run for it, dashing back onto the airplane and asking for asylum, but he knew it was hopeless. Even if they didn't shoot him down in the terminal, they'd just come on board and drag him off. He almost didn't notice that he was going along with them peacefully.

The first leg of his trip was all of fifty feet, just around the corner to a tiny office with a couple of chairs and a desk. "Please have a seat here," a soldier said. "We'll get this straightened out as soon as possible."

They closed the door and left him sitting there in a hardback chair. Alone.

Staring down at him from his perch over the door was a portrait of General Manuel Antonio Noriega.

The bastard had won.

Out on the concourse, beyond the baggage carousels, Tomás Muñoz fought the urge to pace. It had been over an hour since he'd cleared Immigration, and there still was no sign of Kurt. Something was definitely wrong.

The word "shopette" rolled around in his mind. He and Kurt had devised the evacuation code together over a year ago—a simple word to be transmitted if one of them was ever arrested. The Noriega prisons were famous for their tortures, and under those circumstances none of the conspirators harbored any doubt that even the strongest among them would break and reveal the names of their partners. They needed a word that would never be used on the radio except in the direst of circumstances, and at the very moment that Kurt and Tomás had been discussing the issue, they happened to have been passing in front of the small base exchange on Albrook Air Force Station near the Canal Zone—the Shopette.

If ever that word were broadcast, the instructions were clear: they were each to drop whatever they were doing, gather their families, and head to Fort Clayton, home of the U.S. Army Southern Command, where they would seek asylum and protection with the U.S. government.

Even as he considered that maybe this was the time, Tomás found himself putting the brakes on his imagination. There were a hundred reasons why Kurt could have been delayed an hour. So how come he couldn't think of any of them right now?

Shopette.

It was not a signal to be broadcast lightly. When the panic button was pressed, there was no turning back; it meant a one-way trip out of the country, never to return. The U.S. intelligence community in Panama was so riddled with moles that the instant any of them showed up at the gate, Noriega would know each of their names. They might as well come wearing "We Are Fugitives" sweatshirts.

There was time, Tomás told himself. It was too early to panic.

Perhaps it could all be settled with a phone call. He knew that Kurt's daughter, Kimberly, was waiting at the house by herself. He'd never met the girl, but Kurt talked about her all the time. She had a good head on her shoulders. All he had to do was call over there and see if Kurt had arrived home. If the answer was yes, then Tomás could relax and have a little laugh. If the answer was no . . .

Perhaps the question should come from a voice she would recognize.

2

The ceiling fan churned the air, stirring the humidity without cooling a thing. As music from the Arosemena's party down the street filled the night, Kimberly Muse desperately wanted to go to bed, but biology beckoned. The midterm was coming, and if something didn't click soon, she'd be in big trouble. Her notes lay strewn across her desk, the corners curled by the tropical moisture.

She scooted forward in her chair, hoping to find a cool spot on the seat, but they'd all been turned hot a long time ago. Here it was going on midnight, and she was still sweating, wearing nothing more than cutoffs and a T-shirt. It was the pink Esprit T-shirt that always ticked off her dad. He was so out of touch. What was wrong with showing off a little midriff, for crying out loud?

Daddy had become a real grouch recently. Everybody noticed it, even her cousin, Joanna. Aunt Carol and Uncle David were pissed at him, and so were Nana and Papi, and between that and the politics that made him such a madman, she wondered when he might just explode.

He should have been home hours ago. Navigating customs was always an adventure at Torrijos Airport, and she should know better than to worry just because he was running late. But honestly, it shouldn't ever take *this* long. Kimberly tried to tell herself that there were a thousand things that might have gone wrong to delay him and that he was probably just stuck on the plane on some tarmac where he couldn't get to a phone.

The fact was—and she'd never admit this out loud—Kimberly wasn't keen on being home alone at this hour. Okay, so she wasn't exactly alone—Lala, their maid, was there, too—but let's face it, if Jason Voorhees or Freddie Kruger decided to pay a visit, Lala would be of precious little help. Of course, there was always Gretel, but the very thought of siccing the pet boxer on an intruder made her laugh. She'd be better off throwing a teddy bear at the guy.

There was something creepy in the air tonight. She'd been jumpy all day.

Of course, it could just be that she hated biology. A party raged within earshot, and Erik was having fun at the Prietos' house, and Mom and Dad were jetting off to the States, yet she was stuck here in the house studying frog guts. Where was the justice?

Finally, she heard a car in the driveway, and she stepped outside for a peek. Even as the oldest child, she still didn't rate an air conditioner, but at least she had the terrace. With the doors open, it was the rare night that didn't offer a pleasant breeze. What a shame that this was one of them. Walking carefully on bare feet, she slid the door open and stepped out into the night. At least the heat hadn't done anything to spoil the view.

The car she'd heard was nobody, just a nondescript Toyota using their driveway as a turnaround. As the last house on a dead-end street, they got a lot of that. People got lost in Panama City all the time; it was a way of life. There were no addresses, at least not in the sense that they had them in the States. All the mail came to the post office, and if you wanted a pizza delivered, you gave directions via landmarks—go past the old rendering plant, turn right at the pink house . . .

In fact, when Dominos Pizza first started giving away pizzas for free if they weren't delivered within thirty minutes, Erik had used the confusion to cash in big time. He'd order a pizza when he got home from school, knowing full well that the driver would get hopelessly lost on the way. He thought he could eat for free. Kimberly thought the plan was brilliant, but when their dad caught wind of it he went ballistic, claiming that they were stealing from the pizza guy. Kimberly liked to think of it more as exploiting a loophole than stealing, but the gambit stopped immediately.

She stayed on the terrace long enough to watch the Toyota find the party, and then headed back inside, even more pissed off than before.

It was official: Everybody in the world was having a better time than she.

She decided to study on the bed for a while. As she gathered her book and notes for the transfer, she couldn't help but smile at the pictures that adorned her walls: the world's most complete collection of anti-Noriega political cartoons, plus a few drawings of her own. It was her nod toward civil disobedience, and her dad loved it. Call it their bonding moment.

So long as Noriega's *sapos* never saw them.

Or Papi. Papi didn't believe in meddling in local politics. He seemed not to believe in a lot of things that were important in Kimberly's house.

Things were not good between Dad and Papi, and from what she could tell by eavesdropping, political leanings weren't the only issue. Things at the business weren't going well, and even though Daddy outranked him, Uncle David was somehow being treated better. It all had something to do with Mom's job with the U.S. Department of Defense (DoD). Kimberly didn't pretend to understand the details, and she knew better than to mention anything, but she and her family really did enjoy advantages that were denied the rest of her extended family. The DoD connection gave her and her family access to the shopping facilities on the military bases, where there was always ample food at an affordable price. For Carol and David and Nana and Papi, life was just more complicated. These were tough times in Panama, what with the closing of the banks and all. Kimberly even got to go to the American school for free, while her cousins, Joanna and Samantha, had to pay tuition to go to an Episcopal school. And now that Samantha had gone on to college in the States, they were facing an even bigger burden.

Even without the details, Kimberly was sure that this, like everything else with her dad, was ultimately about principle. His whole life revolved around principle, always first in line to fall on his sword. Kimberly couldn't swear to it, but she suspected that Dad had either quit or been fired over this stuff. You'd have to be blind not to see that Dad wasn't going into the office anymore.

Sometimes, she wondered if things wouldn't be easier if they actually lived in the United States—not that she'd ever done that—but the tensions here both inside the house and out in the street made life tougher than it needed to be.

The telephone startled her. She hurried to pick up the receiver before Lala could get it. "Hello?"

"Hello, Kimberly? This is Jorge Quintero. I'm a friend of your father's."

Kimberly recognized the name and the voice. He and her dad knew each other from Rotary. "He's not here right now," she said.

"Oh," he said. It was a single syllable, but it carried a dreadful tone.

"Is everything okay?" Kimberly asked.

"Oh, I'm sure it is," Jorge said quickly. Again, his dark tone belied his words. "There's nothing to worry about. I'm sure everything will be fine."

She'd never thought otherwise. "Mr. Quintero, is there something wrong with my father?"

"No," he said. "Heavens no, not at all. Well, I'm sorry I disturbed you. Good night."

The line went dead. Just like that. No pleasantries, no "how are you doing" or "how's school?" None of the social niceties of Panamanian discourse. It was almost as if he'd been verifying something he already knew.

Kimberly shivered. The night seemed to have turned colder.

Fear had begun to alter Kurt's sense of time.

The PDF guards had quietly loaded him into the backseat of a white pickup truck, and with two other vehicles stationed ahead and behind, they'd taken him to a police substation out in the suburbs near his home. But for the cluster of police vehicles in front of the substation, passersby would have assumed that the squat building was just another house on the block.

Kurt knew the truth of the place, of course, just as he knew the names of many of the officers and their patrolling schedules. Once he'd broken their codes, the rest had been easy. Over the last eighteen months, he'd dispatched quite a few of them on wild goose chases just for the thrill of messing with their minds. He wondered what they would do to him when they found out—as they eventually would—that he was the personification of the giant burr under their saddles.

It had all seemed very funny at the time. The one about the fictitious sniper high on the hill had been a particularly masterful stroke,

Kurt thought. Despite the gnawing fear and blossoming panic of the present, he still drew satisfaction from the memory of the PDF cowards dashing for cover as he spoke directly to them and threatened to shoot if they didn't disperse from the street corner where they'd been busily bashing heads.

That had been just a few weeks ago. Their memory of the incident would no doubt be fresh and clear.

Now, as he walked across the parking lot surrounded by goons, he told himself to stay calm, even as he prayed that Tomás would somehow figure out what was happening and get word back to Kurt's family.

How soon would it be before they, too, were dragged off to some squalid room for interrogation, enduring questions for which they had no answers? Nana and Papi were particularly vulnerable, he knew. Kurt's heart raced as his mind conjured horrid images of what the PDF were capable of, and he tried to settle himself. There were many things that could happen now, and at least a few of the options had to fall short of disaster. They *had* to.

Kimberly and Erik.

The thought was too much to bear. Erik was only twelve! They wouldn't torture a twelve-year-old, would they?

Kurt tried to force the thoughts away. He tried to form prayers in his head for their safety, but even those words wouldn't come. Instead, his mind filled with images of the tortures and depravities of which these animals were capable. Every newspaper in the world had carried the photos of the castrated and beheaded corpse of Noriega rival Hugo Spadafora. Everyone on the streets knew someone who had endured the rapes and sodomies that were a staple of the prisons; everyone had seen the scars that were the prize of merciless beatings. Such were the public relations tools of the regime, designed to instill terror. Why let a prisoner die in a concrete cell when you could send his maimed shell back to his family, where the stories will be told over and over?

Of course they'd torture his children. To extract information or merely to make a point, the PDF would do whatever was necessary. And more likely than not, they'd do it in front of Kurt, where he could see the blood and hear the screams. In the face of that, Kurt knew that he'd beg for the chance to turn on his friends, if only to make his children's agony stop.

The fear in his gut began to bloom, building exponentially. He prayed that Tomás would get to a radio in time to sound the distress signal. *Shopette*. It all came down to two syllables. Would he think to make the transmission? Would he do it in time?

The police station was as hot as a sauna. Clean enough at first glance, the place had a yellow-brown hue to it, testament to the ever-present haze of tobacco smoke. They led him through a squad room toward an office in the back, past a warren of desks and chairs that looked as if they'd been arranged by air drop. Kurt noted with curiosity that his hands were free, that they hadn't cuffed him, and it occurred to him that he was quickly approaching his last opportunity to run. It would be suicidal, but at least it would be on his terms.

The images of his family returned, and the option evaporated. If there was a chance of seeing them again, he'd do everything in his power to make that happen. After thrusting all of this trouble on them, the very least he could do was struggle to stay alive.

His captors led him to a closed door in the rear of the squad room, where the escort on Kurt's left opened the door and ushered him inside. One man sat in a metal, army-surplus chair while three others hovered nearby. A desk sat in the middle of the small room, lit only by a dangling bulb that seemed to have the light of the noontime sun. The heat in the room was off the scale, and every face he saw sweated profusely. They were all looking at Kurt's passport.

One of the armed escorts placed a hand heavily on Kurt's shoulder and pressed him into the hardbacked wooden visitor's chair. "Here he is, Major Moreno," the guard said.

The seated man raised his head to make eye contact. Muscular and wiry, Moreno wore a pastel blue shirt that fit his form tightly. The major's eyes were hotter than the room as they bored through his visitor from behind an ugly, pock-marked face. As he measured Kurt with his glare, his hand fiddled with a riding crop on his desk.

Kurt did his best to return Moreno's glare, but he didn't have it in him. By breaking the gaze, Kurt knew he was projecting guilt.

"You are a spy," Moreno said in Spanish.

Kurt spoke without a trace of a gringo accent. "No, sir, I'm not a spy." *A spy?* he thought. *Why would . . .*

"You traveled to Honduras," Moreno said, indicating the visa stamp on the passport. "Meeting with the Contras, no doubt."

Kurt smiled in spite of himself. "No, sir, I was there on business, meeting with local officials about printing equipment." Every word was the absolute truth. Could it be that they didn't know who he was? How could that happen?

"And the trip to Nicaragua immediately afterward?" Moreno prompted.

Kurt's smile started to fade as he realized that a lie would actually sound more convincing than the truth. "I am a Rotarian," he said. "On my return from Honduras, I visited Managua to attend a Rotary conference. There was no spying involved."

Behind Kurt, a brief knock preceded the swing of the door. A short, trim man in civilian clothes but with a soldier's bearing stepped into the office. "Captain Cortizo is here to translate," said the clerk. On the other side of the glass partition, Kurt could see Cortizo's familiar face and form standing in the squad room. A graduate of West Point, Cortizo was a Noriega favorite, constantly paraded in front of the cameras as an embarrassment to the Americans.

Moreno waved the clerk off. "It won't be necessary," he said. "The prisoner speaks Spanish." The clerk disappeared, and the major turned his eyes back toward Kurt. "You are lying," he said.

Kurt cursed himself for his own guilty demeanor. He knew that from here on out nothing he said would be perceived as truth. "No, sir, I'm not. You can check these things yourself." As an afterthought, he added, "If I were a spy, do you think I'd be traveling on my own passport?"

The question angered Moreno even more. "I will ask the questions," he snapped.

Kurt had pushed too hard. Yes and no would be the standard from now on. His mind raced even faster now. *They think I'm a spy. They honestly don't know who I am. How can that be? If they don't know, then why the hell am I under arrest?*

Movement outside the building caught Kurt's eye through the window. A white crew-cab Toyota pickup truck slid to a halt and disgorged four armed men. Again, no uniforms. Kurt recognized the vehicle as the typical transportation for the Departamento Nacional de Investigaciones (DENI; National Department of Investigation—a corrupt, miserable Panamanian version of the Federal Bureau of Investigation), the dreaded secret police, and their presence seemed to disturb the officers mingling outside. Moreno saw them too, and he scowled. Whatever was happening bothered the major nearly as much as it bothered Kurt. Tempers were running hot, and he didn't understand why.

"Wait here," Moreno commanded. His chair shot away from his desk as he stood, and his minions jumped out of his way as he stormed out of the office into the squad room. "What is this about?" he heard the major yell, but the rest of the heated conversation was garbled by distance and the separating wall. Kurt probably could not have heard the rest of it above his hammering heart anyway.

Moreno was gone for all of ninety seconds before the door opened again. "Stand," he said to Kurt, who complied without question. "Come with us." To the others in the office, he added, "You stay here."

There was a new group waiting in the squad room now, likewise all dressed in civilian clothes. As Kurt followed Moreno to the front of the squad room, and then outside, other soldiers fell in behind him. They led him to the white crew-cab pickup truck. The double-side doors were open, waiting for him. "In the back," Moreno ordered.

Kurt steadied himself with his hands and pulled his big frame up into the vehicle. He had some difficulty pressing himself past the seats as he made his way to the back of the pickup. They closed the doors, and suddenly he was alone. The atmosphere outside buzzed with excited electricity. More officers swarmed around the vehicle, and as they did, many cast sideward glances his way, only to avert their eyes when he caught their gaze.

In the silence of the pickup, he tried again to settle himself down. There was a way to survive this, he told himself. First of all, as an American citizen, he had a certain advantage over regular Panamanians. The paternalism bred from the decades of the Panama Canal Treaty—the American money that helped to keep the Panamanian economy afloat and many of the residents employed—brought an intrinsic deference, despite the increasingly hot rhetoric from the Noriega regime. It was that deference, Kurt figured, that had kept his captors from pinioning his wrists with handcuffs and beating him for information.

All at once, as if on cue, the meeting out in the driveway broke up, and people headed for their vehicles. Six armed men joined Kurt and Major Moreno in the pickup. "Take us to your house," the major demanded.

Kurt's stomach fell. This was it. They were going to get his family. For the first time since the moment of his arrest, he considered spilling his guts. Anything to keep them from harming his children. The emotional side of his brain screamed at him to just start talking, but then the rational side took over. If he talked, dozens of lives would end. Not just his, but all his coconspirators' and all their families'. Every minute that he remained mute bought them another minute to make their escape.

"Straight ahead," Kurt said, pointing, "and up the hill." The total trip would be less than a mile. His mind raced for some ruse that would lead them to a false location, but a lie like that would cause far more trouble than the few seconds it would save. At least for the time being, his PDF captors seemed content not to hurt anyone. God only knew what might happen if he started sending them to far corners of the city. Hell, for all Kurt knew, this was a test to see if they could trust him at all. They had his passport, for heaven's sake, and the passport clearly showed where he lived.

Sitting in the dark in the back of the stifling pickup, Kurt's mind whirled out of control. A precise and orderly man by nature, he found himself overwhelmed by the unknown. Nothing made sense, not even the fact of his arrest. His captors seemed to know only that they were to arrest him on sight, but it appeared as if no one had bothered to tell them why. Clearly, they'd been waiting for him—they knew precisely what flight he would be on—yet the poster for his arrest had been hastily hand written and bore no picture. If he was such an important enemy, wouldn't they at least have taken the time to lift the picture off his identity papers?

If you get caught, you're on your own. Richard Dotson's words echoed deafeningly through his head. *On your own.* Could Richard have known that his arrest was imminent, yet failed to say anything?

No. Absolutely not. He and Kurt had been dearest friends for longer than either one could remember. If Richard had known that Kurt was in imminent danger—if he'd even *suspected* that danger lurked—he would have found a way to warn him.

So, how then? How could the PDF have known to be looking for him?

Kurt checked himself. That was the wrong question. Once they knew *to* look for him, finding him would have been easy. The more appropriate question lay rooted in a day and a time *before* today. Someone would have had to leak the information about his activities to the PDF, but who? Kurt didn't work with strangers, he worked with friends—brothers, for all practical meanings of the word. Kurt ran the faces through his head: Tomás Muñoz, Jorge Quintero, Antonio Martinez, Coronado Samaniego. It simply was not possible that one of them would have turned him in. They'd have died first. But who else knew?

Pablo Martinez. Absolutely not.

Rod Esquivel. Ridiculous. Kurt had saved Rod's life, for crying out loud. There was no way that he could have been the traitor. Who then?

Someone at the Agency? That was always a possibility, given Noriega's infiltration of the American intelligence community in Panama, but Kurt's knowledge of that infiltration was the very reason why he never dealt with any of the operatives assigned to the Panama City Station. Because there were people there whom he disliked and distrusted, Kurt had to assume that there were people who disliked and distrusted him back; but surely not enough to do this. Not enough to risk getting him killed.

These thoughts raced through his mind at the speed of a heartbeat, manifesting themselves as feelings more than rational thoughts. The longer he stayed alive, the less he worried about dying. If they'd wanted to kill him, he'd be dead by now.

But there were alternatives to dying. Things could be done to the human body that would make a person pray for death. No matter how hard he tried to will himself to think reasonable thoughts, the projector in his mind brought him back to the torture chambers about which he'd heard so much.

As their motorcade of five vehicles sped down Avenue Manuel E. Batista on their way to Kurt's house, he couldn't help but think that every turn of the wheel brought him closer to a nightmare.

3

Kimberly stared at the handset before hanging up, and as she did, she had to stifle the urge to cry. The fear in Jorge's voice spread instantly through the phone line.

"Daddy, come *home*," she whispered.

As if on cue, she heard engine noises out front. She knew just from the sound of the engine that it was another false alarm. Her dad's Volvo had a sweet hum to it; the vehicle she heard out front was some sort of truck. A peek through her bedroom window confirmed her suspicion. And then it triggered a bolt of panic.

It wasn't just *a* truck, it was a convoy of them, and they completely blocked the street in front of their house. Down to the left, at the bottom of the street, she saw more trucks. And men with machine guns. They were all looking up at her house.

Suddenly, the stifling night was impossibly cold. She shivered all over and was surprised to find herself crying as she stepped out onto the terrace, just far enough to where she could see the apron of their driveway. A white crew-cab truck blocked the street, parked at an angle, flanked by two white pickup trucks—the standard elements of a PDF goon squad. Wherever they went, they left bloodstains behind.

Her brain screamed at her to run, but her body wouldn't respond. She just stood there, trembling, her hands pressed to her mouth, certain that this was the beginning of something terrible.

She remembered the tone in Jorge's voice, and even though the windows on the crew-cab truck were all blacked out, she somehow knew that her dad was in there.

A few seconds later, the doors opened, and there he was. He stepped out calmly, naturally, and for just a moment she thought that maybe through some weird twist of fate he was just being dropped off. He was dressed in the casual style of Panamanian nationals, in Dockers and a polo shirt, and from this distance, he seemed as if nothing was wrong.

But then the others climbed out to join him. Five, ten, it might as well have been a hundred for all Kimberly could see. For a long time they just stood there, talking. Then, when they moved, they moved together, and for the first time, the horrifying reality hit her: he'd been arrested.

As they walked casually up the driveway, Kimberly tried to disappear; but somehow, her dad knew exactly where to look for her. He tried to appear calm, but his face looked tight—as if he was scared to show his fear.

At the first glance, Kimberly started to sob.

"Sweetheart," he said. "Can you come down and open the door, please?" He stood shoulder to shoulder with five of his captors.

"What's wrong?" Kimberly asked.

Kurt just shook his head. "It's okay, sweetheart, just open the door." He looked ten years older than the last time she'd seen him.

She didn't believe him. Not for a second. These were the Panamanian Gestapo, and they were at her house! She didn't know what to do. Maybe if she ran really fast.

"Sweetheart," Kurt said again, "everything's going to be just fine. I don't have my keys, so please just come on downstairs and open the door for us, okay?"

The world became a blur, an indecipherable swirl of meaningless action and feelings. For a long moment, it seemed as if her feet were glued to the floor, her whole body filled with concrete. Nothing moved but her heart, and it slammed like a runaway drum.

She wanted to run, but there was no getting away from the PDF. Where would she go? Everything she'd ever known was right here at the end of this dead-end street.

She had to let them in. She had no choice. If they started their invasion by breaking the door, God only knew what they'd start breaking next. A heavy fist pounded on the front door. "I'm coming!" Kimberly yelled, dashing into the hall on her way to the stairs. "I'm right here."

This was the end of everything. Don't ask her how she knew, but she did. When she opened the front door, she would cross a threshold from which there would be no return. And she'd be making her journey alone.

Her mom! How was she going to tell Mom? And what about Erik? A thousand thoughts flooded her mind at the speed of panic—a velocity for which there was no measure. Without any conscious thought, she snatched the flimsy, paperback family telephone directory off its table in the upstairs hallway and stuffed it into the waistband of her shorts. Her grandmother's number would be in there.

As her bare feet finally skidded across the marble tile of the foyer, the invaders started pounding again.

Kimberly opened the door, and there was her father, aged yet another ten years.

"Hi, sweetheart," Kurt said. "Don't worry, everything's going to be just fine."

She knew it was a lie.

They invaded the house like roaches, a dozen of them pouring through the front door and spreading quickly throughout the house. Kurt opened his arms to Kimberly and she hugged him tightly, so close that she could hear his heart pounding in his chest.

"Daddy, what's happening?"

"I've been arrested," he said. His voice showed none of the fear that she saw in his eyes.

She pushed herself away far enough to see his face. "For *what?*"

He pulled her to his chest again and stroked her hair.

"Do you have weapons in the house?" one of the soldiers demanded.

Kurt had learned that this one was named Captain Quintero, and he clearly was Moreno's right-hand man. Blessed with movie-star good looks, Quintero wore a wildly flowered blue shirt that seemed entirely incongruous with his military bearing.

"I have two guns," Kurt said. "One is in the closet upstairs, and one is in the living room." It sounded innocent enough, but he knew there'd be hell to pay when they found the M-1 carbine with 300 rounds of ammunition in his bedroom, and his mind was already racing for a way to explain why his 9mm Glock was poised for quick use in the top of a lamp shade near the front door.

While the goons went about the business of rounding up the guns and searching the house, Captain Quintero turned to Kimberly. "Do not be afraid," he said. "We are not here to harm you."

"Let her go," Kurt urged. He was well aware of the art work in her bedroom, and under the circumstances, there was no telling what the fallout might be when it was discovered.

"She can stay," Quintero said. He smiled pleasantly at her. "If she has done nothing wrong, then she has nothing to worry about."

Kurt lowered his voice to a whisper. "Captain, please," he said. "Be reasonable. She's only a little girl. I don't want her to see me like this."

Quintero stewed for a long moment. The way he looked at Kimberly made Kurt wonder if maybe the captain had daughters of his own. Finally, he nodded. "She can go," he said.

Kurt didn't hesitate. Taking Kimberly's shoulders in his hands, he gripped her tightly, their noses nearly touching. "Go," he said.

Kimberly started to cry. "Daddy, what's going on? What are they doing here?"

"Don't worry about that, sweetie. You just move away from here as fast as you can and get to a telephone."

"What am I going to say?"

"You say exactly what happened. You tell Mom that the army came and arrested me. She can take care of everything."

"But she's not—" Kimberly cut herself off before stating that her mother was out of the country. That was probably a detail that the PDF didn't need to know. Kurt sensed it and smiled. She had a good head on her shoulders. She'd find a way to get through this.

Please God, let that be true.

Kimberly stood there for a long moment, staring, searching for something to say that would somehow make this better. But if those words existed, she didn't possess them. In the end, all she had left was, "I love you, Daddy."

Kurt pulled her close to him for one last embrace. "I know you do, sweetheart. And I love you, too. Tell your brother and your mom that my heart is with you all, always."

Kimberly wouldn't let go. If she hugged him long enough, then maybe she'd never have to go away. If she kept her eyes closed, maybe she'd wake up and all of this would never have happened. In the end, Kurt pushed her away.

"Go," he whispered, and he looked away. This was not the time to show the kind of emotion that welled within him. The Muses had never been criers, and Kurt wasn't about to start a new tradition with all these people watching him.

Kimberly understood and stepped back. "Bye, Daddy," she said, and she headed for the front door.

She didn't think it was possible, but somehow the crowd of army and police vehicles had grown even larger outside. Even as everyone watched the front of the house, no one seemed to notice her, a white girl in a pink T-shirt and denim shorts, leaving barefoot through the front door. At first, she tried to keep herself from running, from attracting too much attention. By the time she got to the end of the driveway, though, she didn't care anymore.

She started to run, and as she did, she heard one of the soldiers yell, "*Alto!* Stop!"

The harshness of the order made her run even faster, and as she did, she heard the staccato beat of heavy boots following her.

"*Alto!*" he yelled again, only this time from much closer.

Kimberly didn't know where she was going or what she was going to do when she got there, but she was absolutely certain that above all other things in the world, she wanted to outrun this thug on her heels. She didn't dare look. She didn't dare slow down or change course, because as it was, she was charging headlong down the steep incline, and any sudden move—

She felt herself airborne even before she realized that she'd tangled her feet. When she hit the ground, it was on the concrete, and she hit hard on her knees. A bolt of pain launched all the way up to her thighs as the rough cement tore the meat from her kneecaps.

The soldier was on her in an instant, grabbing her by her arms and yanking her to her feet.

"Get your hands off of me!" Kimberly shrieked. As she yelled the words, she could see the effect they had on the soldier. He was not one of the DENI thugs; he was rank-and-file PDF, just a guy doing his job, and he clearly was not comfortable roughing up a young girl. That she would shout it so loud and draw so much attention made him very uncomfortable.

"You are coming with me," he said to her in Spanish, tightening his grip on her arm. "I have orders to keep you at the house."

"You do not!" Kimberly shouted back at him, in unaccented Spanish with better diction than he. "Your captain said I could go. He said I could leave! Ow, you're hurting me!"

The soldier blushed a deeper red, but his grip did not loosen. "Please do not make this more difficult that it has to be," he said.

Kimberly stared for a long moment, then straightened herself and jerked her arm away. "Okay," she said. "I'm going." Trying her best to be stoic, she silently followed the goon back up toward the house, ignoring the tickle of the blood tracing down her shins. From the foyer, she could see the invaders inside, sifting through all the things that did not belong to them. She hated these men more now than at any other moment in her life. Her dad was nowhere to be seen, already taken into another room somewhere, for God only knew what purpose.

Over near the stairs, Captain Quintero sensed the movement and turned his handsome face to greet her. "I thought you left," he said.

"This goon chased me down," Kimberly spat. "Look what he did to me." She gestured to her bleeding knees, but the captain seemed unmoved.

"I thought she was running away," the soldier said quickly. He sounded as if he were whining. "If you said—"

Quintero dismissed the soldier's concern with a wave of his hand. "Let her go," he said. "She is not important to us."

And just like that, she was free.

This time, as Kimberly ran, the soldiers stepped out of the way to let her pass. As she burst through the cordon at the foot of her driveway, she stopped and gasped as she saw a second cordon forming up at the bottom of the hill. "My God, what's happening?" she asked to the night.

She needed a phone. She also needed a home and a bed and her books for the biology test tomorrow. She needed her mother and her father, and even her annoying little brother. For the time being, though, all she had was the still night air. And her fear.

The party. They would have a phone. She could call somebody from the Arosemenas' house. She could call Mom. She always knew what to do.

The panic started to build exponentially now, and Kimberly found herself struggling for control. She had the phone book, didn't she? Surely the number was there. It had to be; that was why God had prompted her to take it in the first place.

Except for the Muses, it seemed that everyone who lived on the street was related to each other, all of them an offshoot of the Arosemena family: uncles, cousins, grandparents, and assorted friends and hangers-on. When they threw a party, it was always packed to the rafters, and this one was no exception. Desperate for help, Kimberly knocked heavily on the front door.

The girl who answered it, Maria, was a neighborhood acquaintance, and she instantly read the panic on Kimberly's face. "*Dios mio,* what's wrong?"

Kimberly stepped past her into the entryway. "I need a telephone."

Maria looked past the new arrival at the cluster of cars and soldiers on the street, then shot a concerned look.

"My father's been arrested," Kimberly said. "I need to call my mother."

Nicole, a second acquaintance, joined them in the foyer.

"Señor Muse has been arrested," Maria told her, eliciting the gasp she'd no doubt been expecting. "But I'm sure everything will be just fine."

"It's not going to be fine!" Kimberly screamed, bringing silence to everyone around her. She felt the heat of their eyes and in that moment, she seethed with anger. She was angry at all of them for their pity and for the normalcy of their lives. "Now, can I use your phone or not?"

4

It's terrible watching a relative die. The hospice in West Palm did its best to keep the experience manageable, but at the end of the day, it was a place dedicated to death. The slowly decaying shell that Annie Muse had moved into the hospital bed three days ago was not the vital Aunt Elsa whom she'd come to adore. The second wife to Annie's grandfather, who had predeceased her by quite a number of years, Aunt Elsa was a force of nature, always on the go, always doing something at full speed. She still tried, even as the cancer moved from her stomach to her pancreas and beyond, and those very efforts to keep going somehow made it all that much sadder.

At least there was dignity at the hospice—something that hospitals never provided and rarely cared about. The dignity came in the form of honesty. Medical jargon and euphemisms for the inevitable gave way to blunt surrender and acceptance of impending death. The staff was solicitous and friendly, and under the circumstances Annie wasn't sure she could ask for much more.

It had been a long day, and Annie still had much to do. She'd returned to Aunt Elsa's apartment a few hours ago and had spent the evening rifling through the reams of papers that never seem important until the end of someone's life. The apartment was a comfortable one, situated one block from the water on A1-A in West Palm Beach. Annie's Uncle Larry was staying there, too, lending a hand, and it had been kind of fun to spend the evening chatting with him about the old times, even as it was decidedly less fun to talk about the future.

The apartment was designed as a loft, and Larry had graciously offered to sleep on the sofa in the living room, while Annie settled into her grandmother's bed upstairs. Sleep eluded her, though, as she stared at the ceiling, her mind awash in the staggering details of all that needed to be done. It helped that Aunt Elsa was so actively involved in the funeral plans. Ever the efficient manager, Annie had already caught her grandmother sitting upright in her hospice bed with her ever-present yellow legal pad, orchestrating the details of her own farewell. She was particularly emphatic about who could speak and who could not. Catholics could be long winded, Elsa had pointed out, and she didn't want any speeches that went on past people's ability to comfortably endure.

It hurt Annie to think about how much she would miss her when she was gone.

The phone awoke Annie a little after midnight, before she'd even known she'd fallen asleep. The shrill ring cut like a knife, tripling her heart rate. Good news never came at this hour. Assuming that Aunt Elsa had slipped away during the night, she let it ring twice, steeling herself for the bad news.

"Hello?" At first, all she heard was background noise—the sound of a party—but after just a second or two, she also heard the sound of snuffling.

"Mom?"

At the sound of Kimberly's voice, her heart rate doubled again. "Hi, sweetheart, what's wrong?" She worked hard to keep the panic out of her voice.

"There are soldiers at our house. Daddy's been arrested."

The words hit like a lightning bolt. A kick to the stomach. Without prompting, Kimberly poured out what she knew in a continuous, unbroken narrative. She heard all about how Kurt had been running late from the airport, and about the call from Jorge. Annie recognized the name immediately, and with it came full realization of the impending tragedy.

Annie did the math in her head. Kurt's flight had landed around eight o'clock, and now it was after midnight. That was four hours.

Things were spinning wildly out of control, and they'd lost valuable time.

"Listen to me, Kimberly," Annie said quickly. "This is very important. Are you listening to me?"

"I'm scared."

"I know you are, sweetheart, but you have to be strong now, okay? You need to take a deep breath and be strong."

"What's happening? Why are they at our house? Why have they arrested Daddy?"

"I don't know," Annie said, wincing at the lie. "Is Erik with you?"

"He's at the Prietos."

That wouldn't do. He needed to be with the rest of the family. "I need to call them," Annie said. "Where are you now?"

"I'm at the Arosemenas. They're having a party."

Annie nodded. "Okay, fine. Ask Señora Arosemena if she has a telephone book and get me the Prietos' number."

"I have our directory," Kimberly said. "The one from the hall upstairs."

Annie couldn't believe it. "They let you take the phone book with you?"

"They didn't know I had it," Kimberly said. "I stuffed it down my shorts."

Annie laughed in spite of herself. It was brilliant, really. The Latin American machismo would never allow one of the soldiers to search a young girl; certainly not in so inappropriate a spot as her pants. "Good thinking," Annie said. "Let me have the number for the Prietos." She jotted the phone number in the margin of the funeral plans.

"Very good, sweetheart. Since you have the book, I need you to give me one more number." It was a name she was sure Kimberly didn't know.

Why did this have to happen now, when the children were on their own? They'd taken such care to protect the kids from information that could harm them; it seemed unfair that this would befall the family when the children were most defenseless. If only there were real magic in the world, a way to trade places and put them safely in Florida while Annie faced danger that would terrify an adult. And perhaps ruin a child.

Annie would have given her life simply to hug her daughter. But that was not to be. Not tonight. Not until the nightmare was over.

After writing down the second phone number, Annie got her head back in the game. "All right, Kimberly, you have to do something for me now, okay? I need you to call Nana and Papi and have them come and pick you up. They'll take you to their house. Give them my number here at Aunt Elsa's. Can you do that for me?"

"Are we going to be okay?" Kimberly asked.

"You'll be just fine. You and Erik will both be just fine. But I won't lie to you. You're in danger, and you have to move quickly."

"What's *happening*?"

"Later. There's no time to explain now. Just call Nana and Papi. Right now. I'll call the Prietos and have them bring Erik to Nana's house."

"I'm scared, Mom."

"So am I, sweetheart. I'm a little bit scared. But everything will be just fine in the end."

"Promise?"

Annie hesitated just a beat too long. "I promise we'll all work our hardest. How's that?"

It would have to do.

5

Jorge Quintero had picked up Tomás at the airport and driven him home. For the past three hours, they'd been sitting in Tomás's living room, trying to think of what to do. Tomás's wife, Helena, sat with them. What Tomás knew, Helena knew; that was the nature of their marriage.

"If things were normal, he would have called by now," Helena said.

"Things are clearly not normal," Tomás agreed. "But we can't jump directly to the conclusion that he's been arrested."

"Well, we'd better conclude *something*," Jorge said. "It's getting late. If we're in danger, we're running out of time to respond."

They'd talked through the circular logic before, and they knew they'd do it again. On a table near the sofa, the police scanner continued to monitor the radio waves. They were strangely silent tonight. Certainly, there was no mention of anyone being arrested at the airport.

Jorge considered that an encouraging sign until Tomás pointed out that if their network had, in fact, been broken, radio traffic would be the first thing to cease. The PDF weren't the smartest group on the planet, but they weren't idiots.

The entire team had been put on alert. All over the city, the small cadre of friends who had worked so hard for so long were listening simultaneously to their own scanners, while keeping an ear to their portable radios. All of them were working secretly to find out through friends and relatives whether they had heard rumors of something happening, taking care not to raise suspicion in case all of this turned out to be nothing.

Tomás thought back to the beginning of this crazy endeavor, back to the head rush on that hot October night in 1987 when they first signed their own death warrants. For months before, they'd been fooling around with their radios, playing tricks on PDF soldiers, dispatching them on useless missions to dead-end streets. Tomás had been especially fond of singling out an individual soldier, using his radio code name, and berating him for showing such disrespect to his neighbors. Kurt's approach had always been more brash and mean spirited, threatening troops from nonexistent sniper positions, and pulling other pranks that Tomás found to be unnecessarily dangerous.

On October 11, 1987, the fun turned to fear in a single one-minute broadcast.

It had been Tomás's idea. As the owner of a communications company, he'd always been the technical genius of the group. One day while he was diddling with his radio dial, he discovered a weak signal that seemed to be carrying the same words and music as Radio Nacional, the powerful nationwide FM station. But this signal was a weak low-band broadcast. It took him only a few seconds to figure it out, and the discovery nearly made him dizzy: he'd stumbled on the radio link to the repeater station.

In an area as mountainous as Panama, effective transmission required antennas positioned on the highest ground. It was impractical, however, to locate studios on mountaintops, so the stations themselves beamed low-band transmissions only as far as the mountaintop, where the signal was boosted and beamed to the rest of the world on a stronger signal and better frequency. It's a technology used all over the world, and in that moment, an idea bloomed that was so brilliant in its simplicity that he was shocked that it hadn't occurred to him before.

Tomás could still remember the look of excitement on his friends' faces as he detailed his plan. The linking frequency was so weak, he explained, that it could easily be overpowered by a cheap transmitter easily procured in Miami. By overpowering the link, they could hijack Radio Nacional's 50,000-watt transmission, and the government would be powerless to stop them. The only defense would be to take the station off the air completely.

La Voz del la Libertad was about to be born.

The first hurdle was obtaining the transmitter. Unlicensed radio equipment was illegal in Panama. Period. And no radio licenses were issued to anyone but Noriega cronies. To be caught with transmitters—even the portable radios or the scanners that had by that time become permanent fixtures in the conspirators' lives—was to experience the business end of a rubber hose on your naked flesh. None of them flinched at the risk. They were neck deep as it was, after all, and the prize was a valuable one.

Surprisingly, the most difficult hurdle was bureaucratic, not technical. That low-band linking transmission turned out to be a violation of international law. It utilized a frequency that had been set aside for use by Costa Rican fishing vessels, and as such the Miami radio wholesaler wouldn't issue the chips to anyone who was not a Costa Rican fisherman.

Enter Kurt and his family's printing business. Overnight, Tomás and friends printed themselves purchase orders for a fictitious Costa Rican fishing company. Using a credit card and the purchase order, they mailed a request for their chips to be delivered to Annie's APO address on Albrook Air Force Station.

By early October, they were ready to go. At least they thought they were. Truthfully, even Tomás wondered if he hadn't forgotten something. Surely it couldn't be so simple to hijack a nation's national voice. They needed to test their theory.

Using Kimberly Muse's boom box without her permission, Tomás walked down the street from Kurt's house, listening to Radio Nacional's normal broadcast of news and music, while Kurt pointed their new toy toward the repeater tower in the distant hills. At a specific time, Kurt keyed the mike on his transmitter, and for just a couple of seconds, Radio Nacional was off the air.

"Holy shit," Kurt exclaimed when Tomás returned to the terrace. "This actually works. We own the airwaves."

Tomás grinned, as if to say, "Of course."

With the feasibility established, they now needed a date and a text. For all they knew, this one broadcast would be their only shot, and they wanted to get it right. They wanted the biggest audience possible, and that fact alone made selecting the date an easy task.

On October 11, Loyalty Day, Noriega would swagger into a baseball stadium packed with citizens and brag about his power and accomplishments before a crowd who had no choice but to cheer. The speech would be broadcast live throughout the country. The audience couldn't possibly get any bigger than that.

But what would they say? It had to be something good, something that would capture the hearts and minds of the people and cause them to cast Noriega and his henchmen out of office in the next election, some nineteen months in the future. Tomás had ceded the words to Kurt. He was the one with the fleetest tongue, the one who knew how to stitch flowery sentences together. When he was done, the message was a thing of beauty.

Finally, they needed a voice. Kurt tried a couple of takes himself, speaking into the microphone of a small cassette recorder, but he could never get the timbre of his voice the way he wanted it. It had sounded okay to Tomás, but Kurt was a perfectionist on these things, and he was determined to make a recording that sounded professional, while at the same time disguising his voice enough so that he would not be instantly recognized by all of his friends and acquaintances.

Kurt had tried recording under a towel and blanket, hoping to get the reverb in the signal that would make it sound professional, but all he got was a muffled mess. Ditto his attempts to record through a handkerchief. There had to be another way. There had to be a trusted friend with the kind of voice they needed.

They turned to a friend from the Rotary Club, Enrique Fernandez. Enrique was an outspoken opponent of the Noriega regime, and he came from a long line of prominent Panama City residents. He even had a background in radio, as Kurt recalled, with the kind of hypnotic baritone voice to which people loved to listen.

The very nature of a conspiracy such as theirs required that the deepest secrets sometimes be shared. None of them liked it, but all of them agreed that the voice on the tape had to command respect. Tomás and Kurt both shared concerns about Enrique's trollop of a wife, but what she didn't know could never hurt them. Besides, if Enrique agreed to put his voice on the tape, neither he nor Betty would be inclined to point any fingers.

Enrique recorded. It was perfect.

When Loyalty Day dawned, Kurt, Tomás, and Jorge gathered in the apartment owned by Tomás's mother—among them all, the apartment with the clearest view of the mountaintop repeater tower—and they waited for the moment to arrive. As with any major speech, even the U.S. president's State of the Union address, pregame coverage preceded the address, with commentators saying all the right things. Finally, the moment arrived.

The conspirators waited, all of them panting. Tomás remembered it as the most stressful moment of his life. Timing was important here. If they went too early, the government would merely shut down the radio station, and all the effort would have been for naught. So they waited, listening as Noriega glad-handed his way up to the podium.

"Ladies and Gentlemen," the anouncer said, finally, "I now present to you our esteemed leader and commander-in-chief of our glorious armed forces, General Manuel Antonio Noriega." The stands erupted in cheers and applause, and Kurt reached for the button.

"Not yet," Tomás had urged. "Wait till the noise dies down. Wait till he starts speaking."

Like all politicians everywhere, Noriega took his time absorbing the adulation, smiling and waving to people in the crowd. He waved his hand for silence, but of course silence takes time when a crowd is whipped to a frenzy.

At last, the baseball stadium grew quiet. Noriega took a breath. "Thank you fellow citizens . . ."

"Now!" Tomás said, and Kurt pushed the transmit button.

All over the nation, millions of citizens heard a soothing baritone voice intone, "We interrupt this broadcast to bring you a message of hope from the free and democratic people of Panama. Our date with destiny approaches. One day we will finally have an opportunity to cast our vote against the tyranny of General Noriega's dictatorship. It is up to you, and it will not be easy. You know the many tools that the oppressors have to keep us from the polling places. We beseech you to be brave, to persevere. We beseech you to vote. Together we can bury General Noriega's dictatorship under a mountain of ballots.

"Workers, students, professionals, soldiers, housewives, unite! Cast your vote to end the dictatorship. Be courageous. Do not fear them. Remember that we are millions and they are but a few thousand thugs. The end of their dictatorship is near! Together we can run them out!

"The free and democractic people of Panama now return this radio station to its broadcast of oppression."

When the broadcast was over, it was as if no one in the spacious apartment could breathe. On the radio once again, the Pineapple continued to drone on, unaware of the sedition he had just endured.

The next day, the hunt would begin, and within a month, La Voz de la Libertad would be interrupting morning and evening drive-time radio. There was no turning back.

Sitting now in his living room, with Jorge at his side, Tomás remembered the fear in his gut from Loyalty Day. It had returned. They had been betrayed. The others could talk of hope and doubt, but in his heart, Tomás knew that it could be no other way. If Kurt were free, he would have called; if he'd been in an auto accident on his way home from the airport, Tomás would have seen it along the roadside. Arrest was the only reasonable explanation of his continued absence.

When the phone rang, Tomás knew that the end had come. Whatever fleeting traces of hope remained in his heart evaporated when he heard Annie's voice on the other end. She knew little more than he did, it turned out, but she knew for a fact that Kurt had been arrested. Beyond that, the rest was more or less academic. Annie spoke hurriedly yet clearly and was off the phone in a minute or two, promising to call back when she had a chance. In the meantime, if Tomás or the others needed anything, Annie gave him her number in West Palm.

Tomás closed his eyes when he heard the click of the receiver, taking a moment to gather himself. When he opened them again, Jorge and Helena were staring at him expectantly. Tomás wanted to say something profound, but his voice wouldn't work. He pulled Helena into his arms and nodded to his friend.

Jorge looked stunned as he brought his portable radio to his lips and keyed the mike.

In five homes, scattered throughout the city, men who'd pledged their lives to a cause jumped when their receivers broke squelch. They prayed individually for news that would make them all sigh with relief.

Instead, it was Jorge's leaden voice delivering the message that they hoped they'd never hear: "Shopette, shopette, shopette."

Across town, Pablo Martinez jerked awake with a start, his sleep shattered by the sound of footsteps running down the hall of his apartment. Before he had time to put the pieces together, his bedroom door crashed open, revealing the disheveled and unnerved silhouette of his twenty-seven-year-old son, Antonio. The young man was wide-eyed and breathless.

"The DENI arrested Kurt Muse," Antonio blurted. "Jorge just broadcast 'shopette' on the radio. We have to go. Pack your things." Just as quickly as he'd arrived, Antonio was gone, back down the hallway to his own room.

Next to him in his bed, Pablo's wife, Victoria, sat bolt upright. "What is he talking about? Why was Kurt arrested? Why is Antonio so upset?"

Pablo sighed and rested his hand on his forehead. Victoria knew nothing of what they'd been doing. In his role as a leader of the National Liberal Republican Movement, Pablo Martinez did many things about which his wife knew nothing, and if he'd had his way, Antonio would never have been involved, either. But his son was young and wild. Antonio considered himself to be immortal, and when he'd walked in accidentally on a conversation between Pablo and Kurt, he'd put it together quickly and demanded to be made a part of it all. By all accounts, his son was one of the most active members of La Voz de la Libertad. That made him one of the first to be hunted down and killed.

"Answer me, Pablo," Victoria pressed. "What does Antonio mean, 'pack your things'? Are you going somewhere?"

Pablo sighed again, unsure even where to begin. "I'll explain as we dress," he said.

David Skinner didn't know which way was up when he replaced the telephone on its cradle and turned to face his wife, Carol—Kurt's sister. "This is ridiculous," he said, throwing off the covers. "Kurt's finally gotten himself arrested."

Carol gasped.

David padded to his closet in search of a pair of pants. "Apparently, they've got him in custody at his house. Kimberly's by herself and Papi's on his way over to pick her up."

"What *happened*?" Carol asked.

"Who knows? Maybe his junior G-man fantasies finally caught up with him." David had had about all he could take of Kurt and his self-righteous anti-Noriega attitude. Kurt called himself the general man-

42 • Kurt Muse and John Gilstrap

ager of Intergraphic, but he hadn't put in a full day's work in God
knows how long. Even when he was there, he was so wrapped up in
his whispered phone calls that he might as well have stayed at home.
David had lost count of the number of times he'd been counting on
Kurt to take care of some critical detail for the company, only to watch
him sprint out on another mysterious rendezvous.

David had long thought that Kurt was working for the CIA. He'd
always dug the clandestine crap, and David could never forget the time
he happened to see Kurt talking with another American in a parking
lot downtown. The body language alone had told David that it was
something that his brother-in-law should not have been doing. It was
either spying for the CIA or it was a drug habit, and David wouldn't
entertain the latter possibility.

What really frosted his flakes, though, were the endless speeches
about what a scourge Noriega was on the country. It was like sitting
in a reenactment of the U.S. Continental Congress, for crying out loud.
Give me liberty or give me death!

Give me a break.

No amount of ignoring would get him to shut up. And what a wonderful pulpit Kurt had! Here he was, living in a spectacular house sub-
sidized by a generous U.S. government housing allowance (courtesy of
Annie's job with the Department of Defense Dependent Schools), fat
with food bought from the American Commissary in Corozal, and all
comfy cozy in the clothes they bought at the American PX. Their health
care was paid for, and no matter what happened to the Panamanian
economy, Annie's paychecks from the U.S. Treasury would keep coming like clockwork. Who better to make speeches about liberty and
freedom than an ex-pat who hadn't a financial worry in the world?

Meanwhile, people like Carol and David—ex-pats themselves, but
he a citizen of the United Kingdom—had to eek out a living on the local economy. They sent their girls to Panamanian schools and did their
shopping in Panamanian stores. When the banks closed down the previous year under pressure from the Bush administration, Carol and
David had had to do their shopping from the barren shelves of the
Panamanian shopkeepers.

Why was it, David wondered, that political ideologies boiled most
ferociously in the guts of people who had the least to worry about?

"Is Kurt all right?" Carol asked, bringing David back to the present.

"I have no idea," David said, sitting on the edge of the bed to buckle his sandals. "But what do you bet he costs us $10,000 to get him out?"

The soldiers just kept coming, pouring onto their street and invading their house. Kimberly watched numbly from the Arosemenas' front stoop. The party continued to rage behind her, while in the foreground, her world collapsed.

Her phone call had rousted the Prietos out of a sound sleep, and while they seemed nearly as rattled as Kimberly felt, they promised to deliver Erik to Nana and Papi's house. What happened after that was anybody's guess. She just wanted to be with somebody now. Somebody who would know what to do.

When she saw headlights roaring up from the distance, her first thought was that it was another carload of soldiers. As it came closer, it veered to her left, and for a brief moment she thought that the driver was aiming straight toward her. She clambered to her feet, preparing to jump out of the way as the car slid to a halt just a few feet away. It only took a few seconds to recognize the faces. It was Papi and David, and both of them looked mad as hell.

"What is all this?" Papi demanded to no one in particular. With little of the height he passed on to his sons, and none of the girth, Charlie Muse still looked like the paratrooper he once had been. Thin and wiry, his shock of white hair was uncharacteristically disheveled and he needed a shave.

"They arrested Daddy," Kimberly said. She walked toward her grandfather hoping for a hug, but he was locked in on the scene unfolding up the hill.

"Stay here," he said.

Together, the two men walked up the hill to engage the first officer they ran into. Kimberly guessed from the body language that Papi was demanding entry past the cordon. On most days, he was not accustomed to being denied what he wanted, but on this night—or was it morning?—things were different. Kimberly could tell from the look on his face as he stormed back to the car that he was even angrier now than he was when he'd arrived.

"Get in the car," Papi ordered.

Kimberly didn't move. Couldn't move. She just stood there in place, gazing back at the bedlam that once was her home. "What about Daddy?" she asked.

"In the *car* Kimberly," Papi barked.

It was all happening too fast. Kimberly couldn't wrap her mind around it all yet. How could she climb into a car and drive away when her father was up there in the house all by himself? How could she not go back up there and sit with him? He looked like he needed a hug as much as she did.

"Now, Kimberly! We'll make phone calls from the house."

In the end, she had no choice. But as she slid into the backseat of Papi's BMW, she knew that something had changed forever. She knew that for her, childhood had ended.

6

Too distraught to either sit or stand, Kurt found himself pacing; but the pacing made his guards nervous, so he tried to stand still. It was all very disorienting. He was aware of his physical surroundings, but it was as if he were watching it all in the third person. For the time being, he found himself sitting upright in a hardback dining room chair.

They'd been rummaging for the past hour, and he still sensed that they didn't know what they were looking for. He thought about asking if he could help, but decided against it. At best, such a question would make him sound arrogant; at worst, it would put him in a position of incriminating himself. He only hoped that his family and his coconspirators had started to make their way to Clayton.

"Bring Muse up here!" someone yelled. Kurt thought it was Quintero, but he wasn't sure. Whoever it was, he was angry.

In an instant, three soldiers appeared by his chair. One of them poked Kurt in the arm, even as he was already preparing to stand. "I'm going," he said.

It was in fact Quintero. Kurt found him standing in Kimberly's room, fists on his hips, staring angrily at the posters on her wall. "How do you explain this?" the captain demanded.

"Those are political cartoons."

"I know what they are. What are they doing on these walls?"

Now, just how in the hell was Kurt supposed to answer a question like that? What were they *doing*? They were just hanging there. Pictures are inanimate objects, for crying out loud. It was an obnoxious reply, he knew, but it was the first one that formed in his head, and in his head was where he kept it. What the captain truly wanted to know was why did he allow his daughter to hang them on her walls, and Kurt would die before he'd implicate his own child.

"I asked you a question," Quintero demanded.

"I heard you," Kurt said. He tried to keep his tone even. "But I have no answer."

"You'll have one by the time the evening is done," Quintero growled.

A voice from the doorway made them both turn. "What is going on here?" It was Major Moreno. Deep scowl lines traversed his face. He took in the contents of the room in a single extended gaze, then turned to face Kurt. "This is your daughter's room?"

Filled as it was with girlish treasures, there was no sense denying it. "It is," Kurt said.

Moreno's gaze shifted to Quintero. "Then we'll let her answer for it. Bring her here."

Suddenly, Quintero's face darkened. "I let her go, sir."

Moreno's eyes glowed hot. "You what?"

"I let her go, sir."

Kurt suppressed a smile. Quintero reminded him of a schoolboy in trouble.

"On whose authority?"

"My own," Quintero said. "She's only a little girl, Major. I didn't think that she would be important to us."

Moreno's jaw tightened. "You didn't think," he said, tasting the words. "You didn't *think*? You are not paid to think, Captain. You are paid to follow orders. Get her back. Right now."

Suddenly, Quintero looked ill, as if he would rather *be* ill than to say what was coming next: "I can't. I don't know where she is. Sir."

"Idiot!" Moreno boomed. "Suppose we need her for—" He stopped himself, casting a sideward glance to Kurt, and didn't bother to finish the question.

"You are right, Major," Quintero said. "I wasn't thinking. I'm terribly sorry."

Moreno turned to Kurt. "Where is she?"

Kurt scowled at the question. "How would I know? Not here."

"Do not anger me, Mr. Muse," Moreno growled. "You and I have many hours ahead of us. You and I together. This is not a good time to anger me."

"She was scared," Kurt said. "She could be anywhere. Last time I saw her, she was running down the street. It's not as if we had a long time to discuss her plans."

He was being obtuse, and Moreno knew it. The major was not amused. "Where do you think she *might* have gone, then?"

Kurt pretended to think it over for a moment before offering an innocent shrug. "I don't mean to anger you, Major. As you say, that hardly works to my benefit. But I honestly don't know. If I think of something, I'll—"

"Excuse me, Major," someone said from the hallway. Kurt turned to see a soldier with his rifle slung.

"Not now," Moreno barked.

"But I think it might be important, sir." The soldier was a kid, barely older than Kimberly, it appeared, but he carried himself with a military bearing that was unusual for members of the PDF. He was hard to ignore.

"What is it, then?" Moreno barked.

"I'm sorry to be listening, but I believe Mr. Muse's daughter was just picked up by her grandfather."

Oh, shit, Kurt thought.

Moreno's complexion was heading north toward purple. "How long ago?"

"She had been waiting at a friend's house, apparently. Down the street. The house with the party."

"How long!"

The soldier jumped at the eruption, nervously checked his watch. "Ten, maybe fifteen minutes ago."

Moreno whirled on Kurt. "You have no idea, eh? You have no idea where your daughter might have gone, yet your parents live here in Panama City?"

Kurt eased a step backward, sure in his heart that the major was going to strike him. On any other day, one on one, that wouldn't have been a problem; Kurt could have kicked his ass into next week. With this much reinforcement, however, to fight back would mean suicide.

"She's my daughter, Major. What would you do?"

Moreno trembled with rage. Clearly, he wanted to lash out, but for whatever reason, he did not. "Captain Quintero, find out where Mr. Muse's parents live and we will pay them a visit." He turned to leave, but stopped at the door to level a finger at his prisoner. "Bring him along."

Annie felt the panic rising in her gut. It was like a balloon deep inside her belly, and with each passing moment, it grew larger and larger. She'd lost track of the number of phone calls she'd made and received in the past hour. Right now, she had Nana on the line, and she was having trouble getting her to acknowledge the seriousness of their situation.

"You need to get the children to the back gate of Fort Clayton," Annie said for the umpteenth time. "They're in grave danger. So are you and Papi. You need to go with them."

"I'm not going anywhere!" Nana proclaimed yet again. "Not until you tell me what this is all about. Rita and Alex Prieto called and they're scared to death."

"They're on the way with Erik, right?"

"Well, yes, but they don't know what to think. I don't know what to tell them. And now you say that we all have to leave the country without telling me why?"

"I don't have time to tell you right now, Nana. I'm not holding out on you, I just don't have the time. Kurt was working against Noriega, and now he's under arrest. There are other people involved, too. It's big, Nana. If you stay, they'll use you and Papi and the children as a means to get to Kurt. They'll hurt you."

"I don't believe that. Panamanians aren't like that."

Good God almighty, how long could this go on? "The children, then, Nana. Get the children to Clayton."

"Where are we going to take them?"

"To the back gate."

"There are going to be MPs," Nana said. "What do I tell them?"

Good point. Very good point. "Can you call Major Mansfield?" Annie asked. Nana had worked as the secretary to the Provost Marshal of the U.S. Southern Command. Major Alan Mansfield was the Provost Marshal Pacific, and as such, he and Peggy had cumulatively spent hours talking to each other about one issue or another. These days, Mansfield was in charge of the military police units on the Pacific side of Panama. "Tell him that there are upward of twenty people coming to the back gate in the next hour or so. Almost all of them are going to be Panamanian citizens, and they'll all be seeking asylum. It's important that they be taken in immediately."

"Twenty!" Nana gasped. "Good lord."

"More than twenty," Annie corrected. She was guessing here. She knew about the basic six coconspirators, but she didn't know which were married, and she certainly had no idea how many children they might have. They would all need asylum.

"I don't know that he has the authority to grant asylum," Nana said. "Charlie will be back with David and Kimberly soon. Maybe you should talk—"

"Nana, no! We don't have *time*!" How could she make her understand? "I can't emphasize that enough. You are all in danger."

"I don't even know if Major Mansfield is home," Nana said.

Annie dismissed it as irrelevant. He was or he wasn't. She could do nothing about that either way. "Once you're on the post, you need to find a Mr. Chiang. Everyone will know who he is. You find him, and he'll know what to do."

The comment seemed to take the wind out of Nana. She fell silent.

"Nana?"

"You know Mr. Chiang?" Nana gasped. "This is about Mr. *Chiang*?"

Annie heard the realization in Nana's voice. Finally, she understood. Mr. Chiang was the CIA chief of station in Panama City, with quarters on the grounds of Fort Clayton. He had some official diplomatic cover, but such things never fooled people on the inside.

"Now you understand the seriousness of this," Annie said.

"But Kurt said—"

"Nana, please."

"Okay," Nana said. The truth had finally dawned on her. "Okay, I'll get right on it. I'll call Major Mansfield right away. I don't think Charlie is going to want to leave, though."

"Let's just worry about the kids for now."

There was no effort made by either end of the conversation to close with a good-bye. There was so much to be done, and Annie knew that the clock was quickly ticking down to zero. The recognition in Nana's voice when she mentioned Chiang's name gave Annie pause. She herself had never heard of the man until a half hour ago, when she received a phone call from Suzanne Alexander, a long-time friend whom Annie knew for a fact worked for the Agency.

Suzanne had called out of the blue, unsolicited—prompted, Annie was sure, by a plea from Richard Dotson, who was one of the first people Annie called after she got the news. The Alexanders, Dotsons, and Muses had long been good friends and had even vacationed together in the past. About two years ago, though, Suzanne transferred back to Langley, followed shortly by Richard, who was called back for a stint at Foggy Bottom.

However it worked, Suzanne had been very specific: they were to find Mr. Chiang at Fort Clayton. He was the one and only person who could make this work out happily.

With her phone call to Nana complete, Annie placed the phone on its receiver and realized that for the time being she had nothing left to do but wait.

"Is there anything I can do?" asked a voice from the doorway.

Annie hadn't realized that Larry was listening. Come to think of it, she'd forgotten that he was in the house at all. "No," she said, rubbing her temples. "All that's left now is the wait."

7

Kurt squirmed in the back of the van, doing his best to overhear what lay ahead for his family when the caravan arrived. His parents had all the money, the business belonged to them. There was the property on Taboga. All of it was in jeopardy now, and it was all because of him. Noriega had long established himself as a tyrant who assumed that everyone's property was his for the taking. God only knew what he would take from a man whose son worked ceaselessly and effectively to make the general look like a fool.

Please get away, Kurt prayed. It had been nearly six hours since his arrest, plenty of time for word to spread. The uncertainty of it all was killing him.

If Kimberly got in touch with Annie, then everything would turn out fine. Annie could make amazing things happen in no time at all. But if, for some reason, she had not gotten the message . . . He refused to think about it. In three minutes, they'd be at the house. There was no stalling anymore.

The clock on the dash of the BMW read 1:30 when Papi finally pulled to a stop in front of the La Cresta apartment. Carol had already arrived from her and David's place across the street, and Kimberly found the atmosphere electric and frightening.

Nana met them before they were halfway to the door. "When Erik gets here, we have to leave," she said. "The children are in danger. I just spoke with Annie on the phone. She says that we should leave, too. You and I."

Papi didn't want to hear it. "That's ridiculous. This is Kurt's game, not ours."

"Mr. Chiang is involved," Nana elaborated. "That means the CIA is involved."

This only seemed to make Papi angrier. "Dammit," he growled. "He swore to me. He *swore* to me that he was not involved with the Agency. I'm not going anywhere." Papi had roots here that were thirty years old. He had a business to run, a life to lead. He had no desire to get sucked into his son's suicidal politics.

"We have to," Nana said. "When Erik gets here, we have to leave. If the PDF gets a hold of them, Annie is convinced—" she cut herself off, as if suddenly aware that Kimberly was listening.

"What about our lives?" Papi demanded.

"Tomorrow," Nana said. "We'll get to that tomorrow. For right now, we have to get the children to Mr. Chiang's house on Clayton. He's waiting."

It was an unspeakable betrayal of the family. Papi couldn't get beyond the anger. How dare Kurt take such ridiculous chances with his life—with all their lives? His *children's* lives, for God's sake. With emotions boiling this hot, all he could think about was the day of reckoning. Sooner or later, he'd have a chance to speak to Kurt face to face. When that happened—

The thought was cut short by the roar of an approaching engine and the growing glare of headlights.

For a moment, Kimberly thought it was over, that the PDF trucks were arriving, but no sooner had the thought formed than she recognized the Prietos' black Toyota Pathfinder. In the backseat, in the dark, she could just barely discern the outline of her little brother. He looked as if he might be asleep, but when the door finally opened, she saw that he was more than awake. Barely dressed, with his auburn hair on sideways, he seemed to be stranded in a netherworld between anger and fear.

As the Prietos discharged their passenger and his luggage, there was more talk about what her dad had been doing. Why on earth would the DENI be arresting Kurt? He was an American citizen. He had ties to the Defense Department. It was all the same stuff over and over again. This time, though, by eavesdropping, Kimberly learned the additional detail that her mother was very distraught over this.

For the first time, Kimberly had a very real sense of the danger that she herself was in. Up till now, her fear had all been about her father. Now it was personal. Now it was about herself, Erik, and her angry grandparents.

Nana cut the discussion short. She thanked the Prietos for their help, but then started herding the family toward the car. Erik was here now, there was no need to wait. If Annie's suspicions were correct, the goons would be here momentarily, and then all options but surrender would evaporate in a heartbeat.

Kimberly didn't hesitate. She was ready to be moving. She was ready for the arguments to stop and for life to return to normal. As she sat with the car door open, she listened as an argument erupted between her brother and Papi.

"No!" Papi barked. "Absolutely not. There's no room for that thing in here."

Erik had recently taken up skate boarding, and it had become his number-one passion. "I'm not going without it," the boy said. That kind of recalcitrance in the presence of Papi's anger could only be explained by exhaustion.

"Get in the car," Papi said. Standing nearby, Carol looked ready to throttle the boy.

"Not without my board."

"Get. In. The. Car."

Finally, Erik got it. Sanity bloomed like a lifting veil. Realizing that he'd pushed everyone as hard and as far as they would go, he sullenly surrendered and climbed into the back of the BMW while Papi loaded the suitcase he'd packed for his sleepover into the trunk.

One look at his sister frightened him. "What's happening? Where are we going?" he asked.

Kimberly shook her head. "I don't know."

"Where's Dad?"

She hesitated. How much should she share? As the big sister, how much responsibility did she have to keep her worries to herself? "He'll be fine."

"Somebody said he was arrested."

Kimberly looked at him for a long moment and then turned to face front. "He'll be fine," she said again. Repeat it often enough and it would come true.

Outside the car, there was more discussion that this was all a waste of time. Carol and David would wait at Nana and Papi's house until everything blew over and they returned. It couldn't take more than a few hours, after all.

The whole car shook as Papi closed the door, his ultimate expression of frustration and anger. "Where are we going?" he asked Nana.

"To Clayton. The back gate." She pulled the notes she'd taken from her conversation with Annie out of her purse and read them.

"We're to take the children to Mr. Chiang's house. He'll take care of things from there."

Papi pulled the transmission into gear and grumbled something that Kimberly could not hear, something she probably didn't want to hear. Slowly, they pulled out of the driveway and headed down the hill for the other side of the world. She settled into the seat and closed her eyes, hoping that rest might settle the awful churning in her stomach.

Two minutes into the trip, something happened to jolt her upright in her seat. Maybe it was a gear change or a subtle jerk of the steering wheel. Or, maybe it was an audible gasp from someone in the front seat. Heading down a long hill, Papi had to pull far over to the right to let the parade of PDF vehicles charge up the hill in the direction they'd just left. They drove fast and aggressively, clearly on an important mission.

Up in the front seat, Nana and Papi exchanged nervous glances.

When Carol saw the headlights at the end of the street, her first thought was that Nana and Papi must have forgotten something. They hadn't been gone two minutes. Then, when the vehicles kept coming, she realized who it was. The hunters had missed their prey by mere moments. They must have passed each other on the street, she thought.

The vehicles took up the entire street, some of them parking close to the house and others parking farther away. At this hour, crowd control couldn't possibly be a problem, but they seemed to be taking no chances. Carol retreated to the doorway of her parents' home and waited for the lead soldier to approach her. There were no uniforms, she noted, but there was no way to miss the way they swaggered when the moved.

"I am Captain Cortizo," the soldier said. "Please step aside."

"What do you want?" Carol asked.

"Are you Mrs. Muse?"

"I am her daughter. We live across the street."

"And where are your mother and father?"

Cortizo could not have been more polite, yet his questions could not have been more piercing. "I don't know," she said. The transparency of the lie was obvious, yet what else could she say?

The captain's eyes narrowed as he jerked his head for Carol to move aside. She complied as they filed into the house, then followed them inside.

They worked with the zeal of a hungry hoard, spreading quickly throughout the apartment as they searched every corner for something of interest to them.

"What exactly are you looking for?" Carol asked, but no one would answer her. She jumped when the phone rang. Carol picked it up before the second ring.

"Mom?" said the voice on the other end. It was her daughter, Joanna—Joey—and her fear was palpable even through the phone line. "What's happening?"

"Nothing, honey. Stay home."

"It looks like the police."

Shocked that no one had yanked the phone from her hand, Carol tried to speak as cryptically as possible. "That's right."

"I'm coming over."

"No, you're not. Stay where you are."

A soldier had finally taken notice of what Carol was doing and started her way. Carol quickly hung up the phone and tried to look innocent as she smiled at the guard.

"Who was that?" the soldier asked.

"My daughter," she answered, honestly enough. "We live across the street and she saw the commotion."

The soldier gave her a hard look and extended a threatening finger. "Stay off the phone."

Carol nodded, trying to choke down the fear that invaded her chest and throat. From across the room, her gaze found David, who was already looking in her direction, trying to get her attention. With arched eyes and a nod, he asked her silently if she was all right.

She wanted to say yes, but she could feel the tears pressing.

Tomás tried not to think about all that he was leaving behind: his business, his house, his fortune, such as it was. He had his family, and when all was said and done, a man couldn't ask for much more than that. When they reached Fort Clayton, they would be safe; after that, there would be time to manage the other problems. It was all in God's hands anyway, and to date the Creator had never let him down.

Harder to press out of his mind than the personal losses was the terrible dread of lost opportunity. They'd been so close. Just one month before all planning and sacrifices would have been worth it. If they could have continued for just four weeks more, Noriega would have been gone, ousted from power by a liberated citizenry. He couldn't be sure, of course, but that didn't stop him from *being* sure. The seeds of bitterness began to take root in his belly, and he tried to smother them. This was not the time. The Lord had led him and his compatriots down this path for a reason, and a good Christian did not question the unspoken plan of the Almighty.

"Shopette" called for everyone to drive to the back gate at Clayton, and from there to seek asylum. They'd assumed that it would be that easy, but when Tomás and Helena finally arrived, pulling their car off to the side of the road, they found a number of their friends clustered at the outside of the gate, the fear and frustration plainly evident on their faces.

"They won't let us in," Coronado said as Tomás approached. "We asked for asylum, but they won't let us in."

Tomás scowled. Truth be told, no one had thought "Shopette" through to this point; the escape plan had been in place for months, but not one of them had actually considered that they might one day launch it. Surely, if the right people found out that they needed help, then help would come, but that begged a question that now seemed so horribly obvious that he felt embarrassed that neither he nor Kurt had ever thought to ask: Who, in fact, were the right people? And how, precisely, were they to contact them at this hour?

The first name that came to mind was Father Frank—the mysterious operative with whom he and Kurt had met a dozen times to exchange information or to pick up equipment—but that seemed impossible. First of all, Father Frank had no real name as far as they knew, and he seemed to come and go with all the speed and mystery of a ghost.

Tomás did his best to calm Coronado with a hand on his shoulder. "Let me see what I can do." Behind him on the road, he saw another set of headlights bloom and watched as Antonio pulled his car to the side of the road and exited to join his compatriots. Yet another car was close behind. If Tomás couldn't get things straightened out quickly, there was going to be one heck of a traffic jam out here.

As the MP at the gate stepped forward to greet him, Tomás noticed that the second guard was Panamanian, a member of the PDF. It was common for the Americans and the indigenous military to stand guard together at check points, but the second soldier put Tomás in the position of choosing his words very carefully.

"I need to speak to you," Tomás said in perfect, unaccented English.

"So speak," the MP said.

"Alone, please."

The guard shook his head. "I'm sorry, sir, but this is as alone as I'm authorized to get."

Tomás glanced at the PDF soldier, who stepped away as the MP cued him with a nod to do so. Tomás said softly, "We need asylum. We are in danger."

"I understand that from your friend," the MP said, with maybe a twinge of compassion. "But I don't have the authority to grant that."

"Then I need to ask you to find the person who does have the authority."

"I've called my officer in charge, sir. He's aware of the situation, and that's about all I can do."

"Can you call him again?"

The MP answered with a frustrated, helpless look.

Tomás nodded. Clearly, the soldier's hands were tied. Like soldiers the world over, this one could only follow orders. Truly, it was in God's hands now.

Still, as he watched the PDF soldier pick up the phone in the guard shack and dial, Tomás couldn't help but hope that God would act quickly.

*   *   *

Kurt never left the car. Flanked on both sides by silent guards, he watched as the troops swarmed into his parents' house and tore the place apart. What must they think of him, he wondered. How could he ever apologize? How could they ever forgive him?

He prayed that they'd had a chance to get away, that the BMW they'd passed on the way in was them. If it had been, then it had been very, very close. Too close. Finally, the clock had ticked to zero. *Please, God, let them get the children to safety.*

The search was still underway when they made the decision to move Kurt to his next location. Two additional soldiers he didn't recognize climbed into the front seat, and they eased away from the curb.

"Where are we going?" Kurt asked.

No one answered. No one even bothered to cast him a glance.

What could they possibly do to him? Killing wouldn't give them what they wanted. Torture him? He supposed that was possible, but to what end? What would they be looking for? The names of his coconspirators? Perhaps, but that assumed that his captors knew that there were conspirators to be found. So far, it still didn't seem as if they knew why he had been arrested. Clearly, someone at the top of the chain of command must have known, or else there wouldn't be this full-court press; but by all indications, word of the discovery hadn't yet filtered down to the level of the soldiers.

A horrible thought bloomed in his head: Without an endgame for the torture, how would they know when to stop? If he spilled everything he knew about everything he had ever known, how would they know it was enough?

It was a foolish thought, he realized, but foolishness was a close cousin to hopelessness, and he certainly found himself belly deep in a river of that.

No, he told himself, torture could not be part of the plan. He was far too white and far too American to be subjected to the kind of treatment that might befall a Panamanian. And his wife was an American government employee. That had to mean something. Surely the United States wouldn't tolerate the brutal mistreatment of one of its own. Then he remembered the dozens of stories of violent showdowns between American servicemen and PDF soldiers, and how on each occasion, General Fred F. Woerner, the commander in chief of the U.S.

Southern Command, had ordered the Americans to back down. This was a time of turning the other cheek so many times that the bruises never went away. Kurt had referred in writing to the general as Wimp Woerner.

Funny how intemperate words came back to haunt you. Now, as Kurt swirled down the whirlpool that his life had become, he had to wonder just how committed he himself would be, if the tables were turned, to saving the ass of a man who had worked diligently to make him look like a fool.

You can't do this, Kurt chided himself. He couldn't afford to sink this low this early. God only knew how long this was going to take to play itself out. It was foolishness to jump ahead into the darkest conclusions. For the time being, he was alive and unharmed. He had no reason to think that his family was any less safe.

Right now, the worst of it all was the confusion. It was all emotion. No one ever died of emotion. One step at a time.

He'd almost talked himself into a kind of resigned calmness when he picked up something out of the guard's radio chatter that made his blood run cold. A group of Panamanian citizens was seeking asylum at the back gate to Fort Clayton.

8

The drive seemed to take forever. The BMW sliced through the night like a knife through flesh, Papi's anger clearly conveyed with a heavy foot on the accelerator. No one spoke. In the silence, Kimberly was startled by the loudness of her own heartbeat.

She thought about asking where they were headed, but decided not to. Saying anything right now would be a bad idea. Erik was frightened too, his eyes huge even in the darkness.

Why did she have to be alone now? Why couldn't her mother be home? Why did they have to go away at all? Aunt Elsa's timing really sucked.

On top of everything else, Kimberly could feel the exhaustion pressing in on her. She had no idea what time it really was, but she felt as if she'd been up for three days. Sleep, she would find, was still many hours away.

Finally, they arrived at a military gate. Papi pulled to a stop and ran the window down to speak with the MP on duty. Without any preliminary fanfare, the soldier asked, "What's your name, sir?"

"Muse," Papi said. "Charles Muse." He produced some identification to prove it.

Pausing just a moment to peer behind the driver into the backseat, the MP unholstered a Maglite and examined Papi's identity card in the brilliant white glare.

Over to the right, off the side of the road, Kimberly noticed a gathering of people. They all appeared to be locals, and they all looked scared to death. "Who are they?" she asked to anyone who might be interested in answering. Apparently, she was completely invisible tonight.

The soldier handed the card back to Papi and stepped aside, and they were allowed to pass. It was interesting, Kimberly thought, that at this hour, and with this much security all of a sudden, the soldier never bothered to ask what their business was. The military posts in Panama weren't the securest places in the world. Still, you'd think they'd have asked *something*.

Nana and Papi had started talking again, but in tones so hushed that Kimberly couldn't make out the words. They drove slowly, with the high beams on, apparently looking for a particular address. She couldn't help but wonder just how pissed off the person was going to be when he found someone knocking on his door at two in the morning.

"Look over there," Nana said, pointing to the Provost Marshal's office where she used to work. Squat and rambling, the building was lit up like a soccer stadium. "Somebody's working late."

Papi said something, but again Kimberly couldn't make out the words.

She knew they were trying to find a Mr. Chiang's house—that much she had been able to decipher—and from there, Mr. Chiang would know what the next step was supposed to be. Slowly, one street led to another, and finally they pulled to a stop in front of a house—an upper-end house by base standards—whose every light was turned off. It was as if it had been completely swallowed by the night.

"Nobody's there," Papi observed.

Nana shook her head. "He has to be. He's waiting for us. This is the place we were supposed to go."

"You can see the same as I," Papi said. "There's no one home. This isn't the place."

"But it *is*," Nana insisted. Everyone in Panama knew where the CIA chief of station lived. "He has to be home." Perhaps saying it enough would make it come true.

"Have it your way," Papi said. "But it's clear that he wants us to think he isn't."

Nana scowled. "But why?"

" 'Why' is the question of the night, don't you think?"

"So, what do we do now?"

The indecision and the confusion in the car raised Kimberly's fear to a new level. Things that she'd never thought about were happening all around her, and as they tried to fix things, the fixes were falling apart, too.

Please don't hurt my dad. The thought appeared out of nowhere and doubled her heart rate.

"We go home?" Papi suggested.

Nana didn't honor the suggestion with a reply. "Let's go to the Provost Marshal's office. At least there are people there. Maybe I can find Major Mansfield. He should have some suggestions."

"I don't think I need any more suggestions tonight," Papi said. "But I could sure use some answers."

For Marcos Ostrander, the sound of a telephone at night always portended bad news. As the chief of international law and relations for the U.S. Army South, he would come to realize that he was the logical choice for the call, but at that moment, pulled out of a deep sleep, all he felt was a terrible unease. These were tough times in the history of America's relations with Panama, and he'd reached that point in his career where people no longer called him for the little stuff.

He picked up the receiver. "Ostrander."

"Time to go to work, Marcos," said the voice he recognized as belonging to Major Alan Mansfield. "We've got a couple dozen IPs seeking asylum down at Clayton."

"Asylum? What the hell for?" This wasn't Berlin, after all. The borders to U.S. territory—the Canal Zone, for example—were so porous that they wouldn't hold a teaspoon of water. Requests for asylum were anything but commonplace.

"Not on an open line. I need you down here at the fort right now." The line went dead before Marcos could form another question. He didn't work for Mansfield, but he owed the man enough favors that when he said jump, Marcos was airborne.

He dressed quickly in casual clothes and headed for the front door, reminded as he always was when leaving the house, of the morning not yet six months ago when he'd found a headless corpse on his front stoop, a less-than-subtle hint from Noriega for him to straighten up his act. There had been three silver bullets left next to the corpse, along with a note warning that there were other bullets just like them that were meant for Marcos. Just days before, Marcos had learned of rampant corruption in the Panamanian courts, in which judges were being paid off to pronounce guilt on trumped-up charges against innocent people whose only crime was to be an enemy of Noriega. Corruption exposed, it turned out, was corruption defeated, and Noriega had raised graft to too fine an art form to have it defiled by some U.S. Army lawyer.

General Bernard Loeffke, Marcos's boss, had gone through the roof when he learned of the threat against a senior member of his staff. Major Mansfield had been the one to deliver the message to Captain Cortizo, a senior aide to Noriega, that if Marcos so much as developed a hangnail in the immediate future, Noriega would be held personally accountable and would pay a devastating price.

For the next two months, Marcos had traveled like the president of the United States, flanked day and night by armed guards. Noriega took his own sweet time, but ultimately he made it clear that the threat against Marcos had been lifted, and slowly things had returned to being as close to normal as anything ever was in this part of the world.

As in getting up at an unspeakable hour to tend to Panamanian defectors. The very notion still made his head spin.

The Provost Marshal's office was packed wall to wall with people who all seemed scared to death. Outside, Kimberly had noted more guns among the American soldiers than she was typically used to seeing during her occasional trips here to visit Nana. Even the soldiers seemed kind of jumpy. Had she paid better attention, she would have noticed that the office had been purged of all Panamanian soldiers and workers. Some of the frightened civilians looked familiar to her and she wondered why, until she remembered the cluster of people she'd seen outside.

On entering the front door, the Muse family instantly became the center of attention. Soldiers on the inside moved quickly to greet them and then to split them apart. "Come with me," a young soldier said, gesturing for Kimberly and Erik to follow.

"We're with my grandparents," Kimberly said.

The soldier seemed not to hear. Nobody seemed to hear her tonight.

"*Please* come with me," he said. Somehow the "please" seemed to have a threatening undertone.

Kimberly followed—as if there was a choice—trying to catch her grandparents' eye as they moved in another direction. If they saw, they made no indication.

The Panamanians from the gate watched as Kimberly and Erik followed the soldier to a back room, and Kimberly found something creepy in the intensity of their collective gaze. It was as if they recognized her, but none of the faces were familiar. What was happening? The whole night was turning into an episode of the *Twilight Zone*. That kind of attention from strangers was horribly unsettling.

But they weren't all strangers. There in the back of the crowd was a face she did recognize. It was Jorge Quintero, the man who had called to see if her father was home. Just like that, a circuit closed in her brain and the fear ratcheted up another twenty points. All these people—the men, women, and children—it looked like several dozen of them—were here because of her father. Somehow, his arrest had scared this many people, and how many more?

Her mom had told her on the phone that her dad had been into some things, but good Lord, what could cause this much disruption to so many people?

The soldier took the kids to a tiny windowless office and invited them to sit in the available plastic chairs. Kimberly assumed that the soldier locked the door as he left, but because she had no place to go, she didn't bother to check it.

Daddy, what did you do, she asked silently.

9

Marcos Ostrander sat quietly in a chair off to the side of Mansfield's desk while the major tried to talk sense into Charlie and Peggy Muse.

"This is ridiculous," Charlie said for the dozenth time. "This is my home. I have a business here. I can't just go into hiding somewhere."

"I'm afraid you don't have a choice, sir," Mansfield said in a tone that was at once firm and respectful. "In a few minutes, or a few hours, when you step outside this office, I won't be able to protect you. And without protection, you will undoubtedly be arrested."

"On what charge? I've done nothing wrong. We still have laws in this country. We still have attorneys."

Marcos saw the statement as his opportunity to say something. "I *am* an attorney," he said. "And with all respect, the Panama you describe no longer exists. It's no longer about what you did or did not do. Right now, it's about using you against your son, and when they're done doing that, they'll charge you with whatever they want and manufacture the appropriate evidence to convict you. All it takes is a wink and a nod from General Noriega, and a lengthy sentence is guaranteed."

As hard as Major Mansfield was working to be diplomatic, Marcos doubled the effort to be blunt, and the effect on his guests was immediate and obvious. Peggy blanched with fear as Charlie reddened with rage.

"Use me against my son?" Charlie seethed, saying the words as if they tasted like betrayal. "What exactly has he done?"

Marcos kept the eye contact constant and direct as he said, "I can't tell you. But when General Noriega finds out the full scope of it, he's going to be very angry. He'll move heaven and earth to get even. And he'll start with you." There. He couldn't put it more plainly than that.

"What about our daughter?" Peggy asked. "And her husband?"

This was news to Marcos. He shot a look to Mansfield, who instantly snatched up the phone.

Before dialing, Mansfield pointed to another phone on another desk. "Mrs. Muse, I wonder if you could do me a favor and use that phone over there to call your daughter and tell her and her husband—what's his name?"

"David," Peggy said. "Carol and David Skinner."

Mansfield nodded. "Tell Carol and David Skinner to expect some visitors very shortly."

"What kind of visitors?" David asked. Joey had joined them in the living room as they all tried to make sense out of the night.

Carol shook her head. "Nana couldn't say. *Wouldn't* say on the phone."

"What are these visitors coming to do?"

"She wouldn't say that, either, other than to say that we should do whatever they say. David, I'm frightened."

He gathered his wife into his arms gently and held her. "There's nothing to be frightened of," he assured. "We've done nothing wrong."

Even though they were expecting it, the knock at the door still startled them. Perhaps it was the lightness of it—just a tiny rap to let them know it was time to open the door, even as the arrival was kept secret from the neighbors.

Carol could not have described who she expected to see when she opened the front door, but she knew without doubt that this young American with scruffy hair and rumpled clothes was not it. He greeted her with a big smile. "Hi," he said. "We're the good guys. I think you're expecting us."

"Us?" David said cautiously. "There's only one of you."

As if on cue, another one stepped into view. They could have been roommates at Berkeley. "The back is clear," the second one said. Neither made an effort to introduce himself.

"May we come in please?" the first one said.

"Who are you?" David pressed. "Who do you work for?"

The first visitor nodded toward the foyer. "Inside," he said again. "Please."

Carol pulled David off with a gentle hand on his forearm.

"Thank you," the visitors said together. They stepped inside and closed the door. Once inside, they zeroed directly in on Joey, who couldn't have been more than five years younger than they. "Hi there," said the one among them who seemed destined to do all the talking. His smile had the light of an incandescent bulb. He extended his hand to Joey and said, "I'm Ski. This is John. Who are you?"

Joey blushed and bubbled, "I'm Joey Skinner."

"So there's three of you," John said. The two exchanged a glance that Carol and David didn't quite know how to interpret.

"All right then," Ski said, clasping his hands together with a pop. As if as an afterthought, he whirled quickly to offer his hand to Joey's parents as well. "You're Carol and David, I presume," he said.

"We are indeed," David said.

"Australia?" Ski asked, noting the accent.

"England."

"Okay, then." As if a switch had been flipped, Ski turned seamlessly from pleasantries to business. "Here's the deal, guys. John and I are here to take you to safety."

David recoiled at the thought. "Whose safety?"

"Yours," Ski said. "Your whole family. Everybody else is at . . . is safe. You're the last who are not, and I don't know when the PDF is going to realize that they've missed you."

"So you're suggesting we leave?" David said.

"I'm here to offer that option, yes sir."

"But this is my home. We have business here. We have our lives here."

Ski looked to John for assistance. "We can't speak to your home or your business, Mr. Skinner, but that last part about your lives is what's in play. We've been told that this is a one-of-a-kind offer. You don't have to accept, but if you turn us down, there won't be another opportunity."

Carol was stunned, speechless.

Ski sighed. "I understand this is difficult and frightening, but sometimes choices have to be made quickly, and I'm afraid this is one of those times."

"But we don't even know what you're proposing," David protested. "Beyond leaving with you. What's next?"

Ski shook his head. "I don't know."

"You don't know, or you won't tell us?" Carol prodded.

"Does it matter? Either way, the sun's going to be up soon, and when daylight arrives, options start to shut down. I've got a car outside. Are you going to use it or not?"

A long moment passed as the Skinners looked to each other for a definitive answer. Finally, it was Joey who said, "We don't really have a choice, do we? If we go now, we can always change our minds later. But if we don't . . ." She didn't finish the sentence.

Ski forged ahead with the plan as if he'd heard someone agree. "Here's what we do, okay? We go one at a time. We'll start with John, who will just wander out to the car, and then Joey will be next, followed by Carol, David, and, finally, me. Okay? Any questions?"

They all just stared at him like he'd gone over the edge.

"Okay, that was stupid. Any questions I can answer?" He paused, but it was only for effect. "Okay, then, John, you start."

The Berkeley Boy nodded his approval that a plan was finally underway, and he slipped out the front door, closing it behind him. Ski watched from the window. After maybe thirty seconds, he apparently liked what he saw and motioned for the next round.

"Okay, Joey, you're up. Don't run, don't make a scene, just go straight to the car."

Pausing just long enough to shoot a worried glance to her parents, Joey slipped out the door. Another thirty seconds, and then it was Carol's turn. She was still crying, but in a way that led Ski to believe that maybe she didn't realize it.

What he saw was the manifestation of fear. Carol was never much for the unknown. She liked her world ordered and organized. This kind of adventure, sneaking out of the house in the middle of the night, not knowing what the future held, was so far off her radar screen as to be in the realm of things never thought of.

Finally, for the next thirty seconds or so, it was just David and Ski alone in the house, and in that time, David realized that it was an opportunity intentionally engineered by the visitor.

"Look Mr. Skinner," Ski said, his expression suddenly as serious as that of a soldier on a deadly mission, "I don't know how to soften this, so I'm just going to let you have it, okay? Your family are all American citizens, and as such have certain rights for protection under the rules of the Treaty. You're British and don't. You're invited along as a courtesy—as a nod to the head of an otherwise American household. If we get stopped along the way, I will have no authority to protect you from the locals. I will have no choice but to hand you over. Do you understand?"

David stared blankly, stunned by the words he'd just heard and overwhelmed with the sense that all the air had just been sucked out of the room.

Ski gave his best room-lighting smile. "I tell you this just so you know the deal." He peeked out the window again. "Okay, it's your turn," he said.

For Pablo Martinez, it had been another long night on the heels of many other long nights triggered by yet another threat on his life. The difference this time—and it was a *huge* difference—was that this time his family was as involved in the danger as he was.

As the eastern sky brightened, he fought to keep his anger focused where it belonged—on Manuel Noriega—and not on Kurt, who never did realize the size of the tiger whose tail he took such pleasure in pulling. God knew he'd been warned. Pablo had fought like a banshee to keep Kurt from overcommitting to the cause from which, as an American citizen, he could have walked away at any time, but much like Pablo's own son, Antonio, Kurt suffered from the curse of youth everywhere: the illusion of immortality. The incompetence with which Noriega had pursued the perpetrators of La Voz had only enabled them further.

As Pablo and Victoria cruised through the night on their way to their daughter's house in the country, Pablo's mind was preoccupied with thoughts of his family, of what they must have gone through all these years, and of what lay ahead in the unknown. Their other son, Raul, had been shocked to see his parents standing there outside his apartment at such a ridiculous hour of the morning. Raul, of course, had no idea of what his father had been up to with his involvement in La Voz, and he'd been as shocked as Victoria to learn the details. Dutiful son that he was, he naturally offered his parents asylum at his apartment, which they politely refused. It was too dangerous, Pablo explained, for him to remain in the city, and it would have been foolish to involve Raul so late in the game.

Instead, they would travel to their daughter Maritza's house, where they would lay low long enough to assess the damage that had been done by Kurt Muse's arrest. What Pablo had not told his worried son, and what even Victoria did not know, was that one of the illicit transmitters—more specifically, an illicit television station that the CIA had provided, but which they had yet to use—was in fact nestled in an apartment in Raul's building. If Pablo were caught there, the link would be made, and their last, tiniest, chance of success would evaporate like a cup of water in the desert.

"Will the boys be safe?" Victoria asked in the darkness of the Buick.

Pablo nodded thoughtfully. "Raul, certainly, will be fine. He had nothing to do with any of this."

"But if the PDF connect you with Kurt . . ." Her voice trailed off, as if she didn't want to consider the rest.

"The only way for that connection to be made is for Kurt to tell them what we were doing. He will not." He said it with finality, as if it were a foregone conclusion.

"You can't know that," she said. "No one can know what they might endure under interrogation."

It was understood without saying that interrogation meant torture, and that more than any other reason defined why Pablo would never let himself be taken. "Kurt is strong," he said. "He will protect his friends." Of the two of them in the car, he was not sure whom he was most trying to convince.

For a long moment after that, silence prevailed. Then, Victoria said softly, "And I think Antonio will be fine, too."

Ah, Antonio. Angry, compulsive, energetic Antonio. The young man who would always be a boy in his father's mind had fought hard to convince his parents to slip into exile with him, and now that they'd refused, he was really angry.

Of course, to Antonio it was all an adventure, the true initiation into the revolutionary life to which he had so long aspired. Well, God bless him for it. At least he'd be safe in America—safer, anyway, than he'd be remaining here in Panama. No father would ever wish exile on his son, but if it had to come, he couldn't imagine a better circumstance.

For Pablo, though, none of this had ever been about romance or adventure. For him, it was about preserving an ideal of freedom that he once had known, yet his idealistic son had never tasted. Pablo had absorbed too much responsibility to afford the luxury of a romantic view of politics. There was good and there was evil; there was freedom and there was totalitarianism. Those who did not fight for one were doomed to endure the other. Even beyond his role as family patriarch, he was also the general manager of a major insurance company and a powerful influence in both the Rotary, and by extension, in the National Civic Crusade. He shared Antonio's hatred for Noriega, but Pablo had been around the block enough times and was an old enough hand at political activism to know that the anger had to be spread thicker than that.

Noriega had to be removed from power, of that there was no question and no argument—except from the lackeys and goons who were on his payroll. What Antonio's generation seemed to forget, however, and what Pablo rarely endeavored to remind them, was that but for the interference of the U.S. government, Noriega never would have risen to power in the first place.

Like so much of the political unpleasantness in Latin America, Noriega rode to power on the money machine that was drugs. As early as the 1970s, as President Omar Torrijos ran the government, the United States was working with Manuel Noriega—then an upstart nobody with grandiose ambitions to funnel Colombian drugs through Panama so that the pathways could be traced with an eye toward one day disrupting and destroying them. Noriega, of course, had been shrewd enough to report only a fraction of the total traffic, choosing to keep the remainder of the cash for himself. The money fueled his ability to bribe and steal, even as he bought influence and credibility with the United States by providing always-reliable information to keep the drug war engaged. That he only ratted out his enemies while protecting his friends was common knowledge within the U.S. intelligence community, but knowledge was just so much gossip if the community receiving it lacked the political wherewithal to do something about it.

It was the most frustrating part of the American involvement in Panama: while the State Department hated the corruption and the brutality of the regime, and fought valiantly to foment change, the CIA thrived on the information that was funneled to it. More recently, the Drug Enforcement Administration likewise thrived under careful manipulation by Noriega, and as long as he could continue to offer up victories in the never-ending war against drugs, it was certainly not going to get into the way of a little graft. Add into the mix the overwhelming ambivalence of the American people in any events in Central American politics, and the result was one of benign neglect for the people of Panama.

Actually, even benign neglect would have been an improvement. In Panama, the American neglect was purposeful, and it was all designed to make the Canal Zone Treaty run as smoothly as possible. The logic, as best Pablo could understand it, rallied around the notion that taking a moral stand might antagonize a brutal dictator, who in turn might take to the airwaves and say unpleasant things about a nation that was *giving away* the multibillion-dollar investment that but for its existence would have left Panama an unnoticed strip of land on the world's atlases. It was enough to make you dizzy.

But it was the world in which they lived, and it was the world in which they must ultimately thrive. Making sense would only have been the proverbial icing on the cake.

Driving through the night into the countryside, it was difficult for Pablo to fight off the disappointment brought on by Kurt's arrest. Pablo Martinez had been fighting for change in Panama for as long as he could remember, and after decades of minimal progress, he'd thought that this time they might actually have been close. Now, it was all gone. Now, they were back to where they were before Kurt and Tomás Muñoz first approached him with their illicit transmitter scheme.

But maybe it wasn't all gone after all. The transmitters were in place, and they were all on timers. If they could just be left alone for a little while—just another month—then maybe there would be purpose to what they had done, and for what Kurt was about to endure. Even as he toyed with these thoughts, though, he knew that it could never be. Now that Noriega had a face to put to the transmissions that had been making his life so miserable, he would not rest until he found the transmitters. And when he looked hard enough at the engineering, it would be a very short step for him to learn of the CIA's ultimate involvement, and when that little tidbit came to life, well, all hell would break loose.

Perhaps that was a little part of his disappointment as well. When the CIA connection was finally made, the Pineapple would undoubtedly draw the conclusion that this had been an Agency operation all along, when nothing could have been further from the truth. The Agency didn't get involved until after the radios had been online for over a year, and even then it was only because the conspirators could no longer afford to fork out the money month after month for apartments in which to house their transmitters.

Perhaps it would have been different if the U.S. government hadn't been so efficient at transferring their operatives from one place to another. In the early days of Radio Constitucional—the precursor to La Voz—Kurt had been able to maintain unofficial contact with the Agency through long-time family friend Suzanne Alexander, who just happened to be an employee of the CIA, and through whom Kurt would communicate concerns and pass along the occasional intelligence tidbit that they had picked up through their eavesdropping. Between her and Richard Dotson, who worked for the State Department and was therefore able to be openly supportive of Noriega's downfall, the band of conspirators always felt as if they had the ear and the attention of people in power.

Then, both of these conduits were rotated out of Panama back to their respective headquarters, where they were no longer in a position to monitor Panamanian activities, even from afar. As a gesture of friendship and support, Suzanne passed Kurt's name and number on to her replacement in Panama City, an incompetent bitch named Jocelyn, who in a matter of a few short weeks managed to undo the fledgling trust that La Voz had begun to build with the Agency.

Kurt had told the story of the betrayals to Pablo—and others in his presence—so many times and in such detail that Pablo felt sometimes as if he'd witnessed the events himself.

Her first offer was a trade. The Agency had expressed an interest in the code book that Kurt and his compatriots had developed to translate PDF radio transmissions into useable information. In return for a copy of the codes, Jocelyn would provide additional information that La Voz had yet to be able to obtain—the specific locations codes for PDF operating stations. At the end of the day, both groups would have a more complete list, and with it, La Voz would be even more empowered to wreak havoc at its will.

The meeting was set for a day in the late summer, at Jocelyn's apartment in Punta Paitilla, a residential neighborhood in Panama City. It was hardly the stuff of spycraft. Kurt arrived at the appointed time with his code book tucked into one of his socks and knocked on the apartment door. Jocelyn was waiting for him. They chatted for a minute or two, and then it was time to make the exchange. Just as they'd planned, Kurt handed over his notebook of broken codes, and Jocelyn handed over . . . nothing. Not a damn thing. She just took his book and walked away, knowing damn well that Kurt couldn't start shouting in so crowded a building. "Where is the information you promised?" he asked.

Jocelyn smirked and shook her head. "Oh, it turns out that I'm not permitted to share that with you after all. I'd be happy to pay you for your book, though. Name a reasonable price, and it's yours."

Kurt was stunned. "A *price*? You think I'm in this for the money?"

She shrugged. Everyone was in it for the money. What else was there?

He couldn't believe the betrayal. "I'm not your whore," he said. "I don't perform for money."

"Suit yourself. I just had to make the offer."

A long moment passed. Kurt stared, dumbfounded, and Jocelyn smirked. Clearly, the days of cooperation had ended.

The first thing Kurt did at the end of that meeting—the very first thing—was to call Suzanne in her office, on an open phone line, to tell her, "Look, I know we're friends, but professionally, we're through. Don't ever call me for information again. As far as I'm concerned, the CIA is just a class of idiots and thieves. Pass it along to whoever wants to hear that I never want to talk to the Agency again. Never."

So, when the phone rang a few months later with yet another offer from the CIA, Kurt was genuinely and thoroughly shocked. It came on a Sunday afternoon when Kurt was involved in nothing in particular, sitting at home with his family. The phone rang, and when Kurt answered it, the male voice on the other end carried the attitude of long-standing friendship.

"Is this Kurt Muse?" the voice asked.

"It is."

"How nice to finally get a chance to talk to you. We have a common friend of many years. Suzanne Alexander sends her regards."

Invoking the name of Kurt's old friend made it obvious in an instant that the caller was from the CIA, and no one from the CIA ever made social calls. "Certainly send her my regards," Kurt said. "But surely she made it clear that I am not interested in speaking to any of her friends."

"She did mention that," the caller said, "but I don't run with the same crowd as the one you met. I like to think of myself as being above them, spending most of my time in the palace instead of wallowing in the caves, if you know what I mean."

Kurt found himself nodding. He couldn't know exactly what he meant, of course, but it sounded like this friend of Suzanne's worked not at the Panama station at Corozal, but at the Puzzle Palace—CIA headquarters at Langley. Kurt knew for a fact that that was where Suzanne had been transferred. "Well, it was nice of her to have you look me up. Do you have a name?"

"Of course I do," he said. "I'd like to schedule a get-together, if that's all right. You know, to catch up on old times."

Speaking in code like this grew old very quickly and always felt a little silly. Still, in a nation where every phone was tapped, one had to be careful. "I can't imagine that we'd have much to talk about," Kurt said. "For sure, I know that *I* don't have much to talk to *you* about."

"Still," the man said, "how about a meeting? A picnic, perhaps, in Suzanne's favorite spot."

Kurt knew exactly what he meant. There was a spot among the *bohios*—thatched roofed pole tents—at Albrook Air Force Base where the Muses and Suzanne had enjoyed a picnic shortly before she left for the States. She'd mentioned at the time that it was one of her favorite spots. "I suppose I could make time for that," he said cautiously. "Pick a time."

"Tomorrow morning works well for me. Say, around eleven o'clock."

"I'll be there. Do you mind if I bring a friend?"

"Not at all. I'd be surprised if you didn't."

Kurt couldn't decide if the openness of this man was refreshing or off-putting. "How will I recognize you?"

"My friends call me Father Frank," he said. And then he hung up.

It turned out to be all the identification Kurt would need. He and Tomás showed up ten minutes early and hung back in the parking lot, scoping things out before committing full out to the meeting. The whole thing smelled a lot like a setup. Had the mysterious caller invoked any name but Suzanne's, Kurt might not have shown up. And of course, there was always the possibility that this Father Frank had merely dropped the name without permission, and it was a setup anyway. Kurt cursed himself for not having thought to call Suzanne to verify things.

"What do you suppose he wants?" Tomás asked.

"Something we have that they don't, I would imagine. Just like last time." Kurt had always been slow to shrug off past injustices.

"Maybe they've changed their minds and want to help us again."

"I think we're doing just fine on our own," Kurt countered. "You start taking help from Uncle Sam, and suddenly you find yourself at the tip of the tail when you used to be on the point of the nose. I've learned that nothing comes from Uncle without a price."

While Kurt spoke, both of them noted an old man—easily in his sixties—making his way up the sloping grass from the far side of the parking lot toward the *bohios*. "That's got to be Father Frank," Kurt said, pointing. Sure enough, the portly old guy with the bald spot on the crown of his head looked like a cross between Friar Tuck and Father Flannigan. Put him in a cassock, and he'd be right out of Central Casting as a priest.

"Okay," Kurt said with a sigh. "It's show time."

He and Tomás opened their doors together and walked briskly, purposefully on a path that would intersect that of their new CIA contact.

As they approached, Father Frank met them with a beaming smile. "Kurt Muse," he said, extending his hand. He had the grip of a twenty-year-old. "And you must be Tomás Muñoz," he said, offering a set of crushed metacarpals to Kurt's accomplice. "I'm glad you could accommodate me."

"I think it's a little early to say that we're accommodating anybody," Kurt said. "We're here to listen."

Father Frank considered that and nodded. "Of course you are. I didn't mean to be too forward. It's a beautiful day, isn't it?" He rocked his head back and pointed his face to the sky. "I can understand how my colleagues become so attached to this place."

"So you are not from here?" Tomás probed.

Father Frank seemed surprised by the question. "Oh, heavens no. I've been here a few times, of course, but not in a very long time. I guess I've been about everywhere once or twice."

"That means you're from Langley?" Kurt surmised.

Father Frank half shrugged. "Close enough to the truth to not be a lie," he said. "But we're not here to talk about me."

"I am," Kurt said.

Father Frank's eyes hardened; just for an instant, but it was there to see if you were watching. "Well, I'm not. I'm here to patch up some old wounds and to tell you that things are a lot different up north these days. As I'm sure you know, political winds change direction from time to time, and for the foreseeable future, they seem to be blowing in *your* direction."

"For the foreseeable future," Kurt said, tasting the words. "Why does that comfort me so little?"

Father Frank seemed amused. "Ah, a cynic. Well, I suppose we've earned that. And a little well-considered cynicism never hurt anyone. Hell, it's probably kept a few people alive. But as an old hand at such things, I urge you to weigh the phrase 'well considered.' New elections bring new opportunities, and not just in the third world. It would be a mistake to confuse the priorities of the old administration in Washington with those of the new."

"That wasn't an election, that was a rout," Kurt snorted. "The vice president was promoted to president."

"Don't underestimate the title change," Father Frank warned. "President Bush is a Texan. His view of this part of the world is a lot different from that of the Californian who preceded him. This is truly a new day. If I were you, I'd be pleased."

"Then I'm pleased," Kurt said. He was feeling petulant, and it showed.

"What do you want from us?" Tomás asked.

Father Frank shook his head. "It's not a matter of wanting from you," he said. "It's a matter of providing *for* you." He reached into his pants pocket and produced a standard number ten envelope thick with what could only be cash. "Here's a couple thousand dollars," he said, handing the envelope not to Kurt but to Tomás. "Consider it a gesture of good faith. If you need something else, I'm the man to get it for you."

"We don't need your money," Kurt said, noting without comment that the envelope had been handed to the only non-American among them.

"Of course you do. You've got leases to pay, equipment to maintain." He stated this plainly, as the facts he knew them to be. "Surely you're not waiting for DelValle to change his mind." There was that amused look again.

Kurt still wasn't ready to buy what he was selling. "What's the catch?"

Father Frank scowled and shook his head. "No catch."

"There's always a catch with you guys."

"No, there's *sometimes* a catch with us guys," Father Frank corrected, "and this happens not to be one of those times." He paused for a moment to gather his thoughts. "Look. You need to forget about what happened during those former administrations, okay? There's a new sheriff in town, and he gets to decide where there's a catch and where there's not. It's not something I can prove to you before the fact. You're either going to trust me and learn for yourself if it was worth the risk, or you won't. At this stage, all I can do is talk."

"So, what are you telling me?" Kurt pressed. "That Woerner and Chiang have both had a great change of heart just because they've got a new commander in chief? Or are you telling me that for all those years of planting their noses up Noriega's ass they were just reflecting the whim of previous administrations?"

Father Frank seemed committed to avoiding the fight that Kurt was so actively trolling for. "I'm telling you that Woerner and Chiang are both irrelevant to you. They have their chain of command, and I have mine."

"And they all come together at the top."

"But not below the top. That's the point."

And it was a point that gave Kurt a moment of pause. "So you expect me to believe that neither the commander of SouthCom nor the CIA chief of station know that you're here."

There was that smile again. "And if they did, they'd both shit the proverbial brick."

Kurt exchanged glances with Tomás. It still felt too good to be true. "But why?"

Father Frank cocked his head. "Come on, Kurt, you're smarter than that."

"Because Noriega's going down," Kurt breathed, finally connecting the dots.

"I'll say it again," Father Frank smiled. "There's a new sheriff in town." It was an interesting smile, too. Kurt wondered if this new contact truly cared about the politics he was affecting, or if he merely enjoyed the thrill of interfering with things. It wasn't a question he could ask, because it wasn't an answer he necessarily wanted to hear.

"We won't take payment for what we're doing," Kurt said. "I will not be an employee of the Agency."

"That's good, because this isn't a job interview. This is an offer to pay some expenses, and to provide ongoing assistance in the future." With a snort of laughter, he turned to Tomás. "Is he this hard to give a gift to at Christmas?"

"We need a battery backup," Tomás said.

"Excuse me?"

"You said you could provide for us. I need you to provide a battery backup."

"For what?"

"Our transmitters. Every time we cycle them on, the Pineapple gets closer and closer to triangulating on them."

Kurt picked up on the explanation. "I don't know how much Suzanne has told you."

"I know that the good general has brought in Cuban radio guys to look for you. That's very high-profile, by the way. Shows you're getting his goat. Congratulations."

In spite of his desire to dislike this guy, Kurt was finding him to be quite charming. "Well, their new strategy is to wait till one of the transmissions kicks in, and then they start cutting the power grids in the city, one section at a time. When the signal dies, they know which section to start looking in."

Father Frank raised his eyebrows, impressed. "That's actually a pretty smart move coming from such a small mind."

"Had to be the influence of the Cubans," Kurt laughed. "Anyway, they've already come close enough to one of the transmitters that we can't risk using it again. On the others, we're sort of out of business for a while."

Father Frank stewed on the problem for a moment. "So, you figure that with a battery backup you'll keep transmitting no matter what happens with the power." The smile bloomed even larger. "That'll frustrate the hell out of him." The smile turned to a laugh as Father Frank clapped him on the shoulder. "I like the way you think, Muse. I like the way you think. I'll get it to you within a week. Are there any special parameters or technical details I need to know?"

Tomás recited the name and model number of the transmitter from memory, and then did it again after Father Frank had time to muster up a pen and a pad of paper.

"As for the cash," Kurt started.

The old man waved him off before he had a chance to form the question. "Use it as you wish. I don't care. Buy more equipment, pay off a lease, do whatever you want."

Despite having been down a similar road with the Agency before, Kurt noted how different the road actually felt this time around. In the past, he'd always been the beggar, the runt of the litter struggling for a turn at the teat. This time, they had come to him, and the story Father Frank told seemed not only plausible, but sensible. Besides, how could you not trust a man who looked like a cross between Friar Tuck and Father Flannigan?

"All right," Kurt said at length. "We'll take the money and we'll put it to good use."

Tomás did him one better. "When we meet again, within a week, I'll be sure to give you a receipt and a full accounting of where the money went." Kurt nodded his approval as the offer was made.

Father Frank let go with a laugh that seemed to come from his very core. It was a hearty, throaty thing that you might expect to hear from your grandfather after a really good joke. "Oh, God," he said, "please don't do that. This is the CIA, for God's sake. We're spies. We don't do receipts. The last thing we want anywhere in the world is a paper trail." He laughed again as he waved and headed back down the hill. "Thanks for the offer, though."

When the Cheshire Cat departed Alice, he left his smile behind. With Father Frank, it was the hearty laugh that stayed behind. As he watched the old spy walk toward his car, Kurt couldn't escape the feeling that somewhere, an office full of people would be howling at the story of the rookie spies who offered to give receipts.

10

Time for Kurt had ceased to have any meaning. He knew, certainly, that hours had passed, but for all he knew, it could have been days. The disorientation bothered him, and he cursed himself for not paying better attention, but then he realized that disorientation was probably part of a larger design. What he knew of interrogation techniques could fill a thimble. His sources were limited to the spy novels he'd read and the movies he'd seen over the years.

Now, as he lay curled under a desk in a pitch black office in yet another police substation—following to the letter the very specific orders he'd been given—this lack of training and preparation seemed like the most elementary and yet most foolish kind of mistake. Jesus God, what had he gotten himself into?

The first glimpse of reality hit in the twenty minutes or so that Kurt sat in that pickup truck watching his parents' apartment being ransacked. The logic train was as simple as it was disturbing: Nana and Papi would be implicated and indicted on trumped-up charges, or, as time progressed, they would be used as human bait to get Kurt to open up and tell the PDF everything that he knew. Either way, it was a horrible outcome to consider. Papi was strong—stronger by half than any goon the PDF could throw at him—but Nana was not. She was never meant to be. Her strength lay in morality and nobility. The very thought of what they might do to her as a result of her son's antics turned Kurt's stomach.

Would the fact that his parents knew nothing of his operation—truly *nothing* of it—keep them from the interrogators, or would it just make their ordeal a thousand times worse as the torturers tried to extract information that they'd never possessed? He prayed that they'd gotten away in time. If they hadn't, then by definition his children hadn't, and the thought made his head swim faster and faster.

No, he told himself. Don't think like that. You're scared right now, and fear is the breeding ground for all kinds of negative thoughts and feelings. Destructive feelings. He'd only been into this thing for a short while—whether hours or days, it still hadn't been weeks or months. No one had hurt him. No one had threatened to hurt him, at least not in the physical sense. It was far too early to let hope drip away like that.

His family would get away. Tomás, Pablo, Antonio, Coronado, and all the others would get away. They had to. And even if they hadn't, for the time being, Kurt had to believe that they had. He had to believe at every binary option that the preferable outcome had prevailed until proven otherwise.

Down the hall, from another room in the substation, he could hear a harsh exchange of words, and he could hear the sound of crying. The walls were too thick, or the distances long enough that he couldn't make out the words, but he forced himself to believe that the female voice was neither his daughter nor his mother. Nor was it any of his friends' wives. For all he knew, it was just a couple of actors playing out a scene that was designed specifically to make him think the thoughts he was thinking.

It's not them, he told himself forcefully, and then he struggled desperately to find a way to justify the conclusion. It certainly didn't sound like any voice he'd heard, but what does one really sound like when one is being tortured?

Then he got it: If it were his family or friends, the torture would be meted out in his presence, so he could watch and beg for it to stop. When the loved ones were on the brink of disfigurement or worse, the torturers would then turn to Kurt, who would willingly tell them everything they wanted to know, selling out everyone he knew. But since he couldn't see them, the voices were owned by people he didn't know.

That such fragile logic gave him comfort made him realize that captivity had already begun to transform him into a different man.

*   *   *

Kimberly hated being ignored. She hated being locked into a room, and she hated being segregated from all the others with whom she obviously had something in common, even if she didn't yet know what that was.

"What's happening?" Erik asked for the three thousandth time. "Where's Dad? Where are Nana and Papi? What's going to happen to us? Why can't we be with the others?"

The questions went on and on and on, and Kimberly was running out of ways to say, "I don't know" without losing her temper. She didn't know *anything*. So far as she could tell, *no one* knew anything. People just talked quickly, and none of them plainly enough that she could hear what they were saying through the walls of the tiny office where they'd been stashed.

The fear that blossomed in her belly had a physical weight, a gnawing, awful sense that life had irreversibly taken a wrong turn. She found herself worrying about everything. Not just her dad and mom, but Nana, Papi, Uncle David, Aunt Carol, Joey, and all those people huddled in the front room. She worried about what tomorrow could possibly bring when she clearly could not return to the house, and she just as clearly had no other place to go.

As the fear took root, and as the sense of loneliness and separation grew deeper, she couldn't help but wonder what she had done to be punished this way. She could tell in the attitudes of her grandparents, and in the looks in the eyes of those Panamanians out front that she had somehow been cast as the bad guy in a drama where she didn't begin to understand the action, let alone the plot. They should be feeling *sorry* for her, for heaven's sake. They shouldn't be treating her as if she'd done something wrong. She was just a kid! Her father had been arrested, and now she and her little brother were all alone. Where was the sympathy? Where were the hugs? None of this made sense and none of it was fair.

She looked over to her little brother as he asked his latest set of questions, and she held out her arm for him to snuggle against her. The fact that he didn't even hesitate spoke volumes about just how much the world had changed in the last few hours. At twelve, Erik's job—and he did it well—was to bug his big sister. While he loved being with Kimberly, and his need for her attention was insatiable, he hadn't yet discovered an avenue of expression that didn't involve perpetual annoyance. Certainly, it was not like him to show affection or to take a hug, but for right now that seemed to be what was most important to him.

It frightened Kimberly to think that for the foreseeable future, with only three years separating them, she had assumed the role of being the mother, while Erik seemed to grow even younger as he shrank away from the fear.

When she thought about it, actually, it kind of pissed her off. Now, besides all the other burdens of the evening, she had to swallow her own fear so she could put on a face of calm detachment that would keep Erik's own panic from entering the stratosphere.

Oh, God, Daddy, what did you do?

Kimberly watched as the clock on the wall buzzed its way past six o'clock in the morning. She tried to imagine where the time had gone, even as she wondered how it could possibly be less than a week since the time when she was studying for something as mundane as a biology exam.

Another stab of fear jolted through her belly. She was going to get a zero on the exam!

Before she had a chance to wrap her mind around that, the door to their office-prison opened, revealing a handsome American with the physical demeanor of a soldier, but the haircut and the clothes of a college kid.

"Time to go," he announced.

Kimberly and Erik stood together. "Go where?" Kimberly asked.

"Just follow me, please." He wasn't the same soldier who had led them to the room in the first place, but clearly he'd been trained by the same boss. Kimberly marveled at how efficiently and effectively these people could make an order sound like a request.

She wanted to resist. She wanted to dig in her heels and demand that somebody start coughing up answers before she did anything. Then again, she wanted to be at home in her own bed, but that wasn't going to happen, either.

Keeping a hand on Erik's shoulder, she followed the soldier out of the office, through the now-empty main room, and finally to another office where Nana and Papi sat with Carol, David, and Joey in the company of several serious-looking strangers.

". . . can't stay here," a major said to the rest of the family as the door opened. "It's going on oh-six-thirty. In an hour, this place is going to be swarming with employees, Americans and Panamanians alike, and you just flat-out can't be here."

Kimberly didn't like the gravity in the major's voice, and from the look in Papi's face, he didn't much like it, either. But somehow, the arrival of the kids in the room seemed to decide whatever issue was being debated. All eyes turned to greet them, and again, they all showed some mixture of empathy and discomfort.

The major stood and offered a forced, institutional smile. "You must be Kimberly and Erik," he said, offering his hand. "I'm Major Mansfield. We've actually met, although you might not remember. Your grandmother and I have worked together. It's very nice to see you again."

"Where's my father?" Erik asked. "What's happening to us?"

"Your father will be fine," the major said dismissively. "Right now, we need to get you to a safe place."

"Are we in danger?" Kimberly asked.

Major Mansfield dodged the question. "You'll be perfectly safe, so long as you do what I tell you, okay? I know you have a lot of questions, and if I had answers, I swear to God I'd share them with you. But that's not where we are. What we need is to get you out of here and nestled into someplace comfortable—someplace where you can get some food and rest—and then we'll start on the next big steps. Is that okay with you?"

Erik and Kimberly exchanged glances. Neither of them had a clue what the major was talking about, but from the way the question was structured, it was obvious that there was a right and a wrong answer. They nodded in unison.

"Good," Mansfield said. He looked to the others. "We'll let the Muse children go first, okay?" Again, the "okay" at the end of the sentence was clearly a bit of verbal decoration. If someone had said "hell no," it wouldn't have mattered.

With the concession of the extended family assumed, Mansfield went on, "I want you to follow Ski here"—he nodded to the soldier with the long hair—"out to the car that's waiting outside. I want you to move quickly without running, and I want you to slouch down low in the seats once you're there, and stay down low until your driver says it's okay to sit up again. When you get to the place where you're go-ing, we're going to do exactly the opposite. We're going to open your doors for you—don't open them yourselves, okay?—and when Ski tells you it's okay, then I want you to walk quickly without running to the door that will be open for you." When he finished, Mansfield had an expectant look on his face, like a fellow who had just told a couple of kids about the plan to get ice cream after school. "Is that okay with you?"

"Where are you taking us?" Kimberly asked.

"You'll be with your grandparents," Mansfield said. Apparently, he hadn't heard the question.

"No, what I asked was—"

"Kimberly." Papi said her name with a finality that told her it was time to stop talking.

Just like that, the decision was made. Whatever was happening was either so awful or so secret that the people who worked in the Provost Marshal's office had to be kept in the dark. Kimberly still didn't know what that meant exactly, but she knew that none of it was good.

She started to ask if Carol and David and the rest of the family were coming along as well, but opted not to. She didn't recognize the Papi that she was seeing now. She was confused. Ski was standing at the door. It was time to start the rest of her life.

The drive to the safe house was a quick one, just five, maybe seven minutes. That's what they called it, too—a safe house—as if they were in the midst of some witness protection program or something. From where she sat, hunched down in the back of the car—they only drove Toyotas, it seemed—she couldn't tell exactly where they'd ended up, but just from the traffic patterns and the brevity of the trip, she figured it had to still be on post at Clayton somewhere.

"Okay," Ski said, slinging his arm over the back of the seat so he could look at them. "Remember what Major Mansfield told you. Walk quickly, but no running. Keep your eyes forward and just keep walk-ing toward the back door, the one that's open. Got it?"

Kimberly and Erik nodded in unison. The keeping her head down part made her nervous. Were people going to be shooting at them or something?

"Wait for me to come around and open the door."

The kids did exactly as they were told, their hands gripped tightly together, Kimberly lugging Erik's overnight bag. They led the way up a low hill on which sat a single family house that probably had once belonged to a major or lieutenant colonel. It was a pretty good size from the outside, two stories, but nothing like the palaces on the other side of the post where the bird colonels lived. Ski brought up the rear, keeping them moving without having to push. Up ahead, at the back door, stood another scruffy-haired soldier. He stood sort of sideways in the door, his hand hanging awkwardly by his side in a way that suggested to Kimberly that he might have been concealing a pistol behind his thigh. All in all, the trip from the car to the door took less than fifteen seconds. Kimberly barely had time to notice that a nice day was nearly fully bloomed.

The inside of the house smelled like the former occupants, whoever they were. Old cooking smells and the faint aroma of dirty socks hung in the air like a neglected ghost. They entered through the kitchen, which appeared to be equipped with the original appliances. They'd probably been black and white at one time, but now they seemed cepia-toned in the dim light of the rising sun. Chipped porcelain and cracked counter tops told the story of too many rambunctious children over the years. The metal cabinets mounted to the walls had been painted so many times that they looked padded, squishy. The cabinet doors mostly gaped open, in Kimberly's mind speaking of one last sweep to make sure that they'd been thoroughly cleaned out before the family moved away.

"The house is empty," Kimberly said. She'd meant it as a question, actually, but thought it just as well to have come out as a statement. The answer was obvious enough.

Neither of the soldiers answered her.

"Are Nana and Papi coming, too?" Erik asked.

Ski just looked at him with a mix of sadness and curiosity. "Stay away from the windows," he said.

The tone sounded distinctly angry, and Erik shot a look to his sister to see if he'd said something wrong. Kimberly forced a smile and put her hand on his shoulder. She wanted to tell him that everything was fine, but absolutely nothing about any of this was even close to fine.

"Come on into the living room," the other soldier said, gesturing through the tiny arched doorway. Again, they did as they were told.

Beyond the kitchen, they walked through a miniscule dining room that was nowhere near big enough for the table and chairs that their mother owned. The wooden floors showed terrible wear, and Kimberly wondered why people didn't take at least good enough care of their houses to put a rug under the dining room chairs.

Leaving the kitchen, the first thing Kimberly noticed was the darkness of the place. A single overhead light in the foyer carried the burden of illuminating the entire downstairs, and its job was made a thousand times more difficult by the fact that someone had nailed olive-drab bed sheets over each of the windows.

"Stay away from the windows," the second soldier said, obviously unaware that they'd already been given their strict instructions.

"It's dark in here," Erik said.

"They don't want people seeing in," Kimberly explained. It was a guess, actually, but apparently a good one, judging from the expression on Ski's face.

"Where are all the other people?" Erik said.

Never all that expressive to begin with, when presented with a direct question, their countenances grew even blanker. Whether by choice or direction, these guys were obviously not going to be sharing any details.

They cleared the dining room in three strides and found themselves in the foyer, facing a living room with a worn sofa on one wall and bare blue-striped mattresses on the floor.

"Have a seat," Ski said.

He had to be kidding. The mattresses were filthy. God only knew who had slept there last, and Kimberly didn't *want* to know what they'd done on them while they'd lain there.

"I guess I know where you got the sheets for the windows," Kimberly quipped.

Neither soldier smiled, but as the nameless one crossed his arms over his chest, she saw for the first time the holstered pistol on his hip.

Erik pointed toward a shadow in the background behind Mr. Nameless. "Are those stairs? Where do they go?"

"Have a seat," Ski said again. "Please." He could make a simple request sound as menacing as a threat to shoot.

"How long are we going to be here?" Kimberly asked. Somewhere deep in her gut, a gush of anger threatened to douse the heat of her fear. They'd done nothing wrong here. Didn't they have some rights? Could they be treated like this legally? Like criminals of some sort? Wasn't there some recourse? She didn't ask any of these things, of course, but she was able to summon up one of those glares that made it very clear to everyone that she was not pleased.

Before either soldier had a chance to answer—or ignore—her, they were all distracted by commotion in the kitchen. The door burst open, and a voice that could only belong to Aunt Carol protested, ". . . demand to know what you are planning for us. I will not be treated this way!"

Hearing her thoughts verbalized, Kimberly was grateful that she'd limited herself to the glare. As one, Ski and Mr. Silent moved back toward the dining room to receive their latest guests.

As Carol passed through the archway into the dining room, her eyes locked right onto Kimberly and she stopped speaking.

Erik moved closer to his sister and grabbed her hand.

Kimberly felt a new breed of angst, as if she and Erik were somehow being held responsible for all that was happening. Suddenly, she felt like an animal in the zoo, watching as people stared at her from the other side of a cage. Somehow, this had become "us" versus "them" and Kimberly and Erik were trapped on the wrong side of the conflict.

"Have a seat," Ski said to the newcomers, motioning toward the mattresses.

No one moved. They just stared in horror at the terrible furnishings.

Ski said, "It's the best we could pull together on short notice." He then went on to renew his instructions to stay away from the windows.

"I don't understand," Erik said. "Who's going to see us? Who's trying to hurt us?"

No one even tried to answer.

Erik caught the subtext, and his face was like a giant O. "But you'll protect us, right?" he asked, pointing to Ski's sidearm. "That's what the guns are for, right?"

Ski shifted uncomfortably. "If you stay away from the windows, you won't have to worry," he said.

They'd barely made their way to the living room when the kitchen door opened and shut again, and the two soldiers returned to the dining room. An instant later, there were Nana and Papi.

Carol practically ran across the room to greet them. "Oh, thank God," she said. "You did decide to come."

Charlie set his jaw, causing his mustache to twitch. "I didn't decide anything," he said. "But it was pretty clear we couldn't stay where we were."

Kimberly and Erik hadn't moved from their spot in the living room. As the room filled with family, she felt curiously more and more detached from all of them. Even when the rest of the family settled in on their mattresses, the others remained segregated on the other side of the room, talking in clear tones about how irresponsible her father was and how many lives he had ruined. They didn't care that Kimberly and Erik could hear every word. Even when the conversation turned mildly hopeful—"How long could they possibly keep him in custody?"—the words still hurt.

Kimberly couldn't wrap her mind around it. Her extended family had never been one of hugs and kisses, but beneath the reserve, there had always resided a layer of love that was supposed to blossom at times like these. There were supposed to be words of encouragement, soothing tones predicting nothing but positive outcomes. There should at least have been a smile.

Maybe in a case like this, there really was no "should" or "ought." Maybe when stresses ran this high—when exhaustion and fear combined forces—people just reacted whatever way felt best. But God almighty, did they hear themselves, she wondered? Carol was worried about her home and her dog; Uncle David and Papi were worried about their business and employees. She supposed that all those things were bad, but she'd lost her father! She'd lost everything about her life, everything she'd ever known, and they were worried about employees and pets.

It wasn't right. None of it was right.

Under the circumstances, would a comforting smile have been too much to ask?

11

Kurt realized with no small measure of distress that sleep deprivation would be one of their primary weapons, and already it was beginning to take its toll. His head wasn't as clear as it once had been, and he was completely unaware of the time. Curiously, he had a watch, but without a date to correlate to the time, the hands on the timepiece could just as well have been the random spin of a child's toy. As time wore on, he realized that he was forgetting the previous answers he'd given to questions they'd asked him, and therefore he was hesitating a little too long as the interrogations continued.

Clearly, they knew he was hiding something, but they still hadn't been able to figure out what it was.

Hours ago, they'd transferred him yet again, this time to the San Felipe headquarters of the DENI. Even from the outside, the squat, sprawling building looked liked the monument to misery that it truly was. Once inside, though, the misery was trumped by terror.

Gone was the shelter of the desk, replaced by yet another hard-backed chair facing a wall of file cabinets. The questions thus far had been cursory, exploratory. They were still hunting for what they'd actually found in Kurt Muse. Clearly, whoever had betrayed him—and now, he was coming to grips with the fact that betrayal was the only possible explanation for his arrest—hadn't done enough research to report it all. But how could that possibly be? How could the PDF authorities possibly know to arrest him, yet at the same time not know why they were arresting him? And whatever the incentive for the betrayal—it had to be either money or privilege, because that was the backbone of all Noriega betrayals—how could it have been realized without all the blanks being filled? It was a puzzle of the worst kind, and he sensed that he was embarking on a trip that would allow him infinite time to consider the possibilities.

One thing was clear, however: There was something about Kurt, or about his situation, that made these people nervous. He sensed that it had everything to do with some combination of his American citizenship and the fact that Annie was a DoD employee. Under the terms of the Panama Canal Treaty, which the entire Panamanian hierarchy lived in fear of upsetting, local authorities had to treat American dependents with a certain grudging respect. No matter how you cut it, though, it seemed clear that they still had no idea that they'd collared the heart and soul of La Voz de la Libertad. To keep him on edge, to keep him from falling asleep, they positioned a blaring boom box on a table just next to his head. In one of life's great ironies, the speakers sported the broadcasts of Radio Nacionale—the very station he and his friends had victimized so many times.

Kurt nearly jumped out of his chair as the door to the tiny office where he was being held burst open to reveal a tough-as-nails DENI interrogator. He entered the room calmly, flanked by two henchmen. The lieutenant held something in his hand, and his smirk betrayed his discovery of information he thought to be valuable.

"How long did you think you could keep your secret, Mr. Muse?" the interrogator asked in Spanish.

Kurt felt his stomach drop. The way the man was holding the paper, he couldn't see what it was, and he wracked his brain to sort through the possibilities. He decided to stall for time. "I don't know what you're talking about."

The smirk disappeared, replaced by a hard glare. He thrust the paper forward so Kurt could see it. "This," he said.

Kurt recoiled from the sudden movement and had to position his head just so to read what was clearly a list of names. It took him a couple of seconds to realize what he was looking at, and when he did, he had to work hard not to smile. "That's my son's old Cub Scout roster," he said truthfully.

The DENI officer looked stunned, and then angry. "Do not play me for a fool, Mr. Muse. How do you explain this?" He thrust his finger at a notation next to Kurt's name that said PDC. "You are the American coordinator for the Partido Demócrata Cristiano." The PDC—translated as the Christian Democratic Party—was considered by Noriega to be a group of seditious rabble-rousers, and its members were frequently the targets of Noriega's henchmen.

Kurt's relief was so profound that he could not help but laugh. "It's a Cub Scout list! PDC stood for Picnic Day Committee. I was the chairman of the Picnic Day Committee."

The laughter was a mistake.

"You think this is *funny*, Mr. Muse?" The officer's eyes burned hot with anger.

Kurt's smile evaporated. He knew he was in trouble—deeper trouble than he'd been before.

The officer said to his henchmen, "He thinks this is funny. He thinks this is a game. He thinks he can lie to us."

Kurt tried, "I don't—"

The DENI officer boomed, "No more lies!" He drew his 9mm Baretta from its holster as he disappeared behind Kurt.

An instant later, Kurt felt the barrel pressing tightly against the back of his skull, and then heard the sound of the hammer being cocked.

"You think it's funny to lie, I think it's funny to blow your brains out." He pressed the barrel against Kurt's head as if trying to push the weapon through his brain.

The images of Annie, Kimberly, and Erik appeared in Kurt's mind, their faces clear and beautiful. "I love you," he thought aloud.

By late afternoon, the atmosphere in the safe house somewhere in the middle of Fort Clayton had become miserable. A couple of hours into it, an MP had brought by some box lunches for breakfast—chicken patties that had seen way too much time in the deep fryer—and a couple hours after that, a female MP had come by and taken orders for special toiletry items targeted mainly at the ladies. But other than that, nothing but sleep broke the oppressive boredom. With every passing moment, Kimberly felt herself and her brother being pushed farther and farther away from the heart of the family.

Ski and Mr. Silent were clearly there to protect them from any harm, and for that, Kimberly felt a certain grudging appreciation. As uncomfortable as this place was, they didn't even get a chance to sit down. It was a little like they were enduring the same hardships as the people they were protecting, except, of course, that they would get to go home tonight to a house they recognized.

At about 4:30, the front door opened, and five soldiers flooded into the room. Unlike the other soldiers they'd interacted with, these were actually in uniform, unafraid, it would seem, of being recognized as what they really were. In a ritual that Kimberly was beginning to get used to, none of them bothered to identify themselves. The presumptive leader was the one with the clipboard. "Okay," he said. "I need to know once and for all who's going."

"Going where?" Carol asked, rising from the sofa.

The question seemed to knock Mr. Clipboard off balance. "Your next location," he said hesitantly.

"We're not going anywhere," Papi said. David confirmed the sentiment with a nod.

The leader's eyes narrowed as he surveyed the cast in front of him. "Which are the Muse children? The *Kurt* Muse children?"

The rest of the family pointed at Kimberly and Erik before they had a chance to point to themselves.

"Well, you two *are* going," the soldier said. "That's not negotiable. For the rest of you it's an offer that I strongly recommend you take."

"Our home is in Panama," Papi said. Nana nodded her agreement.

"Used to be," the soldier said. "And maybe it will be again, but right now, you are all wanted people. We assume—and so should you—that every Panamanian face out there on the street is an informer, and they'll go instantly to Noriega and tell him exactly where you are. If you walk out of this house and off of this base, you will be on your own."

"I see no reason to repeat myself," Papi said, and he sat back into his chair. For him, the matter was closed.

The soldier nodded. "Respectfully, sir, I think you're making a foolish decision. I don't know what your son did exactly to get in this much trouble, but whatever it was, there are a lot of people being yanked out of bed and working overtime as a result. It was big, is what I'm trying to tell you, and General Noriega doesn't much like big things coming from Americans. This is likely to get ugly, and I have to tell you"—he looked directly at David as he said this—"if I had a daughter the age of yours, I don't think I'd want her staying some place where her life might constantly be in jeopardy."

"You don't understand," Carol started to say, but the soldier cut her off.

"I understand everything I have to understand, ma'am, which is everything I'm told. The rest of it, with all respect, is stuff I don't care about. My heart goes out to you folks. This must be a terrible ordeal to go through, but here you are. Right now, I think you ought to think about what Panamanian prisons are really like, and decide if that's the kind of place where you want to spend the foreseeable future."

There it was, Kimberly thought, laid out as plain and ugly as it can get, and it was as if all the air was sucked out of the room.

"Can we have some time to think this through?" David asked.

"Take all the time you like in the next sixty seconds." With that, the soldier retreated to a corner near the door to give the refugees some distance to talk.

When all was said and done, though, what was there to discuss? Nana and Papi were staying; that was a given the moment Papi made his initial statement. Everyone else was on their way. "Okay," David said, recalling the soldier. "We're going."

The soldier made a note on his clipboard. "Good," he said. "Now I'd like you all to gather in the kitchen, please." As he spoke, he placed a hand on Kimberly's shoulder to usher her in the right direction.

She resisted. "Nana? Papi? You're not coming?"

Nana sat quietly; Papi seemed preoccupied with distant thoughts.

"We've got to go now," the soldier pressed.

"But *where*?" Why was this such a difficult question? Why did everyone refuse to answer? For crying out loud, did they think they wouldn't find out once they arrived? And then a more likely scenario blossomed in her head. She decided that the soldiers weren't answering because they themselves didn't know. She figured that they had orders to come and tell them to leave. It was probably someone else entirely who actually knew where they were going.

Carol started to cry. With Nana and Papi refusing to go, they truly were leaving their lives behind.

Kimberly didn't want to watch. If they didn't want to be a part of her life right now, she didn't want to be a part of their emotions. Keeping Erik's hand tightly in her own, Kimberly entered the kitchen first, and was startled to see the number of people there. There were eight or nine of the plainclothes soldiers, and all of them looked very serious and very nervous. The weaponry had increased as well, the pistols of before were replaced with black, lethal-looking rifles—M-16s, she thought, but she was never much into which rifle had what name.

"We're going to do this just like before," Ski said, finding his tongue again, "only this time in reverse. When I tell you to go, I want you to go very quickly down the hill to the waiting car and get inside as quickly as you can. Understand?"

The young Muses nodded in unison.

Ski allowed himself a smile. "Good." He brought a portable radio to his lips and said, "First package is ready."

Erik scowled at the terminology, but at a glance from Kimberly said nothing. Frankly, neither one of them had ever thought of themselves as packages before.

The Skinners entered the kitchen a few seconds later, and Carol gasped at the number of people.

"Not yet," Ski said to them before they could form a question. "You go second."

Ski's radio broke squelch and a metallic voice said, "Package one, go."

"This is it," Ski barked to the others, and as he held the kids back, the entire cast of soldiers poured out of the kitchen to form a double line leading down the lawn to the cars. It almost looked like an honor guard marking the path to the waiting car for a bride and groom leaving a church, except this guard faced away from the guests of honor, with rifles to their shoulders, looking for targets to shoot.

"Remember what I said," Ski admonished, and then he launched the kids with a pat on their shoulders.

They moved quickly, just as they'd been instructed, despite the urge to take in all the firepower. Erik in particular thought this was pretty cool.

The car was yet another Toyota, this one a black sedan, and the back door was wide open, guarded by another plainclothes soldier who seemed nervous and intent on looking at everything but them. Kimberly let her brother go first, and then ducked into the backseat be-

hind him. Her knees had barely hit the seat cushion before the door
was slammed shut behind them and they pulled away from the curb in
a hurry.

"Stay low," the driver said. Maybe it was the only words they'd
been taught, Kimberly thought.

"Do you know where we're going?" Erik asked the driver.

The soldier behind the wheel shifted his gaze into the rearview mirror. "No, sir, I'm sorry I don't. I only know where I'm going. And
when we get there, I want you to do exactly as I say, all right?"

"Because people are trying to shoot us?"

The driver paused for a beat before answering. "Something like
that. But you'll be okay. We've got a lot of people working to make
sure that you're just fine. You remember that."

Kurt's flash of terror evaporated after just a few seconds. Sitting there
in a straight-backed chair in this tiny file room with a gun to his head,
he'd prepared himself to die, and then just as quickly knew that the
DENI officer was bluffing.

Invoking the kind of logic that can only be born of desperation, he
found himself staring at the flimsy metal file cabinet that stood only a
foot or two from the tip of his nose. If the interrogator pulled his trigger, the bullet and Kurt's brains would be drilled straight through those
all-important intelligence files. There was no way they would risk
damage like that to the files.

The moment lasted for ten seconds—or maybe ten minutes, who
knew?—but finally the DENI officer spat out a curse and gave Kurt's
head a shove with the muzzle of his weapon.

Without another word, he stormed out of the room with his minions, leaving Kurt once again by himself.

12

There's an athletic field on Fort Clayton that used to be used for all kinds of activities, from platoon drills to kids' soccer games. On this afternoon, there were no kids at all on the field. Instead, there were a few soldiers tossing a Frisbee, and a cluster here and a cluster there of soldiers talking. Even at first glance, Kimberly thought that it looked all wrong. Then, when she saw a rifle propped up against a tree near one of the talking soldiers, she knew for a fact that it was all wrong.

The driver piloted the car into a parking lot adjacent to the field and stopped at the edge of the grass, leaving the engine running. A half-dozen other cars were similarly situated all around their edge of the field.

"What are we going to do here?" Erik wanted to know.

"We're just going to wait for the next part." The driver shifted his eyes to the mirror again, and Kimberly could tell from the lines around his eyes that he was smiling. "And I think you'll find the next part to be pretty darn cool."

Kimberly heard the choppers approaching before she saw them. It was a deep rumbling sound, not at all like the whop-whop-whop of the helicopters you hear on television. As the noise crescendoed, she knew they were getting closer. And then she saw them.

Three sleek Blackhawks came in hot and low in a wide banking turn, flying nose to tail, and as they flared for landing on the parade field, all those Frisbee tossers and quiet gabbers were suddenly armed with rifles.

"Your chariots are here," the driver said, and he dropped the transmission into gear. The instant the Blackhawks' wheels touched the grass, their car was moving. "The first one is for you and your family," the driver said.

When the Toyota came to a halt on the grass, a soldier wearing a green flight suit and a green helmet pulled the back door open. "Kimberly and Erik?" he asked.

"Yes, sir."

"Outstanding. You're with me. Let's go."

Kimberly then Erik stumbled out of the car and ran to the side door of the chopper, where another crewman was waiting to help them aboard.

"We get to fly in a chopper?" Erik beamed.

Behind them, all the waiting cars raced across the field to their assigned helicopters. They pulled to a stop, and all the people Kimberly had seen in the Provost Marshal station poured out of the doors.

"Have a seat," the crewman commanded, and the kids planted themselves into the nylon-strap passenger seats in the middle of the aircraft. The crewman helped them with their seat belts, and then he reached over their heads to find a couple of flight helmets. "You two have to wear these," he said.

They were heavy. And huge. "It's too big," Erik said.

"My orders are that you wear them. Nothing says it's gotta fit." Said a different way by a different man, the words might have been offensive, but the crewman's smile pulled it off nicely.

Finally strapped into the seat, and with her helmet in place, Kimberly looked up and saw that Carol, David, and Joey had also arrived and were being strapped into their seats. No helmets, though. Then there were others from the Provost who also climbed aboard. Two in particular, young and good looking with big smiles, sought out the kids first thing. They looked familiar to her.

"I'm Antonio Martinez," said the first one with the biggest smile. "You are Kimberly, right? And you're Erik?"

They nodded. Kimberly couldn't help but return the smile. "This is Coronado Samaniego. You remember we went scuba diving with you and your father."

That was it. That was why they looked familiar. Kimberly and her dad loved to go scuba diving, and she could remember now that these two guys had been on one of the trips.

"Sorry to see you in these circumstances," Antonio went on.

Kimberly nodded. Her throat felt thick with emotion.

"We need everybody to plant their butts in a seat," the crewman said, nudging them along.

"But don't you worry," Coronado said. "Kurt's a good man. He's a hero. He'll come out of this just fine. He's too tough not to."

"*Now*, dammit," the crewman barked.

They had to move along. They took the seats next to the kids. "Don't worry about a thing," Antonio said. "We'll get you through this."

Tears pressed hard from behind Kimberly's eyes. It was the sudden kindness in the midst of so much madness. Finally, there was a connection to someone who admired her father instead of berating him.

As the Blackhawk powered up and the world banked away down below, Kimberly watched the cluttered, twisted landscape of the city of her birth spin away; she searched in vain to find her house among all the thousands of houses down there. It was one more unspoken good-bye, and the beginning of the journey that would change who she was.

Back in West Palm, Annie was desperate for news. She wanted every detail, but would have settled for *any* detail. No one seemed to know anything after eighteen hours in limbo. No one knew where Kurt was, no one knew if her children were safe, and no one knew what the long-range plan was or even what it might be.

All day long, she'd been pulling every string she could find, mostly through Suzanne Alexander at the Agency and Richard Dotson at the State Department, but they seemed to be getting as frustrated as she with all the runaround and shrugged shoulders.

"Just tell me this," Annie said to Suzanne, at the end of a very long conversation. "Is anybody doing anything at all, or are we just sitting around and doing a lot of thinking?"

"Annie, I know you're frustrated. I know how agonizing this must be, but these things are not simple. I'm sure Richard has probably told you the same thing. There *is* a lot of thinking that goes into an action that has been wholly unplanned, and I think it's unreasonable for us not to acknowledge that."

Annie could hear the exhaustion in Suzanne's voice, just as she could feel it in her own body. But God bless it, "I don't know" just was not an acceptable answer when the stakes were this high. *Somebody* knew the details, and she intended to keep pressing until somebody either coughed them up, or they put her in contact with someone who could. She started to express this to her old friend when Suzanne started talking again.

"You know, and there's something else that you might want to consider, Annie. If and when a decision were to be made to implement some kind of plan, I really don't think you'd *want* to know the details over an open phone line."

As Suzanne spoke, Annie felt a flutter in her stomach. The words she spoke made perfect sense; open phone lines were just that—anyone with the smallest amount of technical expertise could listen in at will. But it wasn't the words that caught Annie's attention so much as the way in which they were delivered. If she wasn't mistaken, Suzanne was conveying a kind of subliminal message. Something was happening after all.

13

A PDF lieutenant stormed into the tiny office that was serving as Kurt's temporary prison and stopped abruptly, his chest just inches from Kurt's face. He glared down, but said nothing. Unsure whether it was wise to stand, Kurt remained seated, staring at the floor.

Finally, the lieutenant said, "Stand."

Kurt stood and then retreated to the corner of the room where the lieutenant was pointing. He had no idea what was happening, but there was a disturbing electricity in the room. Kurt sensed that whatever was on the way was going to be big.

The lieutenant kicked Kurt's chair out of the way and it flew toward the opposite corner with a metallic clang. As a continuation of the same motion, he beckoned to the door. On cue, three enormous PDF noncoms dragged a terrified man into the room and made him stand on the spot where Kurt had been sitting. They got right down to business.

"You are selling drugs on our streets."

The prisoner's eyes grew huge. "No!" he insisted in a heavy accent that Kurt instantly recognized as Colombian. "I am no such thing. I am a—"

Before he could complete his sentence, the lieutenant delivered a backhanded slap that knocked the prisoner off his feet. The suddenness and effectiveness of the blow reminded Kurt of a rattlesnake strike, and he could not help but take a step back. He watched as the thug who'd brought the prisoner lifted him back to his feet. Again, they all just stood there.

Confused, Kurt turned his eyes toward the lieutenant, who was staring back at him with the intensity of a welding arc. The officer smiled just a little, then nodded toward the hulking noncoms.

They, too, moved with alarming speed, bum-rushing the prisoner face-first into the block wall. Kurt winced at the sharp crack of breaking teeth as fragile facial structures battled with unyielding concrete.

The soldiers moved in unison from here, as if what followed was a choreographed routine. With the Colombian's face mashed ever harder against the wall, one soldier wrenched the prisoner's right arm around and behind his back, the way countless schoolyard bullies subdue their prey every day, while the second soldier brought the left arm over the prisoner's head and likewise behind his back. The Colombian howled at the unbearable tension in his shoulders as they placed one bracelet of a pair of handcuffs on the right wrist. The howl turned to a scream, though, when the guards yanked in unison to make his wrists meet between his shoulder blades, where the remaining bracelet was applied. When they pulled back on the hands, and both shoulders popped free of their sockets, the sound from the man's throat transformed into something that Kurt had never heard from a human being and that no decent person would tolerate from an animal without putting it out of its misery.

Kurt's stomach flipped, and he looked away to avoid vomiting; but the lieutenant barked in Spanish, "No! You watch. This is your future."

The guards spun their prisoner back around so Kurt could see the blood flowing from his nose and mouth, the impossible angles of his dislocated arms, and Kurt felt a new breed of fear shoot through his bloodstream, this one white hot. This was a demonstration to show him what they were capable of, designed to make him fearful of his life, and it was working like a charm.

But they weren't done. As their victim stood there off balance, moaning helplessly, one of the noncoms launched a full-force, steel-toed kick to the Colombian's testicles, causing the man to crumple like a marionette.

Kurt recoiled in horror.

From there it turned into a frenzy of violence. The choreography was gone, replaced with the savagery of a street beating. As the Colombian fought desperately to cover himself up with his knees, and by rolling from side to side, he begged them to stop, pleading in the names of God and his family. He had children to support, he wailed. Please, he didn't know why they were doing this to him. Each hard consonant was punctuated with a bloody spray from his nose and mouth.

They kicked him ceaselessly for what had to be over a minute, the heavy boots landing with sickening, heavy thuds in his ribs, his gut, his extremities, his kidneys, his groin. As horrifying as it was, Kurt couldn't force himself to look away. He was witnessing a man's murder, and as awful as that was, he sensed that he owed this stranger an unblinking audience.

They rolled the poor man onto his back—onto his pinioned arms—and started in on his face, grinding the heels of their shoes into the flesh of his nose and his eyes, their hard rubber soles mercilessly tearing flesh.

When the guards were finally done, they were soaked with sweat, and the noise of their labored breathing was louder than the diminishing moans of their victim. Kurt had heard of this kind of brutality from the PDF, but until he'd seen it for himself here in this squalid little office that now reeked of sweat and blood, he'd not been able to wrap his mind around what it really meant. These were the same men—whether literally or by association—who had dismembered and mutilated Hugo Spadafora before they finally released him to the peace of death, but until you see the pleasure these goons took in inflicting that kind of agony, you never really understood the face of evil.

That bleeding prisoner at their feet was a human being, for God's sake. Someone's son, who had a life and responsibilities and people who loved him, but to his torturers—to Kurt's captors—he was nothing more than an object of perverse, twisted pleasure.

And the crooked smile on the lieutenant's face confirmed it. Still sharply pressed from having merely observed the beating, he eyed Kurt with open amusement, nodding to the guards to lift the prisoner to his feet. The Colombian barely made a sound as they lifted him by his dislocated arms and propped him up against a wall. When the prisoner raised his head, he looked directly at Kurt, as if to ask for help.

Kurt looked away.

The lieutenant wandered to a file cabinet in the corner, stooped, and withdrew from the space between the cabinet and the wall a long-handled lug wrench that might have come from the trunk of somebody's car. As the Colombian's head lolled against his chest, the lieutenant brought the lug wrench to Kurt and made sure that he got a good look.

"Have you been watching?" the lieutenant asked in a tone so soft that Kurt could barely hear it over the sound of his pounding heart and the roar of blood in his ears. "This is your future." He held the smile for a long moment, long enough to make Kurt look away, but only for a few seconds.

The lieutenant shifted his grip on the lug wrench so that he was now holding it like a baseball bat, and the smile broadened.

Kurt braced for the blow that he knew was coming.

But for today, Kurt would be spared. The Colombian would not.

The lieutenant turned back to the pitiful prisoner, and, issuing a guttural growl that seemed to muster all of his strength, the lieutenant delivered a home-run swing to the center of the prisoner's chest. The Colombian collapsed on the spot and never moved.

Clearly pleased with his work, the lieutenant handed the lug wrench to one of the noncoms and nodded for them to take the carcass out of the room. As they dragged the body, the lieutenant recovered the folding chair he'd kicked into the corner and set it up again in the same spot where it had been before.

"Have a seat," he said to his prisoner. "Relax. We'll be back for you later."

14

It had been hours since they'd first lifted off the parade field at Fort Clayton. That flight had lasted only a few minutes, barely long enough to gain altitude before descending again onto the tarmac of a pristine airfield on what Kimberly would later learn was Howard Air Force Base; still in Panama, but a few miles away from the center of Panama City.

They were on the ground for maybe twenty minutes at that first stop, just long enough to use the bathroom and pick up boxed lunches that someone had stacked up on the kind of folding table she had seen in movies from the States that featured cafeterias. She and Erik were still the dirty ones, it seemed, the ones that no one wanted to talk to. Even the soldiers were silent here. And they were much better armed than Ski and his friends had been.

The lunches had been stacked in the great open space of an aircraft hangar that seemed even larger than it was because there was no aircraft in it. Erik, ever the fan of all things military, thought that this was about as cool as you could get. For her part, Kimberly wondered how people could possibly come to work in such a dingy place day after day after day.

With her bladder empty and her stomach not quite settled enough for food, Kimberly passed the time watching the angst and anger that was spreading like spilled oil among her Panamanian counterparts.

Honest to God she tried not to eavesdrop—at least not too closely—but the hangar was such an echoey place that she'd have had to be deaf not to overhear a lot of it. The gist of it was this: The men had been working with her father, doing whatever it was that got him arrested, and the women and children had had no inkling that any such thing had been going on. Now, from what she could tell, they were all facing a choice between death and exile, and they were holding their husbands and fathers responsible.

Seemed reasonable, she supposed. A little harsh, but reasonable. Not unlike the situation with her own family.

After just a little while in the hangar, an American soldier who, Kimberly noticed, had no branch or unit markings on his jungle fatigues (thus making him just a generic soldier), gathered them together in a cluster and instructed them in Spanish on what they were to do next. They were to join hands—no, not in a circle as if they were going to pray, but in a long chain—and stay together as he led them to their next destination. When someone asked where that destination was, the mysterious soldier pretended that he hadn't heard the question.

As the soldier talked, Erik moved in closer to lay claim to Kimberly's left hand. Judging from the grip, he had no intention of being pried free. He looked scared to death. Kimberly wished she had words that could somehow make some of this easier, but those words hadn't been invented.

"Didn't they say we were going to the States?" Erik asked her softly, pulling her attention away from the camouflaged soldier.

"That's what they said."

He stewed for a moment. "They're gonna make us walk the whole way? Holding *hands*?"

The look in her little brother's face, combined with the images his question conjured, made her laugh. She explained that they couldn't possibly walk the whole way. There were rivers to cross. And when he still didn't look convinced, she added, "They can't make me walk too far. I don't have any shoes." That was the logic that seemed to settle him down.

And then it was time to walk. Twenty-four men, women, and children joined hands in one continuous line and started walking, one behind the other, following the mysterious soldier out into the setting sun. As it turned out, Kimberly and Erik were numbers one and two in the line—no accident, because the soldier had called out their names (just their names, as if the others in the group mattered less) and told them to lead the way.

It took some effort at first to get the line moving without pulling or getting their feet tangled, but soon they were on their way. In the distance, out on a runway, a C-130 cargo plane sat on the tarmac with its propellers turning and its enormous back door open.

"Look at the C-130," Erik said, trying to point but abandoning the effort when Kimberly clamped tighter on his hand. "Think that's where we're going?" His eyes glowed with excitement. "How cool is that?"

That was exactly where they were going, and Kimberly didn't think it was the least bit cool. It was stupid. And scary. Didn't Erik realize that there was never any going back from a trip like this? What about school? What about their friends?

What about Daddy?

Inside, the C-130 was as no-frills as it could get. The plane's skeleton was clearly visible where there should have been walls, and the seats, such as they were, weren't seats at all, but rather just strips of nylon webbing that had been stretched across metal tubing. Packages and luggage lay stacked in an unruly pile on the ground outside the aircraft, testament to the fact that this flight had originally been designated for others, who now would have to make alternative arrangements to get wherever they were going.

The unknown soldier handed them off to another soldier who introduced himself as Air Force Sergeant Somebody-or-Other, the loadmaster on the aircraft, and therefore the one and only person they should listen to for the duration of the flight. No, he would not tell them where they were going, and no, he would not share with them any details of anything other than this speech he was making. They would sit where they were told, stand when they were told, and otherwise suit his every whim or else they could get off of his airplane and walk.

"I understand that you've already had a chance to use the bathroom," he concluded, "but if the urge strikes in the middle of the flight, we do have facilities available." He pointed to a chemical toilet toward the rear of the aircraft whose version of privacy was an olive-drab shower curtain that didn't even reach the floor.

They'd taken off from Howard hours ago, and for the entire flight, no one had said a thing to anyone else. No one but Antonio and Coronado, that is, who both seemed very interested in making sure that Kimberly and Erik felt like they had friends. For them, this all seemed like a great adventure. It made sense for Antonio, she supposed, who was here by himself, and seemed to have no one else to worry about. But that wasn't true of Coronado. He had a wife and a little baby to be worried about.

But after a while, even they seemed to grow weary of the façade of happiness and they turned inward to themselves.

In retrospect, Kimberly wasn't sure how she'd spent the long hours of the flight. She supposed she must have slept, but it was equally possible that she just stared forward, out into the miles of space that separated her from the only world she'd ever known.

Something changed. Something happened. In an instant, everyone at once seemed to be aware that the world was different, yet no one seemed immediately to know why. It took Kimberly a few seconds to realize that it was the propellers. After hours and hours of a single monotone drone, the pitch had changed, and they had begun to descend. Even without windows it was easy to tell; there's that lightness in your stomach, and the constant popping in your ears.

The consensus was that they had finally arrived at wherever they were going, but consensus brought no comfort. A number of Kimberly's Panamanian counterparts speculated aloud that they were going to jail, that their lives were ruined forever. Children started to cry.

Kimberly said nothing, but those predictions of gloom didn't sound right to her. If they were going to be sent to prison, it seemed a lot easier just to do it and get it over with. God knows there were prisons in Panama. What was the sense of a long plane ride just for that?

Besides, Kimberly had done nothing wrong. She supposed there was an argument to be made that these Panamanians who had apparently violated the same laws as those broken by her father might be eligible for prison, but certainly not she and Erik. She'd figured all along that that was the whole reason for them being on this flight in the first place—to avoid going to jail.

Another panicky theory among the Panamanians was that they were all going to be killed. Again, Kimberly thought, killing them would have been the easiest thing in the world, and accomplishing it didn't require any of this enormous effort.

No, Kimberly was comfortable with the notion that they were being saved from whatever danger had lain for them back in Panama, and she was likewise convinced that what she'd overheard was probably right—that they were all being taken to the United States. Now, what might happen from there was anybody's guess. She could only assume that the plane was going to land somewhere near West Palm Beach, where her mother was staying, that Mom would greet them at the airport, and that the world would once again look like something that was at least close to being normal.

It was funny, when she thought about it, how being normal had had no value to her at all until all semblance of normalcy had been stripped from her life.

The moods of the conspirators continued to sink with each foot of lost altitude. Finally, the loadmaster returned to address the group.

"All right, everybody listen up because I only want to say this once." He had to shout to be heard above the noise of the engines. "We are approaching our final destination. When we land, I will tell you to join hands just as you did before, and I am going to ask you to exit the aircraft in an orderly fashion. You are in no danger, so I'll remind you to stay calm at all times. Are there any questions?"

Hands went up everywhere. Someone asked, "Where are we going?"

The sergeant just stood there, his hands on his hips, looking disgusted. "Are there any questions that I can answer—about the mechanics of getting off the aircraft?"

All the hands disappeared.

Seeing no further questions, the sergeant gave a satisfied nod. "Very well, then. We'll have you on the ground shortly."

And he meant shortly. Kimberly had been on many commercial flights in her fifteen years, but never had she experienced an approach like this one. After some minutes of gradual descent, the pilot nosed the aircraft forward and poured on the power. But for the seat belt cinched across her lap, she might have bounced off the ceiling. Without windows to get her bearings, it wasn't out of the question that they were crashing. About the time that she was ready to concede that that was exactly what was happening, the plane leveled off and the engines throttled back.

They landed as if to leave a belly print on the ground, the impact jarring everyone, and igniting a chorus of frightened screams among them all. A second after the impact, the pilot hit the brakes and reversed the thrust on the props in a deceleration that would have left skid marks if it happened on a street somewhere. Within no time at all, they'd rolled to a stop, and then Kimberly sensed that they were turning around, pivoting on their own axis until they were facing the other way.

Now the fear in her belly bloomed large. Wherever they were going, they'd finally arrived. Dreaming and guessing no longer mattered. All that mattered now—all she had to cling to now—was the simple truth of reality. Frankly, it sucked.

But there was precious little time to think about it. Seconds after they'd stopped, the rear cargo door started to lower, introducing a new level of noise to the already deafening humid air, and Sergeant Somebody-or-Other reappeared.

"Up!" he shouted. "Come on, everybody up. On your feet." He repeated the command in fractured Spanish.

They all stood.

"All right, ladies and gentlemen, boys and girls, link up again, hand in hand. Everybody gets a partner, nobody gets left behind." As he spoke, he walked to Kimberly, who, because she was first to board, was closest to the front of the aircraft. He put a hand on her shoulder and escorted her past all the others, back to where she was first in line again. Erik hung on to her tightly.

"When I say go," the soldier continued, "this young lady will lead the way out. Do not stop, do not slow down until you are at least fifty yards away from the rear of the aircraft. Stay together, don't break the chain, and everything will be just fine. Any questions on what I just said—and I swear to God I'll smack anyone who asks where we are."

They all knew better. What would be the point? Questions never brought answers anyway.

"All right then. Go!" He gave Kimberly a gentle push; not a shove, really, but enough pressure on her shoulder to let her know there was more where it came from if she decided to resist.

Still barefoot and wearing only the shorts and T-shirt that she'd had on since she couldn't remember when now, Kimberly had to walk carefully on the steel ramp to keep from stubbing a toe or even losing her balance. It seemed steeper on the way out than it did on the way in.

She led the way into total darkness. The immediate area was lit like daylight from floodlights shining down from the back of the C-130, but beyond that, there was nothing but night. And it was a chilly night, at that. Much colder than an evening in Panama. But the humidity was all there. With the lower temperatures, the humidity felt like a chilled, wet wool coat.

At the bottom of the ramp, she found what must have been a runway. It was a paved surface, certainly, and despite the cold darkness, it still radiated the heat of the day. As soon as they hit bottom, Erik tried to stop, but she jerked him along. "He said we have to keep walking."

"To where?" he demanded. It was dark out there. And not dark the way it got in Panama City in the nighttime; this was dark like in a cave. At night. With a blindfold on.

"There must be something," Kimberly said. "They wouldn't send us out here if there was nothing." As she spoke the words, she wondered whether she even believed them herself. Turning around, she saw that they were all still together, every one of the people she'd seen in the waiting room of the Provost Marshal on Fort Clayton was still with her, the farthest away already halfway down the ramp.

Kimberly kept walking, just as the sergeant had told her to do. All she saw was night, and all she heard was the roar of the C-130's engines.

Maybe the sergeant would come clean with some details once they got settled out here.

Where was the sergeant, anyway? Still walking, she turned around to face the crowd to see if she could catch a glimpse of him. What she saw made her heart seize. She could see him, all right. He was still on the plane, apparently still keeping an eye on them, as the back ramp started to close again.

She stopped cold, right there on the sandy tarmac, nearly causing a chain-reaction collision with the others.

"Kimberly!" Erik protested. "What are you—" His eyes followed her gaze and his grip tightened. "They're leaving us?" The others turned around, too, their faces unbelieving.

The C-130 started rolling even before the ramp was all the way closed. As the propeller blades bit into the air, the entire atmosphere seemed to rumble with the power of the engines. The prop wash created a hurricane of blowing sand and debris, causing all the refugees to shield their eyes, but none of them could stop watching.

The plane moved surprisingly fast for such a big bird, shrinking in size as it raced away from them. As the nose rotated up for liftoff, the giant flood lights in the rear were extinguished, and the entire plane disappeared, leaving only the quickly diminishing sound of its engines.

Soon, the absolute darkness was joined by absolute silence.

15

After the torture of the Colombian in his presence, they'd left him alone for a while in that tiny office, facing the cabinets, with the ever-present boom box blaring. Soon, they came for him again and escorted him out onto a balcony that overlooked a walled prison yard, where gaunt, forlorn prisoners gathered for what might charitably be called recreation. Maybe fifteen by twenty feet in size and topped with coils of barbed wire, there was no room for any real exercise even if it was empty. As it was, however, cramped with thirty or forty filthy men wearing the tatters that might once have been clothing, there was nothing to do but pace and smoke foul-smelling cigarettes.

The message here was every bit as simple as the message delivered by the torture. This was Kurt's future. In a few short hours or days, he would be one of these men, and the thought terrified him. As the prisoners in the yard looked up and made eye contact with him, it occurred to Kurt that these men were no longer men at all, not in the traditional sense that civilized people view such things. The humanity had been drained from them all—or beaten or starved out of them, perhaps—and all that was left was the basic survival instinct. As they gathered below to stare at him, they pointed and talked among themselves. Kurt couldn't help but think of buzzards circling the sky, waiting for a crippled animal to finally expire.

That would not happen to him, he told himself. No matter what, he would find a way to preserve and maintain his dignity, even in this place of rapes and cavity searches, where dignity was a relative thing.

It was impossible, under the circumstances, not to dwell on the peculiar brand of violence that defined prison life the world over. That ultimate violation when the choices became binary, between death or defilement. When faced with it himself—*if* faced with it himself—how would he choose? At the end of the day, which was indeed the dignified choice? Certainly, there was no honor in a hideous death at the hands of these jackals, yet how could one continue to live in the aftermath?

It was well known among the informed citizens of Panama that Noriega employed rape rooms for the punishment of prisoners. In an effort to break down resistant political prisoners, Noriega fed them to wings of prisons that were populated by homosexual predators. It occurred to Kurt, sitting here on the balcony witnessing the incarnation of hopelessness, that such could perhaps be the ultimate torture. Over time, one can recover from the crooked limb or the missing eye, but how could one ever heal the wounds of prison rape?

They kept him there on the balcony for an hour, he supposed, maybe more. He just didn't know. Fear and exhaustion were taking their toll. Reality was beginning to slip from his grasp. It was daylight; he knew that much. But as for which day, he was less than sure.

His next stop was likewise in the guts of the DENI station, this time to a larger room, and from what he could tell from the enthusiastic buzzing of his escorts, they had found some treasures they wanted to show him.

The room was filled with Kurt's personal belongings. They had his clothes, guns, books, and record collection. They had everything. All the stuff from his home and garage. What he worried about most, though, was the crew who was hovering around his Apple computer. They were in the early stages of setting it up, and when they finished, he would be sunk.

When he thought about all the data that was stored in that computer—the code books, the fake purchase orders, all the toys and all the paper trails they needed to tie him and all the others directly to La Voz de la Libertad—he wanted to kick himself for being so stupid. He thought of all the attention—the lip service, as it turned out—they'd paid to operational security, and wondered how he could have been so stupid as to record every transaction right there on the computer. He didn't even try to encrypt it for God's sake.

Stupid.

A PDF captain pointed to a chair and desk. "Have a seat," he said in Spanish.

Kurt sat.

"If there's something you want to tell us, now is the time to do it," the captain said. "It's so much easier if we learn from you what you know we will find on our own. It will feel like a goodwill gesture."

Kurt's mind whirled. Could he actually help his cause by coming clean up front? Would it really make a difference?

As soon as the questions formed in his mind, he conjured the answer. Of course it would make a difference. He forced himself to remember the promise he had made to himself just hours before: he would preserve his dignity at all costs. If they found the answers, so be it. What would come from that would flow of its own weight and accord. But he wasn't going to hand them any simple answers. He hadn't fought the noble fight for this long just to cave in under the pressure of exhaustion and fear. No, his one last battle against the Pineapple would be to make him figure out his own damn answers the hard way.

"I don't know what you're speaking of," Kurt said. "I have done nothing wrong. I have nothing to tell you."

The captain eyed him for a long moment. "Are you telling me the truth, Mr. Muse?"

Kurt tried to look nonplussed. "Why would I lie?"

The captain held his gaze for another moment, then leaned a little closer. "Let's start with the password for your computer."

"There is no password," Kurt said, instantly confused.

"Don't lie to me."

"I'm not. I swear to you that there is no password."

"My technicians tell me that there is."

In a flash of inspiration, Kurt understood what the problem was. Apple computers were pretty new technology then; the PDF didn't realize that they were dealing with an entirely different operating system. DOS-trained technicians could work for a week on Apple technology and never get past first base. "Then it is your technicians who need to be reprimanded for lying." He found himself suppressing a smile.

The captain's face reddened as his jaw locked. Kurt wasn't sure what he would do if the captain commanded him to boot up the computer for them, but he didn't think it would be a problem. To ask for assistance like that would be to cede some of their power, and Kurt didn't see this particular PDF goon ceding anything.

The captain decided to change tacks. He reached into his desk drawer and withdrew a sheet of paper, which he slid across the desk. "What is this?"

Kurt tried to keep his face impassive even as his pulse pummeled his temples. "It looks like an apartment lease," he said. Instantly, he cursed his own words. This was not a time to be coy. Of course it was an apartment lease. It said APARTMENT LEASE right at the very top.

"That's what it looked like to me as well," the captain agreed. From his smirk and his tone, it was clear that he knew he'd caught Kurt off guard. "Why would a man with a home as beautiful as yours have an apartment as well?"

Kurt lowered his head and dropped his voice, drawing the captain closer to hear. "It's for my mistress," he said without dropping a beat. He had no idea where that lie came from, but it was a gift, made all the more valuable because many men of standing in Panama had one or more mistresses, both here and in the States. Soon, he was sure, they'd find other leases, and when they checked out the addresses, they'd find that this first apartment was the exception because it was empty. In three others, they'd find that the sole resident of the apartment was a radio transmitter with a battery backup, set to begin broadcasting at their appointed times.

The smile disappeared from the captain's face.

Kurt expounded, "I pay for her apartment, and she, well . . . you understand."

The captain looked stunned, as if he'd been slapped. Clearly, this was not the direction he thought the conversation was headed. He stood abruptly. "Very well, then." He motioned to one of the guards, who materialized in an instant. "Take him away."

The guard escorted Kurt to the next office; a closet, really. From there, he could listen in on the technicians' efforts to break through what they thought was his secret encryption code. Kurt allowed himself to bask in this tiny victory, even though he knew it was short lived. The PDF were idiots, but they weren't stupid. Sooner or later, one of them who had been to the States in the past few months would recognize the different technology, and when they did, it would all be over.

Sitting by himself in that tiny office, he could easily work himself to a corner from which the work room was plainly visible to him. He could see all his stuff, and he could watch to a certain degree all the goings on out there, and as he did, his mind wandered to pondering the impossible.

Suppose they never were able to open those files? Suppose, somehow, the files got destroyed, and they never did find out the details about what they'd stumbled on and whom they'd captured? There was a possibility, he thought, that maybe his plot could live on even in his absence. Without the files, they'd never get the details of La Voz's long-term strategy. They'd never have the details of the broken codes, and they'd never have all the lease addresses.

Without those computer files, all they'd have would be conjecture and accusations. They'd have the testimony of whoever had betrayed him in the first place, and he would have the protection of the U.S. government. Maybe the plan was still alive after all. So he had to make sure that they never opened his computer files.

But how?

When he saw them examining the 5¼-inch floppy disk with the damning files on it, he knew exactly what he had to do. If he could somehow destroy the magnetic surface of the disk drive—it wouldn't take much, just a good scratch across the face—then he could be home free. It might be a little tough on him physically—they'd undoubtedly give him a sound beating—but wouldn't it be worth it at the end of the day?

Yes, it would. Talk about maintaining your dignity. Talk about keeping the upper hand even after you'd been soundly trumped by the other guy. This could be just the thing.

But again: How?

Almost without conscious thought, his hands moved to the pen in his shirt pocket. He'd had it all along; they'd never taken it from him, just as they'd never cuffed his hands, and they continued to bring his suitcase from location to location as they interrogated him. He didn't understand their thinking, and it certainly wasn't a question he intended to ask. Best he could figure out, it still had something to do with the fact that he was an American citizen, as much as they wished otherwise.

For whatever reason, he still had his pen, and it occurred to him that sitting here in this chair, pressed up against the concrete wall, it wouldn't be all that difficult to rub the ball point hard enough and aggressively enough to give it a pretty good point. With a pointed pen—a pointed piece of metal—he could do all the damage he needed to, to keep them from opening his files and learning everything.

Hoping to draw as little attention as possible, he slowly but deliberately slipped his hand to his shirt pocket and withdrew the pen. There was something else in there, too, a piece of paper. The instant he felt it, his heart sank. It was the damn Holiday Inn receipt from Tyson's Corner, Virginia, where he'd met with Father Frank the night before his arrest—the night of the party at Richard Dotson's house. Christ almighty, *Tyson's Corner*—the CIA's backyard, at the intersection of Chain Bridge Road and International Drive. This was why amateurs shouldn't be allowed to play spy games.

How the hell was he going to get rid of a hotel receipt? He'd told the interrogators that he'd been in West Palm Beach with Annie, visiting her sick relative. If they found this on him, God only knew what would happen.

Able to think of nothing else to do with it, he quickly stuffed it into his mouth and started chewing. Let them sift through his bowel movements if they wanted incriminating evidence.

While he chewed, he let his hand with the pen dangle naturally at his side. He clicked it open and felt with his thumbnail to make sure that he in fact had the ball point exposed. Still working only by feel, even as he tried not to stare at anything in particular, he found the rough surface of the wall and started rubbing. A few strokes, and then rotate, just a fraction of a turn, then another few strokes and rotate.

He needed to hurry, but there was no reason to rush. They would be working on that computer for a while, he knew. But success here depended on getting to the floppy disk itself, and who knew how long they'd have it out on the table like that? Who knew how long it would be before they packaged it up for review by somebody else?

He increased the rhythm of the scraping.

Kurt tried to play the entire scenario out in his mind. Once he was ready, he would have to go quickly. He'd have to bolt from his chair and dash to the work table. If things went perfectly—and when do things ever go perfectly?—he'd take the eight or ten running steps that were necessary, and he'd jab the pen like a dagger into the surface of the disk. With a dent made, he'd scrape and scribble on the fragile surface for as long as it would take them to pull him off and do whatever would be the result of his act of madness.

And that's what it would be, too: an act of madness. That's how they'd play it in the press anyway, but Kurt would know differently, just as his friends and his immediate family would know differently. They would see it as an act of courage, an act of patriotism. All he had to hope for was a certain hesitation from the guards that would keep them from shooting him on the spot. He actually thought he could tolerate all the rest—the beatings and the torture—but there was no escaping death.

The images of Annie and the kids tried to invade his consciousness, but he pushed those thoughts away, choosing instead to concentrate on the next few minutes. This wasn't a time to think about the dark side of his actions. It wasn't a time to think about the suffering of family members. Now was the time to think about the present, about the mission at hand. This was bigger than his family. This was about the survival of God only knew how many people. He needed to keep his thoughts focused. His world had taken on entirely new definitions in the past hours. The future no longer comprised years and decades. Now, the future was defined as whatever was coming next, in ten- and twenty-minute blocks. And this next little portion of the future was going to be very, very interesting.

As he saw it, he'd have one shot at this, and one shot only. If he blew it, it was blown forever, because even the PDF, in all of its idiocy, was too smart to make the same mistake more than once. If he was underguarded now—he only counted two—then after he made his move, he'd be overguarded for sure.

After what felt like forever, his thumb told him that he had enough of a sharp point on his pen to make his move.

He set his mind on his mission. He tensed himself, easing forward on his chair. He said a quick prayer. Then he launched himself.

He sprang from his chair, as if ejected, and sprinted toward the table. All he saw was the disk. All he thought about was destroying the magnetic surface—until he cleared the threshold between the doors. Then all he thought about were the three extra guards he hadn't seen from the other room. He thought about their rifles, too.

16

The darkness wasn't absolute after all, not after Kimberly's eyes adjusted, but it was darn close. The world was a jumbled collection of opaque shadows. The runway was a black stripe against the lighter black of the chest-high elephant grass, which itself was offset from the purple night sky. Black silhouettes of her fellow refugees moved about against the purple tableaux as well, their features completely concealed in perpetual shadows.

The silence wasn't absolute, either. With the noise of the airplane engines gone, the songs of the nighttime insects, frogs, and other creatures was nearly deafening. Only nearly because there was no drowning out the sound of people crying. One woman in particular seemed convinced that they had been taken someplace to die.

"Where is this place?" Erik whispered, his grip on Kimberly's hand so tight that he was causing real pain.

She shook her head. "I don't know," she said. "I have no idea." But it was a place she wanted to leave, and quickly. She pulled her brother closer and tried to think it through. They were in the middle of a desolate place, all by themselves, with no means of transportation, and no means by which to take care of themselves. Kimberly didn't know about the others, but she didn't have any money, not even enough to buy a hamburger someplace. It wasn't exactly the ideal circumstance from which to launch an escape.

Kimberly wanted desperately not to be scared. She wanted desperately to be one of the very few refugees in the crowd who kept her wits about her and did not sink into the desperate fear in which so many of her new companions were wallowing, but it was hard.

No, it was impossible. Nothing is more terrifying than the unknown, and never had Kimberly Muse found herself in a circumstance that was less known than this one: No home, no parents, no money, and no idea of what lay ahead. It wasn't *fair*.

Her mind started to take a very dark turn when Tomás Muñoz stepped from the middle of the crowd and tried to get everyone's attention. Because he was Tomás, and because there was no one else to turn to, people quieted down enough to hear him speak.

It was silly, but what Kimberly wanted to hear was a monologue on how everything was going to be fine. She wanted to hear someone with an authoritative presence say aloud that no matter what was going on, no matter what lay ahead, that they could all feel comfortable that no harm was going to come to them. No matter how hollow the words, no matter how contrived and empty, it would have meant something, she thought, just to hear them uttered.

But Tomás did nothing of the sort. Instead, he led them in the Lord's Prayer. "*Padre nuestro que estás en los cielos, Santificado sea tu Nombre. Venga tu reino Hágase tu voluntad En la tierra como en el cielo . . .*"

Some joined enthusiastically, while others mouthed the words and mumbled, their hearts lagging behind their heads. For Kimberly, the sudden arrival of prayer startled her. Frankly, it was the furthest thing from her mind in that particular moment, but then, as she let the words pour over her, she found strength from them that she'd never experienced before.

When Tomás transitioned into the Hail Mary, the words started to flow more easily, and soon she found her fear balanced by hope. "*Dios te salve, María, llena eres de gracia, el Señor es contigo. Bendita tú eres entre todas las mujeres, y bendito es el fruto de tu vientre, Jesús. Santa María, Madre de Dios, ruega por nosotros, pecadores, ahora y en la hora de nuestra muerte. Amen.*"

It was a moment of beauty ensconced in the madness and confusion of events spinning out of control. It wouldn't occur to Kimberly until many years later, but that moment in time, awash in all the fear and uncertainty, was one of the most spiritually peaceful moments of her life. Having no choice but to surrender herself to powers beyond her control, she found the peace and clarity of faith for which many people spend their entire lives searching.

Lights on the horizon broke the reverie and once again introduced an element of fear. At first, she couldn't tell what they were, but after a few seconds, after her ears adjusted to a new generation of sound, she realized that they were vehicles, and that they were approaching very quickly.

Kimberly's first instinct was to run, but as she turned, she could see that the vehicles were coming from all directions. She had no idea how many. Five? Seven? They approached from every compass point, and as they drew nearer, the lights that preceded them became blinding. The refugees all huddled together, perhaps out of fear, or perhaps just to escape the piercing glare of the headlights.

After a few seconds, though, it became clear that these weren't headlights at all, at least not in the sense of lights mounted in the grill of a vehicle. The lights were too high in the air. As they approached even closer, she could see that they were all mounted on the roll bars of some kind of backcountry four-wheel drive vehicles.

The vehicles slowed as they closed to within twenty yards and stopped when they'd formed a circle that was maybe thirty feet across.

Kimberly had never felt so exposed, so vulnerable. Whoever these people were, they could do anything to them now that they wished. Why hadn't she run? Why hadn't she made some effort to get away?

The refugees stood there like that for the better part of a minute, with no one moving, until finally they could see movement in the shadows.

A lone man walked in their direction. At first, he was only a silhouette against the headlights, but as he moved closer, it was possible to see some of the details emerge. Kimberly's first thought was that he was *old*. He was this little bald old man, and as he approached, she could see that he had a very kind expression.

"Does anyone speak English?" the man asked in overly pronounced English.

As a chorus, the refugees said, "I do." Tomás took a step closer to the man. Able to see facial details now in the glare of the headlights, Kimberly noted a confused expression in Tomás's face. She didn't know him well enough to interpret his features, but her thought was that it appeared to be something between relief and recognition.

The stranger smiled. "Hello, Tomás," the stranger said. "Welcome to the United States of America. Welcome to all of you." He paused a moment to let it sink in; to let those who needed translation receive it. He went on, "I'm here to make sure that you're well taken care of. My friends call me Father Frank."

The endless night finally terminated in a block of rooms that had been reserved for the refugees—there were officially twenty-four of them in all—at the Howard Johnson Motor Lodge in, of all places, Panama City, Florida. More than one of the new fugitives had been startled to see the road sign announcing their first stop.

The rules, as explained by Father Frank, were exquisitely simple. The U.S. government was picking up the entire tab for the next few nights. They all had unlimited access to the Waffle House on the far side of the parking lot; they had only to say that they were "with Frank."

That said, they also needed to be keenly aware that they were still in Florida, only a thousand miles from their homeland, and a part of the country where Noriega spies flourished with the abundance of Palmetto bugs. "I don't have to tell you," Frank said, there on the unnamed tarmac in the middle of nowhere, pausing for the Spanish translation, "that Mr. Noriega is a vindictive sort, and if he finds out where you are hiding, he may well take extraordinary actions to hurt you—either here on the spot, or after a ride back to your homeland. We can give you a start here in America, and we can be there to help you with some of the challenges associated with a relocation such as this, but we cannot provide you with protection. I urge you to understand and be aware that every time you step outside, there is a certain risk of you being seen and recognized. As time passes, the risk diminishes, but some risk will always remain.

"Please keep this in mind as you make certain lifestyle choices. You can choose, for example, to be loud and boisterous in a crowd, or you can choose to be quiet and refined. One is far more likely to draw inordinate attention, and I will leave it to you to figure out which."

Kimberly didn't know what to make of this man, this Father Frank.

On the one hand, he appeared to be kind and grandfatherly, while on the other, he seemed to be all-business in a business that frightened her.

Kimberly had no idea what time it was when they finally arrived at the motor lodge but she knew that it was late—or early, she supposed; two or three in the morning. The keys were all ready for them. They didn't have to go to the front office or anything. Nondescript people in nondescript clothing were there on hand to pass out the keys to the preassigned rooms. The Panamanians, Kimberly noted, were kept separate from her and her family. As before, at Howard Air Force Base, and again on the flight out to the United States, everyone seemed particularly officious in their pampering of Kimberly and Erik.

The motel itself was the same layout as a thousand others of its ilk, laid out in a giant two-story square with interior rooms that faced a courtyard and the swimming pool, and exterior rooms that faced the parking lot. The Muse children were assigned a room facing the parking lot. Father Frank opened the door for them and ushered them inside.

"This is your home away from home for the next couple of days," he said. "Relax and get some rest. You'll be perfectly safe. We have people outside whose job it is to make sure that everything is perfectly safe."

"Thank you," Kimberly said. The beds looked impossibly inviting. For the first time since the ordeal began, she felt the weight of exhaustion pressing down on her.

"Sleep as late as you want," Father Frank said. "We'll be sure to get you fed." His eyes fell to Kimberly's filthy outfit and her bare feet. "Tomorrow we'll get you some new clothes, too. There's a store right across the street."

Kimberly scowled and leaned out the door, past Father Frank to have a look for herself. "Where?" she said.

"Where what?"

"Where's the store?"

Father Frank seemed confused. Could it be any more obvious? "Right there," he said, pointing to the brightly lit store on the far side of the parking lot.

"What, the K-Mart?"

Father Frank nodded. "They're open all night, but I thought you'd prefer to get some rest."

Kimberly gave him a look that made him wonder if maybe he'd grown an extra nose. "K-Mart," she said, tasting the very concept.

"They've got pretty good stuff."

Kimberly snorted, "I am *not* shopping at K-Mart." Before Father Frank could say a word, she closed the door.

The next day, they went shopping at the mall.

17

Back in Panama, nearly forty-eight hours had passed since Kurt Muse had been spirited away from the airport, and no one in the American government had any idea where he was. It was as if he had evaporated. Feelers had been put out through diplomatic channels, but they'd turned up nothing. In Washington, D.C., people in high places were waking up other people in high places trying to find the string to pull that would locate him.

Primary coordination for all these activities on the Isthmus fell to the provisional lawyer Kurt didn't yet know he had: Marcos Ostrander. And he was getting pretty pissed about being jerked around.

18

Kurt never had a chance, really. The extra guards had arrived without him knowing, and their reaction as he came bolting out of his closet—raising their slung rifles to their shoulders, ready to fire—convinced him to break off his charge early. In the process, he saved his own life.

Sheepishly, without saying a word, he retreated back to his closet, sat back down in his chair, and returned the pen to his pocket. Outside, in the main room, two guards positioned themselves just outside his door and stayed there. The general consensus, from what Kurt could glean from overheard conversation, was that he was cracking under the pressure of confinement.

Maybe they were right. He'd been stupid to try something so bold. Vowing to be more careful in the future, he wrote it off to overexuberance. From now on, he'd be much more staid.

Perhaps if they'd allowed him to sleep, even a little, his head would be clearer about these sorts of things. The couple of times he had started to nod off, someone had poked him in the head with a pencil to wake him up. They played blaring music from a boom box whenever he was alone. He was discovering how effective an interrogation device sleep deprivation really was.

But he had other concerns to think about. He'd been chewing on this damn hotel receipt for a half hour now, and it refused to reduce to a size that he could swallow. They must have made the paper out of plastic!

He had to do something with it, though. The time was coming when they were either going to move him, or notice that he had something in his mouth. The receipt itself was incriminating enough; imagine how quickly their interest would peak if they discovered that he was trying to swallow it.

He had another wild thought. The corner of the room where he was sitting was constructed of concrete block, right? Well concrete block—he'd always called them cinder blocks when he was growing up—had thousands of little nooks and crannies in them. What perfect hiding places for soggy, spit-drenched pieces of a Holiday Inn receipt.

Removing the spitball from his mouth, he went to work tearing tiny bits of paper off the wad and stuffing them into the irregularities of the wall.

It took every bit of half an hour, and more than a few of the paper crumbs fell out of their crannies onto the floor, but he finally got the task done.

Hours passed before they finally summoned him again.

Your mind starts to play games with your body when exhaustion is unrelenting, and for Kurt, the most debilitating symptom of exhaustion was a deepening sadness over all that had transpired in the past several days. His mind kept sinking back into that crushing sense of guilt over all that he had wrought against his family and friends.

He tried to fight the darkest of the thoughts, but the exhaustion would not let him silence them altogether. Every time he felt that he might be getting a handle on rationality, the relentlessness of the boom box somehow wrenched it from his grip. He knew he was losing his edge, and he feared that there was nothing he could do about it.

The door to his closet flew open, startling him. He could tell just from the expression on the guard's face that there had been a significant development. "Come," the guard said.

It occurred to Kurt for the first time that they had started to address him with the same words and the same inflection as the one he used for his dog. The room tilted a little as he stood, but he didn't stumble. He did his best to stand tall as he followed the guard back to the office where his last confrontation with the captain had taken place.

As he stepped across the threshold, he felt the color drain from his face. They had the gym bag. That meant they had everything.

It's amazing what you never think about when you think you'll never be caught. From the earliest days of their clandestine operations, Kurt had kept all their tradecraft tools (such as they were) stuffed in a black athletic bag, which he in turn kept well hidden under the backseat of his Jeep. In it were his two-way radio, the PDF code book, the keys to all the apartments where the transmitters were stored—everything they would need to nail him to the wall.

"From the look on your face, I presume that you recognize these toys," the captain said.

Kurt didn't bother to respond. What could he say?

The captain motioned to a chair. "Sit," he said.

Kurt sat. The charades and the gamesmanship were all over. Now it was only the darkness of the future.

The captain produced two more signed leases and dangled them in the air in front of Kurt. "How many mistresses can one man have?" the captain asked.

He was toying, and Kurt chose not to rise to the bait.

Next, the captain displayed the radio, the code book, and a set of apartment keys. "I'm sure that these have something to do with your mistresses as well? The time has come for you to start talking openly and honestly with us, Mr. Muse. With your help or without it, we will match these keys with the appropriate apartments, and we will know what you are hiding. Make it easier on yourself by making it easier on us."

Kurt's heart felt as though it had been gripped by an invisible hand. What would stalling for time do now? How much time could it possibly buy? Two, three hours maybe? Surely his friends and family had had the time to get away by now. There are elements of chess in every negotiation, and as in chess, there comes a moment to surrender.

"I am Radio la Voz de la Libertad," Kurt said.

The captain did not appear to be surprised.

Kurt went on, "Those leases and those keys are for the apartments I rented to house the transmitters. Give me the keys and I'll tell you which keys go to which apartments."

The captain made no effort to hand the keys over. "Who else is involved?"

The invisible hand made a fist. "No one," he said.

The captain's eyes narrowed. "Don't lie to me."

Kurt looked away. He'd been a terrible liar his entire life. Whenever he'd tried, people always knew. His only defense was to cast his eyes downward. No matter what, he would not betray his friends. He would not give out their names.

"You work for the CIA," the captain said.

Kurt's head snapped up. "No."

"Yes," the captain said. "Your computer uses a different operating system. Did you really think that we wouldn't find out?"

Silence.

"Answer me, Mr. Muse."

"I never gave it much thought," he said, honestly enough. "It's an Apple computer. Right off the shelf."

"Provided to you by the American CIA."

"No!"

"We know that you are a spy, Mr. Muse. We know that they have been supplying your equipment."

"I am not a spy," Kurt insisted.

"You are an employee of the CIA."

"I am not!" His voice climbed an octave in indignation. "I am an employee of Intergraphic, Incorporated. It's my family's company."

"That is your cover."

This was absurd. "You're out of your mind."

The captain slapped the desk. "Don't lie to me!"

"I'm not lying! I do not—"

"Explain this!" The captain reached to the floor behind his desk, out of sight, and lifted a cardboard box, displaying it as if doing a commercial.

Kurt recognized it instantly. It was a box for one of the three battery backups that Father Frank had provided to them after their meeting in the park. "That's a box," Kurt said. He could hear the petulance in his own voice.

"We found it in your garage."

Kurt shrugged, continuing to look indignant. "There are many boxes in my garage."

"Indeed there were," the captain said. Kurt did not miss the use of the past tense. "We've determined that this box held radio equipment. A battery backup."

It would have been more impressive detective work had the box not said BATTERY BACKUP. "It's for the transmitters," Kurt explained. "I already told you that."

The captain rotated the open box to display a label that had been affixed to the bottom, and in that instant, Kurt understood.

"What do you read here, Mr. Muse?"

Kurt dropped his head, thoroughly deflated, thoroughly defeated.

"Read it," the captain said.

Kurt cleared his throat. "It says, 'Program Development Group.' "

"I'm sorry, Mr. Muse, I couldn't hear you."

"It says 'Program Development Group.' " This time he nearly shouted the words. Jesus God, he couldn't believe the stupidity. The entire world recognized the Program Development Group (PDG) in Corozal to be the euphemism for the Central Intelligence Agency in Panama. They all knew it because Manuel Noriega was so thoroughly ensconced in the daily doings of the PDG over the years that he probably knew his way to all the coffee pots in the place. Noriega's primary currency with the United States had been his ability to tap every phone in Panama, and as a result, he'd accumulated countless millions in his personal fortune. What the Agency thought it was hiding when it addressed items to the PDG was beyond Kurt.

His mind raced back to the day just a few weeks before when they'd taken delivery of the battery backup from a go-between sent by Father Frank. Kurt had blown his stack with the CIA operative when he'd found half a dozen PDG labels all over the box. Kurt had torn them all off by the fistful as he chided the go-between for having been so reckless. "We're trying to keep a low profile here," Kurt had ranted. "This kind of shit can get people killed, you know? Suppose I had this box in my car and some goon pulls me over for a traffic stop. You want to see me get arrested? My God. This is precisely why we've never done business with you in the past."

Well, apparently, he'd missed one of the stickers.

"Why don't you sign this, Mr. Muse, and we can let you get along with your life, such as it will be."

The captain slid a confession across the desk. For the first time since he'd started interrogating Kurt, he was smiling.

19

Kimberly was beginning to feel human again. She had new shoes, a shirt and a pair of long pants, plus some underwear and just enough makeup to let her feel like a girl. But by the end of the second day in Panama City, Florida, she was ready to go someplace where the Waffle House was not, in fact, the most happening place there was.

Their keepers—Joey Skinner insisted that they were CIA, and that sounded right to Kimberly—were still jumpy about letting them go anywhere or do anything. They acted like assassins were lurking around every corner waiting to take them out. They also wouldn't let them contact their mother by phone. They said that she was aware that they were safe, but that for some reason they *weren't* safe to use the telephone. It didn't make any sense to Kimberly, and frankly she was getting tired of hanging around all the gloomy cloak-and-dagger types.

She'd been watching the news a lot these past few days—what else was there to do?—hoping to hear some kind of story about her dad, but there was nothing. With all this hullabaloo and all the activity surrounding their escape from Panama, you'd have thought that the story would have at least been big enough for some mention on CNN.

Yet, there was nothing.

At the end of their second day, Father Frank announced to them that it was time to leave. He reviewed some security concerns: it was important that they all stay together, that they keep their conversations to a minimum, that they not speak of where they are coming from or where they are going, and in general that they should strive to be as invisible as they could possibly be.

Kimberly found herself respecting Father Frank for not even asking them if they had any questions. He acknowledged up front that he had no information to share with them. Unlike the others, though, it wasn't a matter of not knowing; it was merely a matter of keeping the secrets secret. At one level it was annoying as hell, but on another it truly was irrelevant. They were going where they were going, and when they got there, everyone would know what the plan was. Knowing before then was just so much icing on the cake.

They drove in the Jeeps to the airport at Fort Walton Beach, avoiding all the normal travel procedures—Immigration, boarding gate, the whole nine yards—and instead boarded the Boeing 727 via the exterior stairway that led to the Jetway. It was not lost on Kimberly that on a commercial flight headed to Atlanta the first twenty-five seats in the coach section of the aircraft were empty while the rear of the aircraft was packed with travelers.

If there had ever been any doubt that the CIA was involved, that fact alone made the doubt go away.

As they settled into their seats, Erik asked Kimberly why they were going to Atlanta when their mom was in Florida, but Kimberly told him to be quiet, citing the security speech they'd received at the hotel. The truth of it was she had no idea. Still, the one thing she was beginning to learn was that their handlers were most concerned about making sure that she and her little brother ended up where they were supposed to be, on a schedule that only the handlers understood.

The flight to Atlanta was entirely uneventful. Father Frank sat across the aisle from the Muse children, and as they flew, he seemed completely comfortable lounging back in his seat and reading the in-flight magazine. This whole ordeal seemed as normal to him as just another day at the office.

On final approach into Atlanta's Hartsfield International Airport, though, he started to show signs of unease, shifting in his seat and checking his wristwatch two or three times a minute. His nervousness raised Kimberly's anxiety as well, but not enough for her to share it with Erik or the family. Clearly, though, something interesting was about to happen.

They touched down without incident, and after the pilot deployed the reversers and the brakes to bring the 727 to a halt, they taxied not to the terminal itself, but to a spot on the tarmac that was out of the normal traffic flow. When they were at a full stop, Father Frank stood in the aisle and made an announcement to the passengers.

"Ladies and gentlemen, I'm sorry for the delay, but at this time I need for the passengers who arrived with me to move forward and deplane to the waiting cars. Everyone else, please stay in your seats, and we'll have you to your gate shortly. Thank you very much." Typical of everything about Father Frank, the directions were short and to the point.

As one, the group of refugees, who were still little more than strangers to each other, thanks to the isolation in which they'd been kept, rose and headed through the first-class cabin to the aircraft's front door, where an internal stairway that Kimberly didn't even know existed on these airplanes had been deployed. They walked down to the tarmac, where a line of four black vans sat waiting, their engines running. Kimberly and Erik entered first, as always, followed closely by the Skinners, and then by various other refugees, just so many strange faces.

As soon as all the seats were filled, the van began to roll.

To Kimberly's eye, the driver didn't appear to be that much older than she herself. She had blond hair and a bright smile. "Hi, everybody, how are you today?" Her voice seemed oddly cheerful under the circumstances and had a southern twang to it.

The response from her passengers was mostly a grudging silence.

"Well, I understand you've had a tough couple of days. I hope you all enjoy your time in Miami."

So that's where we're going, Kimberly thought.

"Whoa!" said a voice from the back of the van. "What do you mean Miami?"

Kimberly turned with the rest of the occupants to see a man in a business suit sitting among the refugees. He clearly was very American, and now that she thought about it, Kimberly realized that she'd never seen him before.

"I'm not going to Miami," the man said. "I'm going to Chicago."

All the cheer drained from the driver's face. "Excuse me?"

The guy in the suit copped an attitude. "You said we were going to Miami. I don't want to go to Miami. I have to be in Chicago."

The driver's eyes narrowed. "Are you part of the special charter group?"

The guy shrugged. "I don't think so."

The driver looked to the rest of the group. "Is he with you?"

Kimberly shrugged. She'd been surrounded by so many refugees and handlers these past couple of days, she didn't know one person from the next.

The guy in the suit seemed to sense that he'd stirred a hornet's nest. "Look, I didn't mean to cause any trouble."

"Didn't they tell everybody who was not part of this group to stay in their seats?"

The guy shrugged. "I don't know. I guess maybe. I was in the middle of a book. I saw people get up, so I followed."

The driver cursed under her breath and spoke into a portable radio, the speaker for which was plugged into her ear. She listened to the response, stopped the van, climbed out her door, and walked to the passenger door on the right-hand side. She pulled it open and motioned to the party crasher. "I'm sorry, sir, but I'm going to have to ask you to get out of the van."

The man's face formed a giant O. "*What?*"

"You're not supposed to be here. I need you to exit the van."

The guy looked around to get his bearings. "We're in the middle of the runway!"

"No, sir, we're in a taxiway, and someone will be by to pick you up shortly. Now I have to ask you to leave."

Kimberly could see the leading edges of panic invading the guy's face. "You can't do that."

"Please don't make this ugly, sir." She positioned her arm in such a way as to show that she was armed.

"This is outrageous!"

"Now, sir."

"Okay, I'll go to Miami."

"*Now*, sir. You can spend the night tonight in Chicago, or in a jail cell in Atlanta. You need to choose right this instant."

The last Kimberly saw of the man in the suit, he was cursing himself purple, shaking his fist, and kicking the pavement in the middle of a remote taxiway.

It helped to know that someone was having nearly as bad a day as she.

20

Frustration levels within the intelligence, diplomatic, and military communities in Panama had climbed off the charts. The official line from the Noriega regime still maintained that they'd never heard of a Kurt Muse and that they certainly did not have him in custody. It was as if the man had disappeared into the ether.

But he hadn't, and people with jobs significantly above the pay grades of anyone in Panama wanted to know exactly where Muse was, what charges he was being held on, and when the regime intended to give him back.

Marcos Ostrander had been named for the moment as Kurt's de facto lawyer, and he was doing everything he could to keep the heat turned all the way to high, but there was only so much one could do when the party on the other side of the bar refuses to admit that it has custody. He was expressing his frustration with a midlevel official of the U.S. embassy when the discussion turned to the injustice of it all. Here, these PDF goons get to travel at will, protected by the U.S. government, passing in and out of Miami as if it were a suburb of Panama City on visas that were virtually guaranteed to be granted, yet those same people had the audacity to physically hide an American citizen from his lawyer.

It'd be a hell of a thing, they said, if these bastards were stuck in their own country for a while. Cancel those visas—cut the PDF power structure off from their mistresses and shopping sprees—and by God they bet there'd be action pretty soon.

The words hadn't finished echoing in the room before the two men looked at each other. Who exactly did have the authority to cancel visas to the United States?

Well, certainly the ambassador, but he himself answered to the very highest levels of the government, where political concerns often trumped practical ones. Short of him, neither Marcos nor his midlevel friend knew for sure.

The good news was, if they didn't know, then Noriega probably wouldn't know either. A plan was hatched. On his own authority—presumed, but never granted—the staffer picked up the phone and made a call. Just like that, all Panamanian visas to the United States were canceled. From president to peasant, every Panamanian was stranded in their own country until Noriega coughed up Kurt Frederick Muse.

It actually only took a few hours.

The following morning at 10:00 the PDF organized a press conference in which Kurt Muse was presented to the world as a spy for the U.S. government.

PART 2

"No One Walks Out Alive"

21

At forty-six, U.S. Air Force Colonel Jim Ruffer had lived enough lives for two people. Born in 1943 to an Army cryptographer, he had spent his early years in Hawaii, and finally followed his brother into the Marine Corps, where he joined the famed Black Sheep Squadron and flew ninety-two combat missions over Vietnam. When he was done with that war, he spent five months in Japan before finally deciding that what he really wanted to do with his life was to become a doctor.

While attending med school in Mexico, he met Margarita, with whom he quite literally fell in love at first sight. They married, and after he became a physician, Ruffer longed for the action again and rejoined the military, this time as a Navy flight surgeon. He found the job fascinating, but after five years at sea aboard aircraft carriers, he decided that his real love was waiting for him at home, enduring the long separations that made Navy life so difficult for everyone who chose that line of work.

Discharged honorably, he and Margarita moved to Idaho and Jim hung out his shingle as a private practitioner. It was everything he expected from life as a small-town doctor where practitioners of the medical arts were few and far between. In fact, it was much, much more. Day after day, night after night, the phone rang constantly with citizens of his community in need of help and hand-holding. The psychological rewards were tremendous, even if the financial ones were not, but when it finally occurred to him that after months of private practice he had never once completed an entire bath without being interrupted by a phone call, he realized that it was time to move on yet again.

The U.S. military had been good to Jim in the past, and when the time came for him to seek greener pastures, he didn't search for green at all, but rather for Air Force blue. After eight months of private practice, he once again found himself in the role of a flight surgeon, this time for NASA's Voyager program.

For Margarita, however—the patient one who had endured so much time as a loving wife without a husband—it had been too long since she'd lived in a Spanish-speaking country, so when an opportunity arose for Jim to take a position at Howard Air Force base in the Canal Zone, he jumped at it.

The duty in Panama was unique, to say the least. Besides routine medical chores, he also found himself serving as understudy to Command Surgeon Mike McConnell, and in that role, Jim Ruffer found himself often in the company of senior command officers attending meetings and strategy sessions that were much more complex and highly classified than anything he'd attended previously.

He also found himself investigating illnesses of a nature he'd not encountered in the past. For example, in an effort to protect Howard Air Force Base from intrusions and security penetrations, the commanders had planted boonie rats on motor bikes in the jungles to keep an eye on the various trails and clandestine routes of entry. Over the course of just a few weeks, fourteen of these soldiers were attacked by vampire bats. Not deadly in the Bram Stoker sense of the word, the bats were nonetheless a huge morale problem and not an insignificant threat for the transmission of rabies and other diseases.

Thus, working with the epidemiological section, Jim Ruffer, MD, soon became an expert on the elimination of vampire bats.

The solution was not one to garner the support of the animal rights movement, but it was very effective: They staked out a goat that had been smeared with the blood thinner coumadin (which is also a component of rat poison). When the bats attacked, they took the coumadin back to their caves with them. As the critters would preen each other, the drug would get into their system and they'd bleed to death through their gastronitestinal system.

It was amazing, sometimes, where military medicine took a guy.

On April 13, 1989, Jim Ruffer was on the second floor of Gorgas Hospital, the former French hospital on the hills above Chorrillo, the worst conceivable section of Panama City, when he received a phone call from Lieutenant Colonel Robert Perry of the Treaty Affairs office. An Army guy and a fellow Mormon, Rob Perry had always given him the feeling that he was an intel guy at heart. After brief pleasantries, Perry said, "So, Jim, do you have a little black bag with medical stuff in it?"

Is the Pope Catholic? "Sure."

"Okay, I want you to do me a favor and grab it and meet a car out front in ten minutes."

This didn't sound right. "What's up?"

"We can talk in the car," Perry said. "Ten minutes, right?"

"I'll be there."

Nine minutes and sixty seconds later, an Army staff car pulled to the curb in front of Gorgas, and Jim Ruffer climbed inside. Next to Perry sat a young State Department staffer who was all business and impressed Jim as an up-and-comer on the diplomatic front.

"Here it is," Perry said, getting right down to it. "Kurt Muse, an American citizen and DoD dependent, was arrested six days ago and has been kept under wraps. Since his arrest, the PDF has maintained that they know nothing about him or his whereabouts, and now, suddenly, after we canceled the bastards' visas, they're coughing him up for some bogus press conference. We want you to take a look at him and tell us if he's been treated all right."

"He's been there for six days?" Jim asked, making sure he'd heard correctly.

Perry nodded.

"Then he's not all right."

Kurt knew something was coming, but he didn't know what. The DENI headquarters was buzzing with a new excitement, and he could see out the window on the far end of the room that people were gathering in large numbers. He had an idea that it was about time for his perp walk, the parade in front of the television cameras for the world to see—

What, exactly? A local businessman who helped to bring shame and dishonor to a dictator who considered himself the owner of an entire country. His fears were confirmed when a new player entered his tiny room. Kurt recognized him right away as Lieutenant Colonel Nivaldo Madriñán, the chief of the DENI, and a neighbor who lived not a hundred yards from Kurt's house in El Avance.

"So, Mr. Muse, you are the spy I've been hearing so much about."

"I'm not a spy." This exact exchange had happened so many times now, with so many different players that it was beginning to feel programmed.

"You are in a lot of trouble."

"I can see that. Are you planning to file charges against me any time soon?"

Madriñán's eyes narrowed. Clearly, he was here to ask questions, not answer them. "We have arranged a press conference. We will make a statement, and we will present you to the cameras, but we have instructed the reporters not to ask questions, and I am now instructing you not to answer any questions. Have I made myself clear?"

"What are you afraid I'll say?"

Madriñán's eyes grew hotter. "Do you suffer from high blood pressure, Mr. Muse?"

The sudden change in subject was a little unnerving. "No."

"How about insomnia?"

"No."

A hint of a smile appeared on Madriñán's face. "Well, you're soon going to suffer from both."

Robert Perry girded himself for battle as they drove toward DENI headquarters. It felt like he'd done nothing but gird himself for battle over the past two years, and in his case, it was a 360-degree battle front. On the one hand, as the Treaty Affairs officer and the cochair of the Binational Joint Committee provided for in the Panama Canal Treaty, he was charged with protecting the interests of U.S. forces and their families in Panama; on the other hand, he had to deal with General Woerner, the commander in chief of the U.S. Southern Command, whose overarching mission in life seemed to be focused on turning the other cheek. The fact that the State Department was continually putting pressure on Congress and the president to stomp on Noriega and his abuses didn't help a bit. The more dogmatic State became, the more entrenched and resistant the push back from DoD.

Caught in the middle of the clashing political titans was Robert Perry, who just wanted the abuses to stop. A year before, in the summer of 1987, he'd sent a letter to Woerner detailing Perry's deepening concern over the treatment of military personnel in Panama. Woerner didn't buy it; he wanted hard data that he had to know was unavailable. Statistics notwithstanding, Perry had been stationed in Panama before, and he knew what he knew; he saw the changes. The fact that Woerner didn't want to hear it didn't change a thing.

Noriega constantly fanned the flames of anti-American sentiments among his troops, boasting publicly and privately that he had President Bush's "balls in my pocket." As the conditions deteriorated, the PDF became steadily bolder. In one recent incident, an American citizen had been arrested for smoking pot, and rather than following through with the normal flow of the judicial process, the PDF goons had beaten the guy to a pulp and thrown him into the trunk of his car. Because that hadn't been enough fun, they'd taken turns sexually abusing his wife while he listened helplessly to her screams. Perry couldn't stand it.

It had been several days since Perry had gotten the call that an American citizen had been picked up for running the illegal radio station, Voice of Liberty. When word got to Woerner, the general was pissed and ill-inclined to get involved. As far as he was concerned, it was just another case of the CIA conducting ops on his facilities without him being aware of it. If the Agency got itself into a bind, then it could by God get itself out of it without involving Army resources.

But it wasn't anywhere near that simple. First of all, Major Alan Mansfield of the Provost Marshal's office had moved heaven and earth to accomplish some amazing feats to spirit Muse's family to safety, and through that activity, an Agency operative from Langley had taken up residence on Fort Clayton and was stirring as many pots as he could find to get a grasp on exactly what was happening.

Trouble was, if the reports were true that this Muse fellow had in fact violated Panamanian law on Panamanian soil, then there wasn't a hell of a lot that Treaty Affairs could do for him. Then came the bombshell that nearly blew Woerner out of his chair: Muse was a DoD de-

pendent. His wife was a teacher in the DoD school system, and that relationship brought Muse directly under the jurisdiction of the Panama
Canal Treaty, thus invoking many of the rights afforded to American
citizens on American soil. Habeus corpus was among the most basic of
these.

Woerner was angry; he wanted nothing to do with a man and his
toy radio. The last thing he wanted, he said to Perry, was to get involved in yet one more tussle that was going to justify more harassment of U.S. forces by the PDF. Nonetheless, he was in a corner legally,
and he grudgingly stopped blocking Perry's efforts to take care of the
CIA spy.

The first step, of course, was getting the bastards to admit that they
had custody in the first place, and the PDF was in no hurry to produce
him. In fact, Perry's cochair on the Panamanian side of the Treaty Affairs Commission had made it abundantly clear that the powers that
be were none too pleased to hear of the Treaty jurisdiction. It was safe
to assume that they had had some interesting and awful experiences lying in wait for Mr. Muse and that a good deal of the fun would be de-
railed because of Perry's involvement.

Perry was grateful for the opportunity. He knew what Muse was
going through, what hellholes Noriega's interrogation pits could be.
Nivaldo Madriñán was one very, very bad man, who was more than
capable of unspeakable tortures. The sooner they could get in contact
with Muse, the more likely it was that they could intervene in some
meaningful way.

Which, of course, was the last thing the PDF was inclined to see
happen, thus all the denials and delays. The cancellation of the visas
had been a masterstroke, he thought, and he couldn't wait for the opportunity to shake the hand of the man who had come up with it.

So now they were holding a press conference to show off the man
of whom they continued to deny that they had custody. Who the hell
did these people think they were? It was time to play hardball.

The U.S. government car arrived at DENI headquarters. "Okay,"
Perry said to his entourage. "We go in there like we own the place, understand? They're not going to be happy that we're here, and I could
not care less."

The three men moved as one, out of their vehicle and through the
front doors of the station. They waded through the crowd toward the

office marked COMMANDING OFFICER. They were still twenty feet from the doorway when an armed guard stepped forward to block their path. Perry didn't slow down until his nose and the guard's were separated only by inches. Perry said in flawless Spanish, "We're here to see Kurt Frederick Muse, an American citizen in your custody."

The guard was joined by others. "I cannot let you pass."

"Then I demand to see the commanding officer."

A second guard, the latest to join the little clutch of uniforms, said, "Colonel Madriñán is not here."

"You're lying. He's conducting a press conference, for God's sake."

"He is not here. I need to ask you to leave."

Perry recoiled at the thought. "You can ask whatever you want, but we're not going away until we speak to Colonel Madriñán."

"He is not here." This time the guard's tone was heavy and threatening.

Perry eyed the guards for a long moment and then pushed past them. There wasn't a scenario he could think of that would allow a PDF nobody to shoot a lieutenant colonel in the U.S. Army. He went to the heavy wooden door to Madriñán's office with the intention of marching right in, but he found it locked, and he pounded with his fist.

The guards moved in close, to threaten him, but they kept their hands to themselves. "Stop!" they commanded.

But Perry kept pounding.

Finally, the door opened, and there was Nivaldo Madriñán, his face red with rage.

Perry gave his most officious smile. "Good afternoon, Colonel. I'm glad to see you've returned. We're here to see Kurt Muse."

Madriñán snorted, "You have no right."

"I have every right. He is an American citizen and a dependent of a U.S. military employee. Do I need to show you the Treaty?"

Madriñán's eyes burned with rage. He knew that Perry was right.

"This needn't be ugly, Colonel," Perry said. "But I won't hesitate to make it so."

Madriñán stewed for a moment and then nodded. "Come back in one hour. You can see him then."

"After the press conference?" Perry said.

"In one hour."

Madriñán closed the door, and that was the end of it.

22

Kurt did not expect the press conference to be as intimidating as it was. The room was packed wall to wall with people. He figured they must be the representatives of the press, but truthfully, he didn't realize that there were this many reporters in Panama. In a sense, he was right; of the dozens of reporters crammed into the room, none were from any Panamanian newspaper. This was the foreign press. The Panamanians got their news directly from Noriega's propaganda machine. After so many sleepless hours, the flashes of the camera strobes and the commotion of the shouted questions made him feel disoriented and dizzy, and the resulting images showed it. Only, in the pictures he didn't look tired and disoriented; he looked frightened and guilty as hell.

They brought him in from the side, after reminding him of the ground rules: no questions and no answers. He was to stand there and be a puppet for their outrageous accusations. Along the front of the room, they'd lined a table and the floor with what appeared to be everything that he owned. There were the various transmitters, three of them in all, plus the boxes they'd been sent in. They had his computer, two-way radio, scanner, and various notebooks. The guns they'd taken from the house were also prominently displayed. Honestly, if it had been different circumstances on a different day, he himself would have been impressed with the size of the cache. He'd never seen it all gathered in one spot like this. He and his gang had done one hell of a job.

Madriñán made the presentation. Kurt Frederick Muse, it turned out, citizen of the United States of America, was an employee of the U.S. Department of State and had confessed his direct participation in a destabilization plan involving clandestine television and radio stations. The American government had provided him with this $300,000 worth of clandestine electronic equipment, the purpose of which was to bring harm to the free and independent peoples of Panama.

It went on from there, and Kurt found himself stunned. First of all, last time he'd heard, he'd been a Yankee dog working for the CIA, and now he'd learned that he was a Yankee dog working for the State Department. Who knew? And if he'd known that he could get anything close to $300,000 for the $5,000 or $6,000 worth of gear, he might have cashed out a long time ago.

This whole show was a sham, and deep in his heart he knew that the people who mattered to him would know that every word they heard from the podium here was a lie. Of course, a press corps that agreed to ask no questions of the accused would clearly ask no questions of his accusers, so the Latin American press would believe everything—even if they knew better. This was how this part of the world operated. The truth was important, but staying alive was better.

The entire press conference, such as it was, lasted all of ten minutes. It was a diatribe about the evil influence of the Yankee imperialists on the beneficent and peaceful leadership of Manuel Noriega. When Madriñán was done speaking, he turned to leave the podium, and the guards closed in around Kurt to urge him to follow.

Kurt had nearly reached the exit door when an American reporter rushed forward and shoved a microphone under his chin. "Mr. Muse, do you work for the U.S. State Department?"

Kurt didn't drop a beat. "No."

"Have you ever worked for them?"

"No, I have never worked for them."

It was all they could get on the record before the reporter was pushed out of the way.

Across town, in the comfort of an apartment he hadn't left for five days and surrounded by enough firepower to repulse a small army, Pablo Martinez watched the press conference on television. The man he saw on television was a mere ghost of the man he had known for so many years as Kurt Muse. Unshaven and clearly unshowered, he appeared to have lost ten pounds. There was an ashen quality about him, and a deer-in-the-headlights stare that spoke of some form of abuse while in captivity.

But through the gaunt exhaustion, Pablo also saw a measure of defiant strength. Whatever he had done, and whatever he had signed, he hadn't crossed the line of betrayal.

His suspicions were confirmed as Pablo listened carefully as Colonel Madriñán read Kurt's confession. The words themselves were irrelevant; he assumed them all to be lies. What he listened for were key phrases. He heard, *Kurt Muse did this* and *Mr. Muse did that.* He heard about the involvement of the State Department (imagine how surprised the diplomatic corps will be!) and he heard about the attempt of one man—a hated American—to bring down the Noriega government. He heard it all, but never once heard the word "conspiracy." He never heard a mention of a "them" at all; it was all about what Kurt had done.

As inconceivable as it was, Kurt had withstood the misery and depravity that the PDF had thrown at him and never once mentioned the names of the people with whom he had worked so closely.

If he hadn't broken yet, Pablo figured, he never would. He realized that it was safe to come out of hiding.

23

It seemed important to Madriñán that Perry and his entourage—a little larger on this return trip—see the cache of equipment they had on display in the room that was now devoid of reporters. The guards deliberately took a long way around to the commander's office, presumably for the express purpose of making sure the equipment was seen and noted. Of particular interest, Perry thought, was the prominently displayed label on one of the boxes showing the shipping destination to be the Program Development Group at Fort Clayton. He also noted that the shipping address was an APO box, which meant that it had been shipped on military aircraft, presumably without Woerner's knowledge or permission. The general was going to shit a brick when he found out.

As they walked, Perry fell back in the line to tell one of the junior officers in their party to take a close look at the radio equipment and write down any serial numbers he could find. There was no telling what kind of justice Kurt Muse was likely to see in this armpit of a place, and it seemed like the least they could do to make sure that the evidence itself was not tainted.

In the sixty minutes that had passed since their last meeting, Perry had thought through their strategy one more time. According to the ground rules established by Jimmy Carter during the negotiations that would hand over one of the world's most valuable assets to one of its craziest citizens, the entire deal could be queered by even minor treaty violations during the interim period. Being robbed of billions of dollars had to be one of Noriega's greatest fears, and Perry figured that the Pineapple's orders to his underlings had to make that point abundantly clear.

And that was the pressure point on which Perry and his entourage would focus. The treaty was very precise in its language governing the treatment of Defense Department employees in the custody of local law enforcement officials, and Perry was going to see to it that the i's were dotted and the t's crossed.

With the one officer left behind, Perry and Jim Ruffer eventually arrived at Madriñán's door, which the guard opened without knocking, and ushered them inside. Madriñán sat behind his huge wooden desk, which itself was dwarfed by the cavernous size of the room. He rose grudgingly to greet his visitors and scowled when he counted their numbers.

"Where are the others?" he asked the guard.

Perry answered for him. "They're back in the other room, looking at the radio equipment."

Madriñán looked horrified. He shot a glance to the guard for confirmation.

"We're just noting the serial numbers," Perry said, as if it meant nothing. "I don't think you have to worry."

"Stop them!" Madriñán commanded to the guard, who seemed suddenly frightened. "Right now. Go out there and stop them." The guard damn near turned himself inside out leaving the office.

"I'll remind you that this is my office, not yours," Madriñán said.

Perry tossed off a shrug. "Are you prepared to produce your prisoner?"

You could almost hear the wheels spinning in Madriñán's head as he considered his options, which were essentially zero. He'd seen the treaty, and by now, after all these days of nonstop interrogation, he surely knew that its provisions were relevant to Muse's case. Finally, Madriñán nodded to a henchman, who in turn opened a side door and ushered his prisoner into the room.

Jim Ruffer was appalled. The man he saw entering the room clearly had been worked over. He was taller than Jim had been expecting, and he walked with the shuffling gate of someone who had been shackled.

He kept his hands to his sides, and his eyes cast downward, until he saw the American uniforms and then his face brightened.

One of the DENI guards pointed to a chair at a small table, and the prisoner sat down, his hands folded in front of him.

"Are you Kurt Frederick Muse?" Perry asked.

Kurt nodded. "Yes, sir." His eyes were bloodshot, Jim noticed, and he appeared to be very, very tired.

"I'm Lieutenant Colonel Robert Perry, and this is Doctor Jim Ruffer. I'm the Treaty Affairs officer here in Panama, and we're here to make sure that you're treated properly under the terms of the Panama Canal Treaty." He went on at some length, explaining Kurt's right to legal representation and to fair treatment, but Jim had the sense that the speech was more for the benefit of the DENI officers than it was for their prisoner. When he was done with the legal details, Perry said, "We're working to arrange a Panamanian lawyer for you. I brought Doctor Ruffer along to assess your health and to make sure that you have not been mistreated."

Ruffer took that as his cue and stepped forward. "I need some privacy, please. I'd like to be alone with my patient."

Madriñán's face remained grim. "That is not possible," he said.

Jim looked to Perry for support.

"He's legally entitled to medical care," Perry said.

"Indeed. Examine him. But nowhere in the treaty is he entitled to a private room while the examination takes place."

Perry's posture alone told Ruffer that they'd lost this one. He sat down next to Kurt and opened his doctor's bag. As he did, he noticed that the official party moved away from them. Rhetoric notwithstanding, nobody likes to stand too close to someone else's medical exam.

"How are you?" Ruffer asked, keeping his voice as low as he could.

"Not bad," Kurt said.

"Do you mind if I examine you?"

Kurt shrugged. "I suppose not."

"We just want to make sure that your overall health is good." Jim slipped a blood pressure cuff onto Kurt's arm and inflated it. "Your eyes are red," he said. "Have you been crying?"

"No." And if he had been, he wouldn't have admitted it.

"What about your interrogations. What have they been like?"

"Lots and lots of questions."

"Have you been beaten?"

"No, sir."

Jim noted that each answer brought definite eye contact, reassuring him that Kurt was telling the truth. "Any mistreatment at all? Don't be afraid to tell me if there has."

The fleeting temptation to report the murder of the Colombian evaporated the instant it appeared. This was not the forum, and nothing would bring the man back. "Just lack of sleep," Kurt said. "I haven't slept in days. I haven't washed or changed clothes, either. I bet I'm getting pretty rank."

Actually, he was. "Your blood pressure's normal," Jim said, his voice even softer than before.

"They told me that my family is in danger," Kurt said.

"They lied." Ruffer said this with a wink and a smile. Perry had anticipated this question and told him to assure Kurt that his family was perfectly safe. "Don't ask for details because I don't know any, but your family is perfectly fine."

"Are they still in Panama?" Kurt whispered.

"They're fine," Jim repeated. Subtext: We're not discussing this here. Kurt understood. "Please make sure they know that I'm okay."

"We don't know that yet, do we?"

"Tell them anyway, no matter what."

Ruffer didn't commit one way or the other. First of all, he had no idea whether he'd ever be in direct contact with the Muse family, and even if he would, he had no idea what he'd be empowered to say. He put the BP cuff away and removed another tiny medical kit from his bag. This was the lighted scope he used to examine a patient's ears, nose, and mouth. It came housed in a case, and as he opened the top, he turned it so that Kurt could see the inside of the lid. There, Jim had taped a piece of paper with a snippet of a William Wordsworth poem:

Our birth is but a sleep and a forgetting. —Wordsworth

Jim shined the light into Kurt's left ear and leaned in close to take a look. "Read the lid, Kurt," he whispered. To anyone else, it looked like a normal ear exam. "It may feel sometimes as if you are alone, but remember that you never really are. We're going to work to get you someplace safe, and hopefully get you out of here entirely, but these things can take time." He pulled away and crossed behind to examine his right ear. "If bad things happen, if they beat you or abuse you in any way, you need to let us know."

"How?"

It was a good question. "That will become clear in a while." That was a total bluff. Jim had no idea how they were going to communicate after this meeting. "Do you need anything now?"

"Clothes," Kurt said. "I have my suitcase still, but nothing for the heat."

"I'll see what I can do. Anything else?"

Kurt thought for a moment, keeping his sights focused on hittable targets. "Just make sure that Annie knows that I'm safe and that I'm being strong."

Jim nodded and winked. "Done," he said. "Now watch this."

Dr. James Ruffer, Lieutenant Colonel, United States Air Force, snapped his examination kit closed and stuffed it into his medical bag. He snatched the bag into his hand and strode over to the official party. His demeanor and gait drew their attention immediately.

"I see you've worked him over pretty good, Colonel," he said to Madriñán. "How dare you treat an American citizen with such utter disregard." Turning to Perry, he gave his official report. "He looks terrible, Colonel. His blood pressure is high, he's clearly suffering from exhaustion, brought on by the unrelenting interrogation pressure and denial of rest. This clearly is a violation of the Treaty."

Those were the magic words—the ones that Noriega most feared. Madriñán seemed confused, but the fact that he didn't argue told Ruffer that through a little fabrication, he'd landed very close to the truth.

"Unacceptable," Perry said. "Utterly unacceptable."

"I fear for Mr. Muse's continued safety," Ruffer said. Without any preparation or rehearsal, he and Perry seemed to be building to the same point.

To Madriñán, Perry said, "The Treaty clearly states that we have a right to see any American citizen in your custody, and we have a right to monitor his medical condition."

Madriñán thought about that. "We have no objection to a reasonable number of visits."

"Every other day," Ruffer said, out of nowhere. "I must see him every other day to properly monitor his condition."

Madriñán's jaw dropped. "That's ridiculous!"

"It's our demand," Perry said. "Unless you want to turn this into an issue of Treaty violation."

Madriñán's face reddened, but clearly he understood that he had no cards left to play. "All right, then. You can see him in Modelo Prison beginning the day after tomorrow. I will provide you with a schedule and from there—"

"No, Colonel," Perry interrupted. "I will provide *you* with a schedule, and you will make every effort to honor it. Now, when do you plan to file formal charges against Mr. Muse?"

Madriñán glared. He was not used to being bossed around, and he didn't like it one bit. "In due time," he said. He nodded to the guards to take Kurt away. To the remaining guards he said, "Please help our visitors find their way out."

24

Carcel Modelo—Modelo Prison—was as famous in Panama as Sing-Sing is in the United States as a place of misery and perpetual torment. Located in the Chorrillo section of the city, it loomed as the worst of the worst circle of hell. It was a place where people entered but never left. For the residents of Chorrillo, the dirty-beige walls and orange roof stood as grim reminders of the fate that awaited them if they stepped out of line.

High walls surrounded the sprawling compound, which itself was bordered by graveyards on two sides, and the Comandancia on a third—the headquarters for the PDF, and the site of Manuel Noriega's executive offices. In the months to follow, Kurt Muse would come to see the proximity of the graves to the Comandancia as a fitting metaphor to Noriega's entire regime.

They drove Kurt in the back of a white pickup truck that had been fitted with a kind of paddy wagon. It was unspeakably hot, and as he drew closer to his final home, he felt a sense of defeat settling on him like a blanket. Two DENI guards accompanied him—one of them a woman, a sergeant—but they said nothing to him. He was not even shackled, and as they approached the roll-up metal door that served as the prison's gate, he was vaguely aware that the next seconds would be his last for a decent shot at getting away. What were the chances, he wondered, of hitting these guys and bolting out of the truck? Even if he got away, what were the chances that he could run farther than a block before he was shot down with all the compassion of a picnicker smashing an ant?

The question would remain forever rhetorical. Just a few seconds after they stopped, the door rumbled up and they entered the compound. From the gate, it was a short drive to the front door of the prison itself. As they closed those last yards, Kurt looked up through the window of the paddy wagon and saw hundreds of desperate faces staring down at him. His stomach knotted as he observed the number of faces per window: six, seven, eight in some cases. How many people could possibly be housed in a single cell? A physical giant by Panamanian standards, and certainly no weakling, he still wondered if it was possible for one man to keep at bay the violence posed by so many against him?

Dignity, he told himself again. Dignity would be the last casualty, no matter what. That was his promise to himself. And to preserve it here in the opening moments of his incarceration meant sucking up the fear and being a man.

He could to this. He *had* to do this.

No more than ten seconds passed after the truck came to a stop when the back doors opened and his captors escorted him out of the daylight and into the darkness. If he'd known how long it would be before he would see the sun again, he'd have turned his face upward to absorb its rays.

Inside, the hallway was a monument to black-and-white tile. It was everywhere, a checkerboard pattern that started on the first step inside, and traveled from there into forever.

His guards led him up a short flight of stairs to an office on the left. The sign on the door identified it as the warden's office, and the warden as one Major Correa.

The office wasn't much, certainly nothing close to the opulence of Madriñán's digs in Ancon. There was a small metal desk, two chairs, a threadbare sofa, and on the wall the glowering image of General Manual Noriega.

I'm screwed, Kurt thought. But that didn't hurt half as much as the thought that that bastard had won.

But the victory was not complete; at least it didn't feel that way. As he met with Correa and went through the details of in-processing, he had the sense that he was not the only person in the room who was nervous. It seemed as if they'd been expecting him, and they were not happy about it. There were several references during that brief initial meeting to his status as an American citizen and to the provisions of the Panama Canal Treaty, and for one brief moment, Kurt almost had the sense that they were trying to be nice to him, to set his mind at ease.

"Mr. Muse, if you obey the rules and do not cause trouble, we will cause no trouble for you."

Kurt nodded but remained expressionless. If he tried to smile, it might seem as if he were mocking them. If he tried to speak, he was certain that his voice would betray his fear. He was nothing now. Nobody. His future was entirely in the hands of other people, and there was no one in the world to blame for his predicament but himself.

Good God, what had he done?

25

David Skinner had been genuinely touched by the reunion of Kimberly and Erik with their mother. Even days later, the memory of that long embrace in the airport lingered on as a fine, fond memory.

But under the circumstances, no amount of warmth could begin to trump the anger that boiled in his belly. When he thought about all that he'd left behind in Panama—Nana and Papi and the business—and when he thought that it had all been wrenched from his hands because Junior G-Man Kurt Muse couldn't keep his head in the game, it was all he could do to keep from exploding.

The CIA had found them reasonable hotel accommodations here in Miami—they were staying in a Holiday Inn with all the trimmings—but the Agency reps refused to answer any questions that had anything to do with the future. How long would they be allowed to stay as guests of the U.S. government? How was he supposed to find work once they parted ways?

There was some talk among the others that the government dole would continue for some time—perhaps without end, or at least until the situation in Panama was stabilized; but that talk was all overheard gossip. The truth was, the Skinners were not accepted as equals among the other refugees. The Panamanians were already being called patriots and heroes by their government handlers. He was merely a relative, and the clear disdain he felt for Kurt's shenanigans did nothing to ingratiate him.

For them, from where David sat, this was turning into a kind of impromptu party with an unlimited expense account. There was talk among them of unseating Manuel Noriega in the coming elections and of a bright future for Panama. David thought that was all lovely, but for the life of him he could not understand their sense of optimism. Did none of them have business to return to? Did none of them have family who might have been jeopardized by what they'd been doing?

As his thoughts turned in these dark directions, he knew that he had to wrestle them back. He had no right, he realized, to criticize their political activism. They were, after all, Panamanians, born into their nationality as surely as David was born into his allegiance to the United Kingdom. Passions ran high when national priorities and sympathies were in play. He understood that. He respected that.

What he could neither understand nor respect was the fomenting of such passions by outsiders, by guests of a host country. It was something for which he would never forgive Kurt. Who did he think he was, subjecting his extended family to this sort of strife? The Agency still was not allowing them to make phone calls and was still stressing the necessity of keeping a low profile to stay invisible in this place that was allegedly replete with Noriega informers.

Of course, despite all the pep talks and scare tactics, who was the one who chose to up and disappear from the hotel, causing a huge hullabaloo? None other than Kimberly Muse—she of the shoes and the makeup. While the rest of them were huddling in their rooms, lurking naked under the covers one at a time while their clothes were washed in the sink, there she was wandering the beach, off the hotel grounds, just like she belonged there. It was infuriating.

These last days since arriving in the United States had been a whirlwind of activity. Irrespective of the manner in which a person enters the country, an immigrant is still an immigrant, and the keepers of immigration records cannot be ignored. Over the past seventy-two hours, they'd pencil whipped paperwork that took other people months to complete, and, thanks to whatever strings could be pulled by Father Frank, approvals that normally would have taken weeks or months came in just a couple of days.

And what about Father Frank? Who was this old man with all the answers? What was he really about? And if he was such a superspy, how was it that he traveled on his own name and that he'd been foolish (or addled) enough to leave his boarding pass stuffed in a seat pocket where it could be (and was) picked up by one of the refugees? They all knew his real name now, but they'd decided among themselves to keep that a secret, perhaps as a hole card, or perhaps because it moved them one step closer to having some measure of control over their own lives.

Truth be told, there was something off-putting about the old man. David and Carol had talked about it at some length. It was the way he looked at you, the way he dismissed questions without so much as a moment's consideration. Whatever it was, it was yet another wedge between the Skinners and the rest of their party.

David weighed these thoughts as he rode the elevator down to the pool level to meet with Father Frank. He'd been summoned, and the tone in the old man's voice had led David to believe that it was something serious.

David saw Father Frank from across the lobby, standing exactly where he'd promised that he would be, near the pool, but far enough away to be immune to errant splashes. David hadn't closed half the distance when they made eye contact. The old man waved, but made no effort to close some of the gap himself.

When they were close enough, David allowed himself a smile. "Good morning," he said.

"Good morning to you," Father Frank replied, but there was no smile. No frown either; just a businesslike tabula rasa. Reaching into an inside coat pocket, he produced a thick white envelope and handed it to David. "This is for you."

David hesitated, his stomach tumbling. "What is it?"

Father Frank answered by bouncing the envelope once in the air. "Please, take it."

He did take it, and as soon as he felt the heft and the thickness, he knew that it was cash. He peeked inside and saw a stack of hundreds. He scowled.

"That's five thousand dollars," Father Frank said. "With Uncle Sam's regards. Good luck to you. From this moment on, you're responsible for your own expenses."

It was like being slapped. "Excuse me?"

Father Frank had already started walking away.

"Hey!" David said, louder than he'd thought, and much louder than Father Frank had anticipated.

The old man turned. If it was possible, his expression had turned even more bland. He looked utterly bored.

"This is it?" David asked. "This is relocation? What am I supposed to do with five thousand dollars?"

Father Frank let the question hang as he pondered not answering it at all. "This is a free country, Mr. Skinner. You've got your green card, you are free to go wherever you wish whenever you wish."

"Except home. Except to Panama."

"No, *including* Panama, but for the foreseeable future, we recommend against it."

"So, you're just letting us all go? Just like that? You bring twenty-odd people away from their homes, into a foreign country, and then hand them a few dollars and you wash your hands?" This was unbelievable. The nightmare only got worse.

Finally, something changed in the old man's expression. It was a fleeting thing, there for a second and then gone, but David saw it plainly. Father Frank started walking away again.

"Wait a second," David said, putting it together. "It's just us, isn't it? It's just my family that's being sent away."

Father Frank stopped again, turned to face David. "You're not being sent away."

"No, we're just being cut off."

"If you wish."

"I *don't* wish. I don't want to be here at all. And I don't understand why we are being singled out among all these people to be dismissed after we've abandoned everything we have ever known."

Father Frank inhaled deeply and scowled. Clearly, he was about to share something against his better instincts. "Mr. Skinner, it makes perfect sense, if you think about it. Please try not to take it personally. The taxpayers of America have saved your life, and that of your family. We've made entry into this country and assimilation into our society a thousand times easier for you than it is for any other visitor, but the fact remains that you are a citizen of neither the United States nor Panama. We have no authority to hold you and no jurisdiction to protect you. You have performed admirably. So have your wife and your daughter. But now it's time for you move on and go about the business of stabilizing your lives, to the degree that that is possible under the circumstances."

David's scowl deepened as he tried to force the words into place in his head. "We have 'performed'? What does that mean? I didn't know that I had a role to play. You guys were the ones who made it sound so damned important that we come here. That wasn't my idea. Now you're telling me—"

Suddenly it dawned on him. "Wait a second. You needed us. For the children. For Kimberly and Erik."

The blankness returned. Father Frank gave a little shrug. "It all went much more smoothly than it might have. Dealing with kids, it's always best to have family around. When the grandparents refused to leave, you were the natural choice. Again, we are all very grateful for your assistance. Try to keep a low profile." He turned one more time and started walking.

This was unbelievable. The very concept of being so deliberately manipulated was larger than David could comprehend. How dare they? How dare they put so much at risk? "Wait a minute!" he called. He had more questions, a thousand of them, but at this moment in time, he couldn't make them form into a coherent mass in his head.

It didn't matter anyway. This time, once Father Frank started walking, he didn't turn back.

26

The unknown is a beast of unspeakable power. When you're deprived of your freedom—when your future is placed entirely in the hands of people who exist for the purpose of tormenting you— the unknown takes on a life as surely and as treacherously as the most venomous snake. As they led Kurt from Correa's office into the bowels of this horrific place, he could hear the beast's growl and feel its hot breath on the back of his neck.

The ghastly faces of those men he'd seen at the DENI jail and here at Modelo peering out of the windows would not leave Kurt's imagination as guards led him up a flight of concrete steps toward God only knew what.

The guts of Modelo Prison vibrated with a misery that was palpable, reverberated with a level of noise that he'd never experienced. There were no discernable voices, nor audible screams, yet the rumble was distinctly human. If Kurt had been inclined to supernatural thoughts, he might have succumbed to visions of lifeless spirits who continued to linger long after their earthly bodies had given in and given up to the tortures of so many decades without hope.

Kurt had actually seen pictures. He couldn't remember the context, but he distinctly remembered pictures from the inside of Modelo Prison where squalid cells were packed with dozens of men wearing the tattered remains of the clothes that had no doubt fit them on the day they

were arrested, but which now hung on their emaciated bodies like bur-
ial shrouds. He remembered the images of the hammocks these desperate men used as beds, and somehow, somewhere, he remembered
hearing how easy it was to kill a man in his sleep under those circumstances. He remembered thinking as he read the article what an impos-
sibility it would be to close one's eyes in such conditions.

And here he was. His future had arrived, and it brought with it the
combined stench of excrement, sweat, and his own fear.

He tried not to show the terror, tried not to give these assholes the
satisfaction, but he knew that it had to be obvious. It *had* to be.

The concrete steps through the middle of the prison took hard turns
at every landing. The heat of the place was stifling, getting progressively worse with each step toward its center.

On the third floor, they turned, and the guard led him down a hallway of heavy closed doors that he would later come to learn were the
officers' quarters and interrogation rooms, stopping finally in front of
a twelve-by-twelve-foot cell whose front wall was constructed of iron
bars. The guard produced a large key, removed the heavy-duty padlock
from its hasp, and ushered Kurt into his new home. Five seconds later,
the door closed, the lock slipped home again, and he was alone.

A filthy thin foam pad on the floor would serve as his bed. There
were no other furnishings in the room. In an odd twist, though, his
suitcase lay on the floor waiting for him, as if placed by some bellman
in a twisted theme hotel.

At the rear of the cell and off to the left, he found a toilet and
shower area. He had his own little concrete apartment.

His suitcase had been ransacked, but the basics remained. He still
had toiletries, socks and underwear, and the kinds of clothes that one
would wear to visit a dying relative and to make plans with government operatives. What he didn't have were clothes that were appropriate for imprisonment in a tropical hellhole.

The windows in his cell—there were three of them in all, along the
back wall of his cell and his lavatory, looked out onto the prison yard,
where inmates walked, played basketball, or talked among themselves.
On the inside of the far wall—the wall that faced Kurt's cell from fifty
yards away—someone had painted a lengthy quote from Manuel Noriega touting the importance of a fair judicial system to the well-being

of a civilized society. Next to that mural-sized quotation, someone had painted the words "Jesus Saves."

It was hard to tell by looking what the population of the prison was, but it had to be in the hundreds. The yard, with its basketball courts and wandering spaces, was perpetually crowded in the way that New York subways were crowded in rush hour, people jammed shoulder to shoulder in some corners as they tried to absorb the best of what could barely be described as fresh air in a place like this.

Looking out the front of his cell, toward the concrete hallway, he could see nothing but a blank wall. As he moved closer to the bars, however, and when he pressed his head against them, he could see wooden doors on the other side of the hall. They were closed now, but he could hear muffled voices.

And that was it; that was his life until something happened or someone did something to change it. Truly, for good or for ill, his entire life lay in the hands of others. He'd done all he could to screw things up of his own volition, thank you very much.

He wandered to the part of the cell that seemed farthest from the bars, pressed his back to the wall, and slid till he sat on the floor, hugging his knees in front of him. It was time to take inventory on the number of lives he had succeeded in screwing up and the depths to which they had been screwed.

A desperate sadness washed over him in that moment, a sense of helplessness that would not be denied. Kurt felt the tears coming, but he willed them away for another time. For the nighttime. Under the circumstances, tears were probably good, and they probably could not be denied, but he would save them for the privacy brought by darkness.

Dignity above all else, he thought. They had his body, and one day they might conquer his mind, but denying the bastards his dignity was the last battle over which he had complete control, and he wasn't about to surrender without one hell of a fight.

Time in prison does not pass. It creeps. One moment evolves into another without form or meaning.

After the first couple of days, Kurt came to envy those hopeless men crowded into the prison yard. They *knew* how long they would have to endure their confinement, and they had other human beings with whom to share the pressures of their incarceration. For Kurt, there was only the vividness of the present, the hopelessness of the future, and the uselessness of the past. He'd cast his whole life aside in pursuit of a ridiculous plan that had never really had a chance to succeed. Now, it was time to atone for his foolishness, and the penalty was unending solitude and the terrible depression that solitude brought. He had no lawyer, and they had yet to officially level charges against him. He had no way of knowing in those early days, but it would be months before charges were filed, and when they were, they would be as meaningless as the pretense of justice under the thumb of Noriega's dictatorship.

Interrogations continued after Kurt arrived in Modelo Prison, but the character of them changed. No longer pressed to find out who the hell he was, the PDF and the DENI were more interested in filling in the details. Where were all the transmitters located? Where were they purchased? And, of course, who were his compatriots? On that latter point, he continued to maintain that he had acted alone.

The interrogations happened mostly at night now, sometime between midnight and four in the morning, and despite the imposing threat of violence, no violence was inflicted on him. Instead, they told him over and over again that his family would suffer as a result of what he had done and that the suffering was made all the worse by his refusal to cooperate. They told him that he would be forgotten here by the government they thought he had once served, and once forgotten, they would be able to do anything to him that they wanted. Major Moreno—the same man who had run the search of Kurt's house on the night of his arrest—conducted all the interrogations. Professional in his demeanor, but with violence lurking behind every expression and word, Moreno would shout and blather, but there seemed to be a line he would never cross, and that was the line that separated Kurt from physical harm.

It was hard not to be swayed by their words and threats. Aloneness is a powerful motivator, and no place is as lonely as a jail cell.

The good news—if there was such a thing under the circumstances—was the fact that Kurt's primary guard, a Lieutenant Dominguez, wasn't a bad guy at all. A career civil servant in the PDF, Dominguez spouted none of the political bullshit of the Noriega dynasty and kept his harassment of Kurt to a minimum. He seemed to have sympathy, in fact, for the misery of Kurt's plight, and while he was no pushover, he was no zealot, either. He greeted his charge every morning with a friendly hello and a smile that seemed genuine. He had a scowl in his kit bag as well, of course, but he seemed somehow uncomfortable using it.

On the fifth day of Kurt's incarceration, Dominguez came to his door in the middle of the day and announced that he had a visitor. They led him out of his cell and down the hall to a small dispensary, a cell that was twice the size of his own, but outfitted with a sheet-draped table and various jars of medical supplies. He was there for maybe a minute when two men entered, one in an Air Force uniform and the other in civilian attire. Kurt instantly recognized the man in the uniform as Dr. Ruffer, the lieutenant colonel who had conducted the brief exam during the day of his perp walk.

Just seeing an American uniform and a friendly face made Kurt's spirits soar. "Hello, Doctor," he said, beaming. "Nice to see you again. I thought maybe they reneged." When he stepped forward to shake Ruffer's hand, neither Dominguez nor the tall dour-faced black man who accompanied him from time to time made any effort to intervene.

"Hello, Mr. Muse," Jim said. "It's nice to see you as well. I'm just sorry for the venue. Nobody reneged. We just got off to a slow start." He gestured to the small man in civilian clothes who stood next to him, "This is Doctor Marcos Ostrander, a lawyer with the U.S. Army South—USARSO. He'll be accompanying me from time to time as I make my visits."

Kurt shook his hand. "Are you a medical doctor?"

Marcos smiled and shook his head. "No, no such luck. I'm just a lawyer."

"*My* lawyer?"

Marcos shook his head. "Actually, no. At least not for the long term. We're having a hard time finding a lawyer in Panama with balls big enough to take on your case. But we're working on that."

"What does 'working on that' mean?"

Jim Ruffer stepped in to change the subject. "Let's get to the business of your physical examination," he said. He ushered Kurt toward the exam table and pulled the privacy curtain closed. Beyond the curtain, Kurt could hear Ostrander begin chatting up the guards. "Take your shirt off, please, and your pants, down to your underwear."

As Kurt complied, and a routine physical exam commenced, Ruffer asked, "How are you really? Are you being treated well?"

"I'm fine," Kurt said. "The food is pretty awful, but I'm making do."

Ruffer nodded and applied the blood pressure cuff. "I see. Do you need anything? Anything that we can bring you?"

"Shorts," Kurt said, without a moment's hesitation. "They left me my suitcase, but I don't have any clothes suited to the heat. Running shorts would be great."

"I'll see what I can do." Blood pressure done, Ruffer moved on to the poking and prodding part of the exam.

"And I want you to tell my family that I'm okay. That's very important to me."

"I understand that," Ruffer said, lowering his voice even further. "That's why I brought Doctor Ostrander along. He's more or less the conduit for communication with your family. When I'm done, you'll have an opportunity to speak with him. You tell him anything and everything he wants to know, okay? Anything that's on your mind."

The physical examination lasted only a few minutes, and when it was done, Ruffer announced that he had continuing concerns about his patient's health and that the frequency of the visits needed to be maintained. He started to make quite a speech, actually, and as he did, Ostrander moved in close to Kurt and began chatting.

"Doctor Ruffer told you who I am?"

Kurt nodded. "You're my conduit."

"Exactly. I'm your voice to the outside world. You need something, you tell me. If I can't be here for some reason, you tell Doctor Ruffer. The United States government is plenty pissed off that you're being held in here without charges being filed, and we're doing everything we can to get you out. These assholes are going to mess with your head in a thousand different ways telling you otherwise—it's what they do—but you have to always remember that we're out there working for you."

Kurt didn't know why this was as big a shock as it turned out to be. "Thank you," he said. "I told the doctor that I want my family to be reassured that I'm doing all right."

"I'll do that. You know that they've all been resettled, right? All of them are okay. Perfectly safe."

Actually, he hadn't been told that in as many words, and the news delighted him. "Where are they?"

"Safe," Ostrander said. "In the States. I'm not sure it's prudent to go into a lot more detail than that."

Okay, that was fine. Kurt understood that. "Listen, if you talk to Annie—"

"*When*," Ostrander corrected. "*When* I talk to Annie."

Kurt smiled. He liked this guy. "Okay, when you talk to Annie, I want you to tell her that we have a ten-thousand-dollar certificate of deposit in the bank down here. If she needs money, she should cash that in. Tell her—"

Ostrander interrupted with a wave of his hand. "That's all right."

"No, she needs to know this."

"No, she doesn't, Kurt. She's being taken care of."

Kurt paused, then scowled. " 'Taken care of'? What does that mean?"

"It means just what you think it means. She won't have to worry about the CD or her life savings. She won't have to worry about rent or a car payment. That's all being taken care of. You can relax on all of that."

Kurt cocked his head. This wasn't making sense. "Well, who's taking care of it?"

Ostrander's features hardened, and so did his voice. "They're. Being. Taken. Care. Of."

He waited for Kurt to catch on. The government? Was that possible?

Ostrander continued, "Now, do me a favor and catch me up on what's been happening. We might not have time for every chapter on this visit, but start at the beginning and tell me about your arrest and your treatment thus far."

Inexplicably, Kurt trusted this man, this stranger. There was something about the way Marcos looked at him, with a combination of toughness and sympathy that made him believe that he could say just about anything to this man. So he started at the beginning and worked in as many details as he could. He told about being picked up at the airport and about the interrogations. He told about being taken to his own house and then to that of his parents, and was about to talk about the beating of the Colombian in his presence when Lieutenant

Dominguez cleared his throat and announced that it was time for the visitors to leave. Somehow, the better part of thirty minutes had evaporated.

Kurt shook hands with both visitors, but Jim Ruffer lingered a bit on his. "We'll see about making the food a little better, okay?"

Kurt nodded, unsure of what he should say. He defaulted to, "Thank you."

He had no way of knowing—none of them did—that this would be but the first of dozens of similar meetings.

27

Over time, Kurt would learn to exist on the routine of prison life, as best he could construct for himself out of the nothingness of solitary confinement. Early on, he realized that mental stability was tied to physical fitness. As a practical matter, meaningful exercise was impossible, but Kurt developed a routine by which he would jog around the tiny confines of his cell. Using a Casio wristwatch that was ultimately delivered to him by Jim Ruffer to replace the gold one that was stolen from him, he would set the timer for fifteen minutes, during which he would run without stop in a clockwise circle around his cell. When the beeper sounded, he would reverse direction and jog for another fifteen minutes. Never a hard-bodied physical specimen, the workout was taxing in the early days of his confinement, made all the more so by his commitment to repeating the regimen three times a day.

It was tough as hell on the knees, too, but as he got better and better at the physical exertion, he realized that he wasn't getting the cardio value that he wanted, so he added shadow boxing to the regimen. He kept his mind occupied during the workouts by singing songs in his head. When he was done, at the end of every set of exercise, a dark trail of sweat on the floor marked his path to nowhere.

A few weeks into his incarceration, a U.S. Army cot had been delivered to his cell, courtesy of Jim Ruffer, and that had greatly improved Kurt's ability to sleep through the long, humid nights.

The food was . . . adequate. When you're hungry enough, anything that doesn't kill you is adequate. The standard prison fare consisted of a kind of rice stew with chunks of meat. It tasted neither good nor bad; it was delivered once a day, and you ate it or starved. Some decisions are fundamentally simple.

It took a few days for Ruffer and Ostrander to make good on their promise to deliver alternative food for him, and it would be years before he learned what a Herculean task it had been to make it happen. Major Correa, like prison wardens everywhere, loathed any changes to routine, and after only a week with Kurt Muse in his care, he'd been forced to endure more change than he'd no doubt seen cumulatively over his entire career. At first, the U.S. government wanted to deliver special meals to Muse three times a day, but Correa shot that one down before it gained an inch of altitude. The final compromise was for USARSO to deliver lunch and dinner to Muse, but both at the same time, one delivery per day. Colonel Perry had objected, of course, but he'd known enough to realize a victory when he'd seen it and he'd backed off.

For Kurt, the first indication that he would have special food occurred to him when it arrived at his cell door, four ham sandwiches on paper plates. It wasn't much, but it was a life-saver. By happenstance, just that morning Kurt had responded to the sound of an arriving truck by peering out the window in time to see the raw materials for lunch being delivered. When the tarp was pulled back from the bed of the pickup truck, he was horrified to see that it was piled high with the heads of cattle. No legs, no center sections, just heads. The mystery meat in the stew turned out to be tongues, eyeballs, and whatever other meat could be gleaned out of a cow's head. It was way more than he'd ever needed or wanted to know about the culinary secrets of Modelo Prison. In the pantheon of exquisite meals Kurt had had over his four decades on the planet—the meals prepared by family and housekeepers and even at the Union Club—none had ever tasted quite as sublime as that first ham sandwich prepared in the kitchens of Fort Clayton.

Soon, however, a problem arose with those sublime meals. Since two meals arrived simultaneously—meticulously picked over by the guards of any side dishes or condiments—he would eat two sandwiches as soon as the plates arrived and save the other two in the bathroom, on the sink, until dinnertime.

Unfortunately, he was not the only species living in his cell, and of all the various critters, he was nowhere near the most ravenous. Kurt discovered on the very first evening when he entered the bathroom to eat his second meal that it was covered with ants and God only knew what those other insects were, to the point that the evening meal was completely inedible.

It was a perplexing problem: How exactly does one go about preserving one's rightful place in the food chain? Certainly, there was no way to keep the ants from doing what they were programmed by nature to do, and it seemed short sighted to gluttonously consume all four sandwiches in one sitting and then be faced with the prospect of no additional food for another twenty-four hours. Besides, what would happen if the Fort Clayton chefs were running late, or if they just plain forgot one day? That twenty-four-hour wait could quickly grow to double that. There had to be a solution.

Surveying his cell and bathroom, he noted that the shower never really stopped running. There probably had been a time sixty or seventy years ago when the flow valves actually worked, but those days were long past. Now, a steady flow spattered the floor twenty-four–seven, keeping the concrete shower floor perpetually covered with a thin layer of water. Where there was water, of course, there were no ants, because even in the jungles of Panama God had neglected to create an amphibious ant. Perhaps he had worn himself out with the flying roaches and vampire bats.

There had to be a way to capitalize on that, Kurt thought. If there was a way to store his meal in the shower, he could protect it from the marauders, but the thought of water-logged bread was little more appealing than eating the ants or the cow's eyes. Finally, inspiration came in the form of the Styrofoam cup they'd given him for drinking water. Using the cup as a pedestal, he could put the plate with the uneaten sandwiches in the middle of the shower stall, surrounded by a protective moat. With no critters able to reach the food by land or by sea, he protected against aerial assaults merely by placing a second plate on top of the first, upside down.

It worked beautifully.

Within the first couple of weeks after his incarceration, as he was falling into the routine rhythm of visits from Drs. Ruffer and Ostrander, a third visitor stopped by, this one sent by Kurt's dear friend and coconspirator, Tomás Muñoz. Father Kane, a Catholic priest and Tomás's confessor, was a rotund, jovial fellow with a beard that was somehow bigger than his face and a laugh that could clear the clouds from a dark day. Kurt met with him on the third floor in the tiny reception area just outside the infirmary.

After the initial pleasantries, Kurt confessed, "I'm grateful for your coming to see me, but you should know that I'm not Catholic."

Father Kane could not have cared less. He explained to Kurt that he was here not so much as a confessor, or even as a spiritual guide, but as a friend of a friend, who wanted to help a member of God's flock to navigate difficult trade winds. That first meeting was made awkward by the pressing presence of two guards, whose job it was, it seemed, to eavesdrop on all of Kurt's conversations, even when the visitor was a member of the cloth.

Father Kane put a stop to that right away by turning prayer into a weapon. "Let us start with a blessing," the priest said. He grasped Kurt's right hand in his left, and with his right, grasped the hand of one of the guards, whom he instructed to clasp hands with the second guard, who then completed the chain with Kurt. "Bow your heads please," Father Kane said, and then he launched into one of history's longest prayers, beseeching the Lord for his guidance in everything from Kurt's health to a continuation of the marvelous weather.

Through it all, the guards squirmed like adolescent boys at dancing class. Holding another man's hand was simply not done in the Panamanian culture, and the priest understood this perfectly. He also understood that these good Catholic Panamanians would cut out their own tongues before they refused a request from a priest, so by the time he was done with the blessing, these guards were forever weaned from their habit of standing too close to Father Kane.

Over time, the visitation routine fell into an every-other-day cycle, with Ruffer and Ostrander visiting on Mondays, Wednesdays, and Fridays, and Father Kane stopping in on Tuesdays and Thursdays. None of the meetings lasted more than a few minutes—forty minutes, at the most—but they became the precious moments that defined the only breaks in Kurt's unending boredom.

Correa allowed no visitors on the weekends. Those were the days Kurt came to dread, when the terrible thoughts would return, and no amount of running or special food could possibly compensate for the crushing knowledge that while the world continued to spin for everyone else, life in prison crawled along one endless second at a time.

28

A different kind of nightmare had settled over Annie Muse. Aunt Elsa was still in the hospice and getting weaker by the day, and the children, while finally reunited with her after that awful week-long separation, were doing the best that they could. Her husband, her love, her best friend was apparently a pawn in somebody's idea of a game, but the stakes were unspeakably high.

Early on, she'd thought it would blow over in a few days, or maybe a couple of weeks on the outside, with ample opportunity for bluster and speech making. After that, she'd assumed that she and Kurt would be reunited. As time passed, however, Kurt was being pulled father and farther away from her. She tried working the phones, but to tell the God's honest truth, it was hard to think of who to call. Her father, John Castoro, was retired from the Operations Directorate of the CIA, and he was doing what he could, but his contacts were mostly old and no longer in power. Suzanne Alexander was pushing as hard as she could from her current post in Langley, and Richard Dotson was raising hell from the Guatemala desk in the State Department, but none of it seemed to do any good.

The Modelo captors had allowed Kurt to write a few letters home, but they were all read by the guards and stamped CENSURADO so many times that some of the passages were illegible. She and the kids wrote to him as well, but she understood from her contacts that many of the letters never got through; or when they finally did get through, they were weeks old. It was terrible.

All Annie really needed, all she really prayed for, was the strength to keep their lives going through this miserable time. She'd started going to Mass three times a week, and while that helped some—helped a lot, actually, in keeping her head high and her heart focused—God only helped those who helped themselves, and she was paddling like crazy up one heck of a fast-moving river.

The whole situation hit the children the hardest, Erik in particular, who suddenly found himself in a household of women, with no one to help him with the sports he loved so dearly. He clearly missed the long talks with his dad about nothing—the talks that used to fill hours on end. The fact that Kurt was such a terrific dad, and such a kind, caring husband, made his absence unspeakably painful, but at the same time their love kept them all focused on the challenge of somehow bringing him home.

Thank God for Father Frank and Marcos Ostrander.

Father Frank had become Annie's mysterious right hand. Thanks to him, she had a car, a house, and some spending money. Whatever they needed—no matter what it was—he would make it appear. He also helped the family cope with some of the nastier decisions that were attendant to a life akin to the Witness Protection Program. They were still in West Palm, and being that far south, it was important to keep their real identities to themselves. For public consumption, Anne Castoro (her maiden name) was separated from her husband, and she would offer no further explanation. For the kids, their father was "away." As a practical matter, Father Frank had explained, people don't push for details on family crises. If you don't offer, they won't ask.

At the end of the day, though, life is about the little things, and Annie had learned that neither Kimberly nor Erik had accumulated enough hours in that school year to qualify for matriculation to the next grade, so as an early order of business, Annie had to enroll them in a local school. For the sake of discipline and structure, she chose a Catholic school not far from their house. Of course, enrollment forms required transcripts, birth certificates, and shot records, and when Annie realized that she couldn't produce them, in swooped Father Frank to save the day. Annie never saw the records, actually, and had no idea if they were the real transcripts or the product of someone's imagination in Langley, but ultimately she didn't much care. Her children were where they needed to be and that was really all that mattered.

Kimberly adjusted relatively well to the new home and school, but Erik was hating every minute of it. His As and Bs from Panama quickly transformed into Bs and Cs here in the States, and that was an area where no one but Erik—not even Father Frank with his seeming superpowers—could do anything to help.

Marcos's role in their lives was that of physical conduit between Kurt and his family. Once every other week, if not more often, Marcos would fly to West Palm and meet with the family, filling them in on how Kurt was doing, and pass along individual messages and thoughts. In addition, they talked on the phone regularly. If Kurt had concerns, Marcos would relay them, and vice versa, the communication taking place in those moments after Jim Ruffer's physical exam.

Through Marcos, Annie and the family knew that Kurt was at least safe. They knew that he was in a cell by himself and that while he was very lonely, he was at least not jeopardized by other more violent prisoners. Marcos would listen to Annie's frustrations and occasionally offer strategic advice on whom to call for action. On the other side, Marcos would help Kurt keep his head straight by passing along whatever hopeful tidbits he could share. Marcos's special gift was to keep stormy seas calm.

One day at a time, Annie told herself over and over again. Life needed to be lived, endured, and celebrated one day at a time.

As April became May, and the Panamanian elections approached, Annie talked herself into believing that once the elections were over, there would no longer be a need to keep Kurt in prison. All indications showed that a new government would be swept into power, with Guillermo Endara at the helm and Vice President Billy Ford at his side. If the populace of the Isthmus were allowed an honest, direct vote, then the outcome was virtually assured.

Of course, Panama had not seen honest elections in twenty years. That fact weighed heavily on the Bush administration as election day neared, and with the looming transfer of the Panama Canal as a backdrop, who better to assign as leader of the official observer delegation than Jimmy Carter—the president who had engineered the treaty in the first place?

As soon as Annie heard that former president Carter had been chosen as the election overseer, she started working the phones, calling everyone she knew, and a hundred people she didn't know, trying to raise Kurt's profile high enough to bring it onto Carter's agenda with Noriega. Surely, under the circumstances, with a simple wink and a gentle prod from Jimmy Carter—the great hero of the Panamanian people—the Pineapple would have no choice but to cough Kurt up, all in the spirit of international comity.

It would have been so simple. But he didn't do it.

29

Moreno sat across from Kurt in the interrogation room down the hall from his cell, his beefy face a mask of concern. "Mr. Muse," he said, "I'm afraid I have some disturbing news for you." In an unusual twist, Major Correa, the warden, was sitting in on the conversation.

Kurt felt his heart sink. His mind went right to his family, right to the darkest scenarios that his mind could conjure. Something wrong with one of the kids, with Annie, or with his parents. And as the dark thoughts marched through his mind, he forced himself to shut them down. This was all a game, as Marcos Ostrander and Jim Ruffer had told him a dozen times. The DENI and their PDF bulldogs would do anything and everything to break his spirit, and he had to brace himself for that.

That kind of girding is a hell of a lot easier to do in the abstract than it is when the long face is staring right through you.

"It seems as if your compatriots at the CIA are growing weary of you," said Moreno. "It seems that you are an embarrassment. Our intelligence sources tell us that they are plotting to kill you."

The thought was absurd at its face, but that didn't stop the fear from being compelling. "Is that so?" Kurt said, stalling for time as he tried to weigh the kernel of truth in Moreno's premise.

"We are concerned for your safety and believe that we need to protect you from those who would cause you harm."

As Moreno spoke, Kurt began to understand the subtext more clearly than the words. What he heard was, "We're tired of dealing with your frequent visitors."

"I see," Kurt said. "And who are these people you would be protecting me from?"

"Your visitors. I do not think that they can be trusted."

"You heard them as clearly as I did, Major. The Treaty allows these visits."

"Of course," Moreno said, his voice the essence of reasonableness. "But if they are in fact causing you danger—"

"I'll take my chances," Kurt said.

Moreno exchanged looks with Correa and nodded. "I understand. If I were in your position, I would likely prefer the visitors as well. Truth be told, I think that it is reasonable for you to trust them. They, in fact, are not my greatest concern."

If the first approach doesn't work, Kurt thought, always be ready with another one.

"According to our intelligence sources, you are being poisoned."

Kurt's jaw dropped. *"Poisoned?"* Jesus, surely they could do better than that.

"Your meals," Moreno said. "The Central Intelligence Agency is lacing the food brought to you from Fort Clayton with poison. They are killing you to keep you from sharing their secrets. To keep you from embarrassing them."

To the Latin mind, this ruse actually made sense. Theirs was a culture where honor and machismo was everything, and where it would be perfectly reasonable to kill someone to protect that honor. This was a stone cold bluff.

"You want me to go back to eating cows' heads? No thank you."

Moreno waved that off as absurd. "We would never expect you to do that. That would make no sense at all. Given a choice between what we serve and my own foot, I think I might choose my foot. I understand that perfectly. No, what I'm proposing is for us to bring your food daily from a local restaurant. They would fix plates for you just as they do at Clayton, and we would make sure you get them every day. Truly, I believe it is the safer option."

Kurt had never heard such a line of crap in his whole life. It wouldn't be two days before he was back to munching on brains and

Kurt's home in Panama City. Initial transmission tests were run from the balcony. *(Author's collection)*

A memento of more peaceful times. Kurt as a sixth grader at La Salle School, Panama City. *(Yearbook photo)*

Noriega addresses the nation. It was during just such an address that Kurt and his compatriots chose to become public enemies. *(Unknown PDF photographer)*

The enemy: PDF goons lurk on a street corner. *(Grover Matheney)*

Vice President Roderick Esquivel.
(Official Panama government photo)

A prewar photo of the
Comandancia (taken by
Delta in preparation for
Operation Acid Gambit).
(Anonymous Delta operator)

Kurt on the night of his arrest, speaking with Attorney General Villalaz, who ended up in possession of the Muse family Volvo. Note the pen in Kurt's pocket. That would come in handy a little later.
(Unknown PDF photographer)

PDF photos of equipment seized from Radio La Voz de la Libertad.
(Unknown PDF photographer)

Marcos Ostrander, chief of international law and affairs, U.S. Army South. *(Photo courtesy Dr. Ostrander)*

Colonel Robert Perry, taken several years after Operation Just Cause. *(U.S. Army photo)*

Lt. Col. Jim Ruffer, M.D., USAF.
(Photo courtesy Col. Ruffer)

The medical kit used by Jim Ruffer to
communicate private messages to Kurt
during medical exams.
(Photo courtesy Col. Ruffer)

These are the stairs used by Delta Force to effect Kurt's rescue. His cell can be seen at the end of the hall on the left. *(Grover Matheney)*

Kurt's home for nine long months.
(Grover Matheney)

Typical living conditions in Modelo Prison. *(Unknown PDF photographer)*

This Delta reconnaissance photo of Modelo Prison clearly shows the cupola that would be their point of entry. *(Anonymous Delta operator)*

Modelo's prison yard. Noriega's enemies were hung by their wrists from the basketball hoop *(lower right corner)*.
(Grover Matheney)

The door to the officers' quarters across the hall from Kurt's cell. Notice the blast damage where the lock used to be. *(Anonymous Delta operator)*

Modelo from the yard. Kurt's cell was on the third floor, sixth window from the right. The damaged roof line marks the spot where a Delta operator rappelled down to take out Kurt's executioner. *(Grover Matheney)*

Guards in this kitchen annex at Modelo made the mistake of trying
to shoot it out with Delta Force. *(Grover Matheney)*

Father Kane stands in the space where Kurt met with visitors. Notice the
impact marks from bullets fired by Delta from the roof. *(Courtesy Father Kane)*

General Maxwell "Mad Max" Thurman, Commander in Chief, Southern Command.
(Grover Matheney)

A Delta operator prepares for Acid Gambit.
(Anonymous Delta operator)

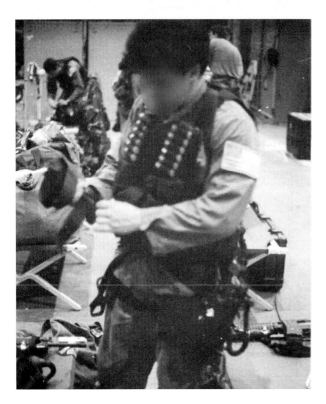

A Delta operator suits up.
(Anonymous Delta operator)

AC-130 Specter Gunship. Once the cupola on the roof of Modelo Prison
was blown, two of these monsters rained hell on the Comandancia.
(Grover Matheney)

This family picture became one of Kurt's most prized possessions. It was in his pocket on the night of his rescue. *(Author's collection)*

Kurt's fatally wounded Little Bird rescue chopper. *(Anonymous Delta operator)*

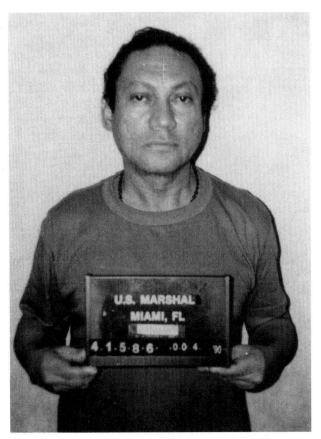

Manuel Antonio Noriega, guest of the people of the United States of America. *(U.S. Marshall's office)*

The Comandancia, Noriega's headquarters, on the morning after Operation Acid Gambit. *(Grover Matheney)*

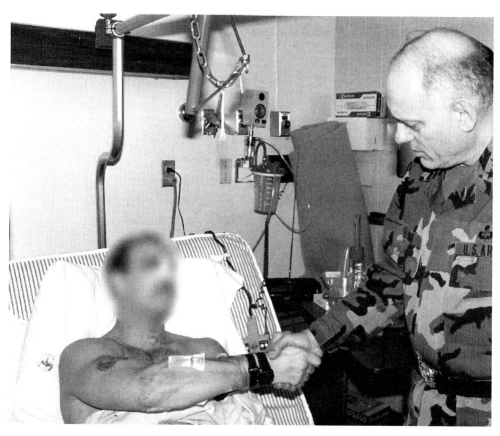

Delta operators recover from their wounds. *(U.S. Army photos)*

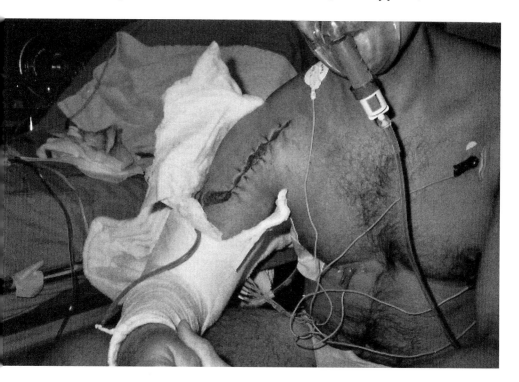

One of Kurt's rescuers receives the Silver Star from
President George H. W. Bush. *(White House photo)*

True to the promise made in his letter to Annie, President Bush receives the
Muse family in the Oval Office just weeks after Kurt's rescue. *(White House photo)*

eyeballs. The bottom line was this: If the U.S. government had wanted to kill him, he would have been dead by now. End of story.

He told Moreno with as much deference and gratitude as he could muster, that he was ready to take his chances and continue consuming the poisoned food.

That night, starting at about one in the morning, the stomach cramps and diarrhea hit him hard.

The first thing Ruffer noticed on his regular afternoon visit was the fear in Kurt's eyes, the uneasiness of his demeanor. Responding to a specific request from Kurt, the doctor had brought along a fluffy green pillow (to replace the rolled up clothes that had been serving that function to date), but whatever was bothering Kurt seemed to trump the pleasure of receiving the gift.

"Somebody's trying to poison me," Kurt said, his voice low. "I was up all night. It was terrible. Diarrhea, vomiting, cramps. Everything consistent with poisoning."

Ruffer tried to set his patient's mind at ease. There were dozens of possible explanations for those symptoms that had nothing to do with poisoning.

Kurt would hear none of it. "No, it's poisoning. I'm sure of it. They told me to expect it."

"They *told* you?"

He nodded. "Yesterday. Moreno was here and he and Correa told me to expect to be poisoned. They told me that it was you guys. The American government."

"But you know better."

"I can't believe that the Agency would do that to me. I mean, there's not a lot of love lost between me and the guys at Corozal, but I can't believe that they'd try to poison me. I think the guys here are trying to poison me, and they're trying to make me think it's coming from you."

Ruffer sighed, took a moment to collect his thoughts. "Kurt, say the word, and I can have the food from Clayton cut off, and you can go back to prison food."

The very thought seemed to horrify Kurt.

"That's what I thought," Ruffer said. "Listen, the PDF is going to do everything they can to mess with your mind, to turn you against the U.S. We're the big bad guys now, you know. But let me tell you this:

never once have they ever killed an American citizen in custody. Never. I really don't think you have to worry about that. Can they make your life miserable by an occasional night of intestinal distress? Sure. But I really don't think they'd even take it that far."

Kurt seemed reassured. At least a little.

"And let's not lose sight of the possibility of coincidence. This is not the most hygienic of places, and you are under considerable stress. It's entirely possible that the discussion with Moreno and the fact of your illness are just freak happenstance." The odds were long, but stranger things have happened.

Kurt considered that. "I guess we can see what happens over the next couple of days."

"If you'd like, I can sample your blood," Ruffer offered. "I can sample it regularly, if you'd like."

Kurt shook his head. "I don't like getting stuck."

Ruffer didn't blame him a bit. If the intestinal issues became a regular concern, then he would take some additional precautions, but for the time being he thought it was best to let things run their course.

"You just need to know that we're here for you if you need something, Kurt. You need to keep faith in the Lord, in your family, and in your country. That's the way to endure this thing."

Kurt gave him a long look. "It's been a month. Any idea how long 'this thing' will have to be endured?"

Ruffer sighed. "It's getting more complicated. There have been several articles in *Republica* with all kinds of outlandish accusations of you being a spy. They've got you connected with DelValle as a subversive. This isn't just about a radio station anymore. They're hanging all kinds of charges on you."

"They're not true."

"Of course they're not true. But that doesn't stop Noriega from padding the list. What I'm telling you, I guess, is you're no longer a criminal. You're a political prisoner. As you know, they've yet to file charges."

Kurt sighed and his shoulders sagged. It was not what he'd been hoping to hear. "Hey, listen, Marcos wants to talk to you about this stuff. I just mention it in case we run out of time. Now, let's take a look in those ears."

Ruffer opened his medical kit and positioned it so that Kurt could see the inside of the lid. There, he'd taped the latest message from Annie: "Read Isaiah 43:1–5."

> *But now thus says the Lord, he who created you, O Jacob, he who formed you, O Israel: "Fear not, for I have redeemed you; I have called you by name, you are mine. When you pass through the waters I will be with you; and through the rivers, they shall not overwhelm you; when you walk through fire you shall not be burned, and the flame shall not consume you. For I am the Lord your God, the Holy One of Israel, your Savior. I give Egypt as your ransom, Ethiopia and Seba in exchange for you. Because you are precious in my eyes, and honored, and I love you, I give men in return for you, people in exchange for your life. Fear not, for I am with you; I will bring your offspring from the east, and from the west I will gather you."*

"I miss her, Jim," Kurt said. "I miss them all. Tell Annie that my words to her are Hebrews 10:33–39."

> *But recall the former days when, after you were enlightened, you endured a hard struggle with sufferings, sometimes being publicly exposed to abuse and affliction, and sometimes being partners with those so treated. For you had compassion on the prisoners, and you joyfully accepted the plundering of your property, since you knew that you yourselves had a better possession and an abiding one. Therefore do not throw away your confidence, which has a great reward. For you have need of endurance, so that you may do the will of God and receive what is promised. "For yet a little while, and the coming one shall come and shall not tarry; but my righteous one shall live by faith, and if he shrinks back, my soul has no pleasure in him." But we are not of those who shrink back and are destroyed, but of those who have faith and keep their souls.*

Marcos Ostrander impressed Kurt as one of those people who could stroll through the middle of a riot and never flinch at the bricks, rocks, and bullets. If the entire spectrum of human emotions could be measured on a ten-point scale, with suicidal depression measured at one and utter jubilation at ten, Marcos's emotions ranged between 5.000 to 5.001. Scrupulously honest and mercifully blunt, he would absorb every dram of information Kurt gave him and faithfully relay every word that Annie and the kids would pass along. All without any written notes.

During their meetings, always on the tail end of the Ruffer exams, Kurt and Marcos would slip easily between English and Spanish, preferring the former for the more sensitive family issues. No matter what the topic, they were always keenly aware that others might be listening.

"You know the elections are coming soon," Marcos said.

Kurt smiled. "I guess we'll see what kind of impact we had, huh?"

Marcos's return smile looked more like a grimace.

"What's wrong?"

Marcos explained that the PDF had already started into their shenanigans to interfere with the vote. Noriega's goons were rounding up as many dissenters as they could find, and they had started to forcibly assemble counterdemonstrations.

Dropping his tone to nearly a whisper, Kurt said, "They took truckloads of prisoners out of here yesterday. During the night, I overheard that they were going out to demonstrate in favor of the Pineapple."

Ostrander confirmed that that was what he had heard as well. Third world democracy in action. "I don't want you to worry, Kurt, but you need to know that things are likely to get pretty hot on election day. Keep your eyes open and your head down. We'll stay on top of these guys to make sure that you don't get sucked up into events here you don't want to be."

30

Back in his cell, his afternoon exercises completed, Kurt considered what Ruffer and Ostrander had told him, occupying himself with watching the activity in the prison yard. Over time, even from this distance, he was able to get a sense of the prisoners' personalities. By and large, these were the worst of the worst when they were out on the street, but once combined in a concrete prison, people had to find their own way. Many, he observed, spent their time in the yard absorbed in studies of the Bible, hoping perhaps that the wonder of eternal salvation might one day compensate for the awful suffering here in Modelo.

Prayer, Kurt had learned, meant a lot when you had nothing left. Always a man of strong faith, his own devotion to God paled in comparison to Annie's. She was a rock in all things, and religion was no exception. That had been more her department than his when dealing with the children, but now that Kurt found himself to be a pawn in a game he didn't fully understand, he found his faith getting stronger by the day. It helped that Annie had sent him an Episcopal Book of Common Prayer with a picture of the family taped inside the front cover. Each day and each evening, as he prayed for strength and guidance, he could look at his family and feel the love they projected from thousands of miles away.

Other prisoners, he'd learned, were not so fortunate. Some simply lost their minds.

A few days ago, he'd been at this very spot, peering out this very window, when the time came for the guard to clear the yard of prisoners. The guard was a fat pig of a man, spilling out of his sweat-stained uniform, and he herded the men as if they were cattle, swinging the length of rubber hose that so many had felt against their skin. "Move along now," he ordered. "Be quick about it. I don't have all day."

As all the men moved obediently toward the cellblock, one prisoner broke free and headed for the middle of the yard. "I am a sinner!" the prisoner yelled. "I am a sinner and a bad man, and I must atone for what I've done!"

From where Kurt stood, Fatso seemed equal parts confused and annoyed. "Back in line, Prisoner!" he commanded.

"I must confess to Almighty God! I am scum! I am a rapist of the worst kind, and I'm sorry!"

Suddenly, it was as if all other activity in the world had stopped, and all eyes were on this one crazed man. Laughter filled the air, but Fatso was not amused. He swung his hose threateningly through the air. "End this foolishness right now," he commanded, "and get back into line before I make God's wrath seem merciful."

"She was young and innocent," the half-wit blathered on. "I watched her and I followed her, and when I got the opportunity, I had my way with her. I raped a little girl."

The laughter turned to taunting now, directed in equal measures to Fatso and the half-wit. They urged the prisoner to continue, even as they urged Fatso to do something about it.

The half-wit continued to rant on and on, sharing the detail that the girl was having her period at the time of his attack, a detail that simultaneously repulsed the crowd and prodded them into a higher frenzy.

Angry now, Fatso came after him. The time for talking was over; the time for a beating had arrived.

The half-wit was in the middle of quoting a Bible verse when Fatso took his first shot, swinging his hose in a wide arc that would have hurt like hell if it had connected. But the half-wit dodged it easily, ducking and spinning away from the guard and running to the far corner of the yard.

Fatso lumbered after him. As the prisoner continued to atone, the guard cursed a blue streak. He had revenge on his mind, but as he tried to run, gravity worked on his trousers, causing him to do an odd kind of waddle as he pulled at them to keep them from falling. When he was within range, he took another swing, but the half-wit dodged that one even more easily than the first.

And so it went, for a solid ten minutes, the half-wit dodging and praying while Fatso worked himself into a lather—almost literally. Even other guards joined the festivities, watching and cheering the action until, finally, the prisoner apparently felt suitably atoned, and then he dissolved peacefully into the crowd. Kurt never saw him again and never heard what happened to him.

From Kurt's special vantage point, he could see much, and many could see him. Off in the distance, but frustratingly close, he could see the seventeenth hole of the golf course on Fort Amador, and just beyond that was the water tower across from Ancon Hill, where Blackhawk helicopters made their final approaches to land. He'd mentioned to Dr. Ruffer just the other day how much he enjoyed seeing that display of American strength, and since then, the chopper pilots had started making their final approaches exclusively on the front side of the water tower, enabling a better view for their audience of one. In prison, it's the littlest things that mean the most.

Today, from his perch in his window, he was watching old friends from the Salvation Army pass out trinkets of mercy to the prisoners in the yard. He couldn't see specifically what they were passing out, but it looked to be toiletries and maybe small gifts of food. All the faces from the Salvation Army were familiar to him. Only six months ago he'd been a member of their board of directors. In fact, it was at the opening of a new Salvation Army school for the blind that he and Tomás had first hatched their crazy scheme to use radios to destabilize a regime.

God, those were good times. Not just the subversive stuff, but the days of good works through Rotary and the Salvation Army. Kurt missed those good works, missed the good feelings that they brought to his heart. Standing here like this, watching good works in progress, he felt oddly ashamed to be on the wrong side of the charitable efforts. Shame kept him from calling out to get their attention.

His anonymity was short lived, however. The only other American in Modelo Prison—a young man named Dana Keith who was serving time for murdering his wife—spent part of his turn with the volunteer workers to point Kurt's location out to them. The ladies' gaze followed Dana's arm, and when they saw Kurt, he gave a little wave and mouthed to them that he was okay.

They started crying so hard that Kurt had to turn away.

31

The May elections in Panama brought unprecedented violence. Despite the best efforts of the international observers, fraud was rampant. PDF goons blatantly stopped vehicles and detained people who were on their way to polling places, even as they hijacked the ballot boxes on the way to the tallying stations. Armed thugs hovered over voters, watching where they cast their votes and overtly threatening those who dared to vote the wrong way.

Toward midday, as it became clear that Noriega was going to prevent a fair referendum, the rightful president and vice president—Guillermo Endara and Billy Ford, respectively—led the people of Panama into the streets where thousands of anti-Noriega demonstrators crowded the avenues and town squares, waving the white flags of the opposition and banging on pots and pans to express their anger.

As the world condemned the elections as a sham, Noriega blamed the United States for meddling in the affairs of an independent nation and declared the results of the election—however they turned out—to be null and void.

As the protestors became progressively more vocal, his goon squads moved into the streets, clubbing and gassing peaceful protestors and arresting anyone who did not instantly disperse when the order was given.

When the would-be vice president, Billy Ford, attempted to intervene in a request for restraint and sanity, the clubs turned on him, creating what became the most enduring image worldwide in the struggle for justice in Panama. *Time* magazine and countless other periodicals around the globe placed on their covers the picture of a dazed and blood-soaked Billy Ford receiving assistance after his brutal beating at the hands of Noriega's thugs.

Powerful people in Foggy Bottom, Langley, and the Oval Office, and on Capitol Hill agreed that that photo, and the moment in history it depicted, was a primary pivot point for the United States' tolerance of Noriega's shenanigans. The Pineapple had ignored the indictments from the U.S. courts, thumbed his nose at justice and decency, done everything in his power to make life as uncomfortable as possible for U.S. troops, and now he was making a mockery of the democratic process in the same hemisphere where the very concept was born.

Manuel Noriega could not be allowed to stay in power.

Staff Sergeant Jim Nelson was the last guy you'd pick out of a crowd as one of the nation's most elite warriors. He favored Hawaiian shirts and blue jeans as his duty "uniform" and his collar-length hair and scruffy beard made him look more like a college philosophy major than any kind of soldier. (Truth be told, the beard remained scruffy because he could never decide whether or not he wanted to keep it; thus, it stayed perpetually at the two-week's-growth stage.) A thorough search of U.S. Army records would show no Jim Nelson on the rolls, but with the right clearances and an appropriate need to know, you'd find his complete military record in the secret Department of the Army Security Roster and see that he was entering his fifth year of service with the First Special Forces Operational Detachment-Delta. The rest of the world referred to the supersecret fighting unit as Delta Force.

On this beautiful May afternoon, as he navigated his vintage Mustang down the back roads of Fort Bragg on his way to the Stockade, he wondered if this day at the office would bring what he was expecting. Having stayed up way too late watching the CNN coverage of the Panamanian polling fiasco, he had a sense that Panama would be back on the radar screen. And as a fluent Spanish speaker, he figured he'd be in on whatever the fallout might be.

It hadn't been that long since he'd engaged the Cubans in Grenada, and he figured that if Uncle Samuel would launch that kind of effort for a group of American medical students, then they'd have to do something about Noriega.

It turned out that he was right; the first order of business this morning was, indeed, about a mission to Panama, but he was surprised to learn the nature of it. This was an 0300 mission—a hostage recovery mission.

The PC—the precious cargo—was some American spy named Kurt Muse.

32

By late afternoon on election day, all hell was breaking loose at Modelo Prison. The first inkling for Kurt was the increased vehicular traffic out on the avenue between the prison and the neighboring Comandancia. Pickup and cargo trucks arrived by the dozen, each of them packed with new prisoners, who were off-loaded and paraded into the bowels of the prison, where the rape rooms and dungeons were located.

Kurt recognized some of the faces: local politicians and businessmen who vocally campaigned against the Noriega regime, and who, it would later turn out, had successfully rallied the Panamanian people to fulfill the crusade that Kurt and his compatriots had launched three years ago. Noriega had undoubtedly lost the election, but the votes would never be counted, and in his panic the Pineapple was making sure that those who spoke against him would never do it again.

Even from his perch in his cell, Kurt could plainly see the terror etched in these men's faces. This wasn't the way it was supposed to work. One of the great fallacies that Americans accept as truth is the deceptive simplicity of democracy. Americans presume that once the votes are counted, the government changes. As a politician, you take your best shot, and if you lose, you step aside and let the opposition slide behind the desk you used to occupy. Americans take it for granted because it was the way it has always been and presumably will always be in the future. In Panama, however, it's the dream that never was, and the Pineapple successfully undermined the entire fantasy merely by refusing to leave office.

And now people would pay with their lives for having dared to pursue change.

One of the politicians, a man Kurt recognized from social occasions, but whose name he couldn't remember, panicked on his way to the prison door and tried to run. He was too old, too slow, and too fat to ever have had a chance. A PDF soldier—there were more soldiers than guards now, given the influx of prisoners—knocked the politician to the ground with a single punch.

On the filthy concrete of the basketball court, the man lay there screaming for mercy, begging for them not to hurt him. He yelled about his wife, family, and business. He swore that he would forever be loyal to General Noriega, if only they would show him mercy. It was a display that turned Kurt's stomach; not for the message, because it was a message driven by terror, but because of the glee the guards and soldiers took in beating this man. They swung their rubber truncheons as if they were axes, great overhand sweeping strokes that landed with the sound of pistol shots on the politician's back, legs, shoulders, and belly as he rolled on the ground and screamed his pleas for mercy. By the time they were done, two, three dozen blows later, his shirt had been completely beaten off his body, and he lay sobbing on the concrete.

They had to carry him into the prison.

The beatings in the prison yard continued for hours, all through the day and into the night. Clearly aware that Kurt was watching, the soldiers and guards wrapped helpless dissenters in American flags and suspended them by their handcuffs from the basketball hoops as they beat them mercilessly with the truncheons. With bitter irony that chokes witnesses to this day, Kurt noted that from where he stood watching, the tortured men were perfectly framed by Manuel Noriega's munificent view of justice on the left and by "Jesus Saves" on the right.

When the beatings were done, the men were allowed to hang there, some conscious, some not, as the pressure from the metal bracelets broke their wrists and ruined the nerves and blood vessels in their hands.

As darkness fell, the tortures moved indoors. All night long, the walls reverberated with the sound of screaming men. It was the sound of agony the likes of which Kurt had never heard, even from wounded animals. It was the sound of pummeled flesh and broken bones, the sound of hopeless lives and approaching deaths.

Just before midnight a new face, Lieutenant Cáceres, a sadistic prick of a guard, paraded a blood spattered American flag in front of Kurt's cell, wiping the floor with it. "Where is your government now, Mr. Muse?" he taunted.

Kurt recognized the gold-fringed flag. He'd been there at Escuela Estados Unitos—Unites States School—when it was presented by the American Society of Panama, a charitable organization whose purpose included the improvement of education available to the residents of Chorrillo. "United States School" was just a name, not an affiliation. Other Panamanian schools carried the names of Mexico, Canada, Costa Rica, and all of Panama's international neighbors. But for Cáceres, mopping the floor, the school and its flag provided a cause.

And the hated bastard asked a good question: Where the hell *was* Kurt's government?

33

Kimberly Muse was impossibly lonely and desperately afraid for her father. She hated what he was going through, and hated that he had to be the brunt for so much anger and political rhetoric in Panama. He'd been trying to do the right thing, for crying out loud. How could the Panamanian papers say such terrible things about him? How could they think that there was anything evil in merely trying to state the truth?

She understood how the Pineapple could think those things, but the newspapers disappointed her. Okay, sure, the editors and reporters were afraid of what might happen to them if they spoke out, but wasn't that the point? Wasn't that how the world changed—by people having the guts to step forward to say what's on their minds? How could debate—honest, open debate—possibly be harmful?

How could they keep her dad in prison without any charges and without any hope of being released, simply because he'd spoken up? It wasn't right.

Life here on the mainland United States sucked. You had to drive everywhere, and if you hadn't known someone since the day you were born, there was no way to ever make a friend. It didn't help that the Muses weren't allowed to say anything to anyone about who they really were.

Things with Mom were a little rocky, too. Not that she didn't love her and respect her for everything that she was doing, but Mom was so damned intent on being strong that she never made it okay to be weak sometimes. Kimberly wanted to cry and sensed that her mom did, too, but crying just wasn't accepted in the Muse house. Not now. They had to stay focused on the goal, and that goal was to get Daddy home as soon as possible.

Kimberly had tried to be hopeful on that note. She'd set milestones in her mind when she might see her dad again. Next week. Three weeks from tomorrow. Within the month. But over and over again, those deadlines had expired, and Dad was still wasting away in that awful place.

Waiting sucked. Florida sucked. Everything about this whole mess sucked. And from what she could tell, there wasn't any change on the horizon.

Everything in and about Panama changed with news of the stolen elections and the violence that followed. Marcos Ostrander brought word to Annie of increasing tensions throughout the country, even as her friends confirmed it all through letters of their own. Time and again, the U.S. military and the PDF would go nose to nose in face-offs that hadn't yet resulted in gunfire, but undoubtedly would, sooner or later.

What was bad before was now many times worse, with CNN and the broadcast news outlets filled every night with footage of Panamanian streets packed with demonstrators waving the white flags of the resistance, only to be inevitably broken up by packs of Noriega's elite Dobermen and his so-called dignity battalion whose job it was to bully the innocent for stating their beliefs.

For Annie's part, now that the kids were out of school and Aunt Elsa had finally passed on, she remained focused like a laser beam on writing as many letters and making as many telephone calls to as many people as possible to win her husband's release. In July, when it finally became clear that Kurt was irrevocably a political prisoner, not a criminal one, she made the decision, with the urging of Marcos Ostrander and the concurrence of Father Frank, to move with the kids to the Washington, D.C., area, where she could have quicker access to the political power brokers and to be closer to her father and stepmother.

On the down side, Annie feared that a move north would weaken the unbreakable bond that had formed between her and Kurt's coconspirators. Through April, May, and June, the group had made a point to see each other at least every other week, providing support, guidance, and love as together and separately they all tried to navigate treacherous, uncharted waters.

She'd grown particularly close to Tomás, with whom she spoke more often than the others. She had come to realize that Tomás in particular had been financially ruined by his ordeal. When it became clear to the PDF that Tomás was involved, they'd raided his business and stolen whatever was of value before destroying the rest. Annie had likewise learned that much of her own property had been seized and divvied up among the PDF elites. Their Volvo, in fact, was now the personal vehicle of Carlos Villalaz, the Panamanian attorney general.

The move to Washington—actually, to the quiet suburb of Burke, Virginia—was also prompted by the promise of occasional telephone calls to Kurt, managed out of the Pentagon. They'd actually been able to complete one call, but between having to pause to say "over" after every statement and knowing that every word was being recorded, the conversation was stilted and ultimately unsatisfying. Kurt had sent word through Marcos that he did not want to do that again. Emotionally, it took Kurt to places he did not want to venture in the presence of his captors. Every perceived weakness could be a weapon to be used against him.

Annie had heard, again through Marcos, that Nana and Papi had eventually been forced to leave Panama for asylum in the States. Apparently, they'd stayed with Major Mansfield for a week or so, but it became clear as Kurt's ordeal deepened rather than resolved that significant danger remained for them in Panama and they were forced to leave the country. Nana had come first, followed a week later by Papi.

Annie had exchanged some very brief letters with them, but there had been no effort at a physical reunion. Frankly, she wondered if that wasn't just as well. This was not the time to open up old wounds.

Richard Dotson continued to be Annie's standard bearer in Foggy Bottom, earning himself an official reprimand from his superiors for continuing to champion a cause that they were not especially interested in pursuing. In Langley, after years of being on the wrong side of Panamanian politics, the CIA was finally taking an interest in the ouster of Manuel Noriega.

Suzanne Alexander, Annie's contact at the Agency, was as much a source of worry for the Muses as she was a source of hope. Even after she'd been transferred to Langley, she'd continued to be so emotionally invested in what Kurt had been doing that she'd developed physical symptoms of stress, manifested by the total loss of her voice. Even though she'd begun to recover, Annie made a concerted effort to keep the pressure off of her.

And Annie was not working alone. Kurt's cousin, Greg Williams, heard of the situation and talked his boss, Senator Connie Mack of Florida, into including a visit to Modelo Prison during his mission as part of the official delegation to observe the Panamanian elections. While there, Senator Mack had managed to whisper to Kurt that he had not been forgotten. Of course, that had been over a month ago now, and reasonable people might begin to wonder after that kind of delay what the difference between forgotten and not forgotten really meant when, at the end of the day, Kurt was still in prison.

Annie forced herself to be reasonable about these things. She told herself that at any given moment there had to be at least a thousand things on the plates of every senior government official and that it would be unreasonable to expect them to just drop everything to concentrate on one political prisoner.

Hers was a war of attrition, wearing down the internal resistance of the government one official at a time. It was a war of countless tiny victories that began with finally talking a secretary into taking her call, and then finally getting the decision maker to listen to what she had to say. Her job, as she saw it, was to be a persistent, friendly, and utterly relentless pain in the neck to as many powerful people as she could draft into her cause.

Ultimately, though, the big breakthrough came not from her hand at all, but from that of her daughter. Annie's letters were written and managed the way these things were supposed to be done. She did the research to find out who was in charge of a particular agency or who the keeper was of some esoteric piece of information she needed and then crafted a delicately worded, politically balanced letter in hopes that it would work its way through the chain of command to the desk of the decision makers. Clearly, she'd had some successes, but she'd suffered nearly as many defeats, and the whole thing was extremely frustrating.

Kimberly, however, didn't know about the etiquette and arcane courtesies of dealing with governmental bureaucrats. All she knew was that she wanted her dad back and that there was one person on the planet who could make that happen. She sat down at her desk, worked through a rough draft, corrected it, and finally crafted her final version, written by hand in the loopy, precise handwriting of a teenage girl:

June 21, 1989

Dear President Bush,

My name is Kimberly Anne Muse. I am writing this letter not for me but for my father, Kurt Frederick Muse. As you should know by now, he is a political prisoner in Panama and has been so for the past two and a half months. I, being a teenager, didn't think there is much I could do but sit around and wait for an outcome. But you know, President Bush, I got very tired of just waiting and watching my father slip away from me. So I decided to go to the top, and besides God, whom I continue to pray to, you're it. I'm asking you now to hear my plea for help.

My dad has lived in Panama for the past thirty five years, so he has naturally acquired a love for the country. Once he saw that this country was being sucked of its life, like marrow from the bone, he decided to try to put an end to it. What resulted was an underground radio station that told the people to stand up for what they believed in and vote. As we saw in the May elections the effort put out by this united group of people worked: The Panamanians voted in record numbers and the opposition won by an overwhelming seventy-five to twenty-five percent. But this happened over one month ago and still Noriega has not left power. Despite numerous treaty violations; the fact that the sixty days allotted by the Panamanian law to gather information for a case has been ignored; and that the Noriega-run government has not charged my dad of any specific crime; he still sits there in prison waiting to be released. President Bush, I want to ask you this: Is speaking up for what you believe in a crime? You don't have to answer that because the answer lies right in our U.S. Constitution. But is life, liberty and the pursuit of happiness only good for Americans or does it pertain to other peoples of the world like China, Nicaragua and Panama, countries that are fighting for these seemingly simple rights.

President Bush, I'm not asking for something as impossible as world peace; but please let's try and get closer by helping my country of birth out of its situation. Most importantly to me, let's try to get the Panamanian government to release my Dad. I know you have a family that loves you as I love my Dad. If anything *were to happen to you they would try their hardest to work out the problem. Because so much time has passed since I've seen my father and no signs of releasing him have been shown, I am asking for your help.*

Mr. Bush I have lost close to everything. I don't want to include my father on that list. I beg of you, from the deepest part of my heart, to please take more serious measures to help obtain my Dad's release so that he may then fulfill his life, liberty and pursuit of happiness with his loving family.

Bless you,
Kimberly A. Muse

A realist, Kimberly understood how households work all over the world, irrespective of how powerful the family. Thus, she sent a second letter to the White House, this one to the First Lady:

June 26, 1989

Dear Mrs. Bush,

Knowing that your husband is such a busy man and that sometimes letters addressed to him never reach his desk I am enclosing two letters. Since I trust and respect your opinion I would be honored if you would read your copy and then deliver the other to your husband, President Bush.

Thank you,
Kimberly A. Muse

It's unclear which letter reached the president's desk, but the letter did arrive in the Oval Office, and as the situation in Panama heated up, there was a personal element to the national strategy that now had the attention of the president of the United States. At the highest levels of the government, a name few people had heard before was suddenly featured in the President's Daily Briefing.

From that moment on, Kurt Muse's welfare became a strategic and tactical consideration in every action taken regarding the Noriega regime.

34

Sept 6, 1989
Time: 9:40

Dear Daddy,

I miss you, and love you. I want you to come back. I'm in soccer. This Friday the 8 of September of 89 and the next day Saturday the 9 of September we have a scrimmage against another school. And Sept 16 a Saturday is our first game. Dad this is just what I wanted. Well I've gone threw two days of school. I met alot of friends. You know that almost every friday the Lake Braddock Bruins play against their oppenants.

Dad I love you alot. Xoxoxoxoxo

Miss you
From Erik
Love you

Sept. 6, 1989

Keep the faith, Musy. God and I aren't resting. I agree that words are cheap . . . I'm not fooled. I'm with you every step of the way . . . and that is not an idle threat.

K & E adore your letters. They need them for strength.

Kimberly is beginning to doubt God's wisdom and love. My message to her was that while we don't understand God's timing we must continue to have faith.

Our house is nice but not a home. It is really quite empty without you. But Kurt you'd be so proud. Erik has become so responsible. He picks out his clothing, does his homework, packs his backpack, collects his notes, money, etc. and makes K's and his lunch.

He does all of this without being asked.

K has taken him under her wing at the new school. He's managing well—getting all of his assignments, being on time, etc.

K is making friends but being careful about just who they are. This puts her under a certain amount of stress. The caliber of kids varies here but I trust her judgment. Any words of encouragement from you—specific suggestions, etc. would be greatly appreciated.

Today we went to a lady orthodontist—a great, honest, capable and pregnant lady.

Kimberly will be finished in 4 to 6 months with a monthly fee only due on her. Erik will need a full 2 yrs new braces, a night brace—so . . . it has to be done.

I paid for the dirty car with the differential problems. That was smart.

I'm working on the red Taurus. With all this leg work it should definitely be a good buy. I'm getting my dad's, uncle's and Timmy's opinion.

I adore you Kurt. We need your letters, too.

Lots of love,
Annie

35

The change in priorities could not have been more obvious to Marcos Ostrander. As the endless hot summer dissolved into an endless hot autumn, the tensions between the United States and the Panamanian regime got steadily worse, with daily harassments of U.S. military personnel by the swaggering PDF forces, bolstered by the unceasing bluster of Noriega. General Woerner, of course, still resisted pushing back, seemingly holding on to the notion that peace at any cost was worth some daily humiliations and the occasional outbreak of violence.

It was getting more and more difficult to get in to see Kurt these days. Checkpoints had been set up on the main avenues into Chorrillo, and any vehicles bearing Americans in uniform were routinely stopped and sometimes detained. Ostrander and Ruffer had adopted the strategy of never making eye contact with the guards as they beckoned for them to stop and to just continue through the checkpoints. It was always a hazardous strategy that occasionally pushed the limits toward a violent clash, but with Perry's concurrence, Ruffer and Ostrander remained unanimous in their commitment to visit Kurt on the agreed upon schedule.

The visits, however, had become more complicated, and not only with regard to their logistics. Ostrander didn't have the need to know, and therefore did not attempt to ask, but it seemed apparent to him that some sort of rescue mission was being cobbled together. Before and after every meeting at Modelo, he was ordered to report to the

Tunnel at Quarry Heights, first to receive a list of questions, and then to debrief a bunch of scruffy-looking men in civvies on what he had been able to discover. They wanted the numbers and composition of the guards, the layout of the interior of the prison, the numbers of steps leading from one floor to another, the type of locks on the exterior doors and on Kurt's cell itself. They wanted to know details on the types of armaments that were visible, and any other information they could find on the names and backgrounds on individual guards.

Kurt himself proved to be a tremendously reliable source for much of this information. Through idle chats he had with the guards, and simply by being ever-vigilant, he was able to funnel out all kinds of personal information about the guards on his floor. He knew which guards were the violent ones and which were mostly passive. They'd learned that Cáceres and Correa were vicious ideologues who would unquestionably lay down their lives for the Pineapple, while Lieutenant Dominguez was merely a passive civil servant whose career ambition began and ended with pacing the halls of Modelo. He didn't participate in the endless political patter that Muse had to listen to every single day.

Ruffer had likewise been summoned to the Tunnel a couple of times, but for him the questions dealt more with Muse's psychological stability. Had he given up yet? Was he depressed? Had he been turned? Of course, all the answers were in the negative. Simply put, Muse was increasingly impatient with the U.S. government's toleration of Manuel Noriega, he was sick to death of "Wimp Woerner," and he was ready to see the country act like the superpower it was and to quit bowing at the feet of a dictator.

Ostrander and Ruffer were careful in their reports to quote as directly as they could and to make their observations as precise as possible. When they were walking, they were counting their steps, and when they were listening to the guards, they were listening to the dialects that were being spoken. Since the elections, they were beginning to pick up more and more Cuban dialects, leading the G-2 guys—the Intelligence guys—to draw all kinds of conclusions, none of which were positive for the Pineapple's future.

For Ostrander, the only conclusion to be drawn from this questioning in the Tunnel was that someone was planning a prison break. He had learned and was later able to confirm that the spooks at Hurlburt

Field in Florida had constructed a three-quarters-scale model of Modelo Prison out in the middle of nowhere and that live-fire exercises could be heard during the night. It pleased him that the plans were that advanced, but of course, the big question would be the timing of any raid. Because this would be a land-based operation, it made sense that when the balloon went up, the execution would fall to Delta Force, a supersecret commando group whose existence was never officially acknowledged by the government, but whose exploits were quickly becoming the stuff of Army legend. If the rumors were close to being true, these guys could crash a building, kill the bad guys, and rescue the good guys before anyone even knew that the shooting had started.

It would have been a mistake, of course, for Ostrander to even hint of his suspicions to Kurt. It wasn't so much that Muse would reveal the plans to the enemy—God knew he had been damned tight-lipped as it was—but more because he thought it unwise to falsely raise any hopes. Planning a rescue operation was a completely different matter from executing one, and for the time being Marcos didn't see the catalyst for armed invasion anywhere on the horizon.

Besides, planning was what Delta did. Again, Marcos had no first-hand knowledge, but the word on the street in the top-secret world that was so much a part of Marcos's life was that Delta started planning a rescue mission the moment it heard that American hostages had been taken anywhere overseas. Of those planned missions, precious few were executed, for any number of reasons, and some were taken more seriously than others. The presence of a faux Modelo somewhere in the Florida outback told Marcos that this was one of the serious ones, but it never made sense to unnecessarily introduce hope into a prisoner's life.

Any doubt Ostrander might have harbored on the issue was more than mitigated by Kurt's impatience to get the hell out of that place. Marcos kept him pretty up to date with the politics of the region, and the more Kurt heard, the more he seemed to be getting frustrated by General Woerner's lack of action. How many indignities did the people of Panama have to suffer before he got off his ass and did something? Kurt knew through Ostrander and Ruffer that the priorities were changing on the Isthmus, so why did Woerner continue to sit on his hands?

In the months that Kurt, Jim Ruffer, and Marcos Ostrander had been meeting thrice-weekly, they'd developed a certain rhythm of communication that suited all of them. If Kurt had something important to say to Ostrander—his political lifeline—he would wear socks to their meetings, and in the days surrounding the elections, there'd been socks for almost every meeting. As a way of sticking his thumb in the eyes of his captors, Kurt had even figured out a way to communicate with his family without enduring the indignity of the official censors.

Marcos routinely brought books in for Kurt to read, everything from *The Hunt for Red October* to *The Count of Monte Cristo*. The books came one at a time. When Kurt finished one, he was allowed to have another. On the way into the prison, Correa or one of his lieutenants would thoroughly examine the book to search for any contraband. On the way out, though, Kurt noticed that the search was always a cursory one, and when Lieutenant Dominguez did the searching, he always held the paperback by its spine and riffled its pages. The outgoing search took no more than a few seconds.

With this in mind, Kurt had taken to jotting long notes to his family in the gutter where the pages met the book binding. The notes would go on for pages and pages, consisting of hundreds of words whose value lay as much in the small victory they represented as they did in the news they passed along to the family. Of course, Annie, Kimberly, and Erik had to refrain from similar tactics for incoming books. For them, the only option was to write the good old-fashioned newsy letter. Truth be told, of the three, Annie was the only one fully cognizant of how crippling the intrusion of censors could be, and as such, her letters tended to be written with fairly stilted language. Kimberly only wished him luck and good things in her letters, while Erik poured out his emotional responses to everything from the Orioles to the Washington Redskins, which he was quickly adopting as his home team.

Ostrander also learned that Kurt had been keeping a journal of his daily activities and travails. As it turned out, the one book that every prisoner was allowed to have, and whose presence was never questioned, was the Holy Bible; in Kurt's case, a five-by-seven-inch King James version printed on onion skin paper. The last twelve pages of Kurt's copy were blank. He didn't know if it was a printing anomaly or if it was intended as a space to write notes, but Kurt carefully tore out one page at a time as needed and wrote his diary in the smallest possible hand. To keep the forbidden chronicle from being found by the guards as they tossed his cell, he stored the pages inside the void space in his stick deodorant tube, where the thumbscrew at the bottom of the tube allowed you to extend the deodorant stick as it was used. Knowing how put off Panamanians were by all by-products of personal hygiene, Kurt made sure that there were always a few armpit hairs on the surface of the stick, so that a curious guard would take only a cursory glance and then quickly put the deodorant down.

By the time September rolled around, Kurt had just about had it with the delays and the lack of progress. Marcos shared with him that the kids were missing him, dreading the start of school in yet another new community, and Kurt was growing impatient with the fact that his parents—his father in particular—continued to be angry at him for having put the family in this kind of situation. He could only imagine what was becoming of Intergraphic. Kurt hadn't heard anything at all from Carol and David, and he knew that that kind of silence could only mean continuing anger. The whole world, it seemed, was turning against him, and still nobody seemed to be doing anything about it.

Kurt wore socks to one of the September meetings, and Ruffer kept his part of their time together short. When it was Ostrander's turn, Dr. Ruffer started chatting up the guards on something soccer-related, and Ostrander had his moment alone.

"How are you today, Kurt?" Marcos asked, careful as always not to speak directly to any issue.

"I'm good," Kurt said. "I'm very, very good." There was a smugness to his tone that made Ostrander scowl.

"Well, I'm glad to hear that."

"This is the secret," Kurt said, handing over a hardcover copy of *The Godfather*. "This is a very good book."

Marcos nodded as he took the book. "I'm glad to hear that. I've only seen the movie."

"Well, you should read the book. You should read it carefully. There's a lot in there."

Marcos turned the book over in his hands. "I'll do that," he said.

"I mean *really*. There's a lot in that book."

Marcos suppressed a smile. Jesus, Kurt had never been much for subtlety. *I got it*, Marcos wanted to say. *You've hidden something in the book. How obvious do you want to make it?*

When the meeting ended ten minutes later, Lieutenant Dominguez gave the book a cursory look and handed it back. Ostrander waited until he was back at the Tunnel before he started searching for the message. It wasn't Kurt's typical message in the gutter space, that was obvious from the very beginning. In fact, as far as Marcos could tell, the book was pristine. It took him the better part of a half hour to notice the small bubble that appeared in the binding when he opened the book all the way. Kurt Muse, king of the void space.

Using a pencil, Marcos probed the space in the binding, dislodging a fan-folded piece of lined yellow paper. It was a letter to President Bush.

Modelo Prison, Panama, Sept. 7

Dear Mr. President:

I've been held in solitary confinement in this prison for over five months, and it now appears I will not be afforded the opportunity to face my accusers. Not only have they denied me due process, the regime's attorney general now informs me that I will continue to be held hostage "until we see how the situation develops." By a most fortunate condition as a dependent spouse of a U.S. Forces employee (my wife is a DoDDS teacher), I'm covered under the Panama Canal Treaties, provisions of which clearly entitle the U.S. to my custody. In spite of a Herculean effort by the men and women of our office of Treaty Affairs to gain my custody, the Panamanian military have now refused to even discuss the matter. A flagrant treaty violation exists, one that by their own admission involves a political hostage. It is my understanding that having exhausted all local means of peaceful compliance, that the CINC Southern Command deferred my case to the Joint Chiefs of Staff for procedural instructions. Mr. President, I've lived in Panama most of my life and in the last 4 years have come to know the regime's workings quite well. Without question I can assure you that Mr. Noriega and his band of thugs will only release Panama from their chokehold when we apply force, military force. When you order that to happen, Mr. President, over two million Panamanians and this U.S. Citizen will be in your debt and free at last.

Very truly yours,
Kurt F. Muse

36

On October 8, 1989, the senior members of Manuel Noriega's military staff staged a coup. When they had the dictator in custody, the coup organizers pleaded with American authorities for protection against a countercoup, even as they tried to protect their deposed leader from penalty or reprisals.

American commanders, however, under the new, days-old command of General Maxwell Thurman, sensed that the Pineapple might be using the new American command structure to set a trap, and insisted that Noriega be delivered to them. Before a solution could be negotiated, the coup collapsed.

Samantha Skinner, David and Carol's oldest daughter, watched the news of the coup unfold on CNN from the safety of her college dormitory at the University of North Carolina, Wilmington, and decided that she needed to see if her Uncle Kurt was all right. She dialed Modelo Prison directly, and someone answered on the second or third ring.

"*Carcel Modelo*," said a man's voice.

"My name is Samantha Skinner," she explained in flawless Spanish. "I'm Kurt Muse's niece, and I'm calling to see if he's okay. May I speak to him please?"

She expected a stern rebuke, a lecture on the inappropriateness of her request. What she got instead was a very matter-of-fact, "We're having a coup right now. He may be home very soon."

37

Kurt's first inkling of the coup came with a spattering of gunfire from beyond the walls of his cell—from beyond the walls of the prison, in fact, from the Comandancia compound on the other side of the street. Startled, he rolled off his cot and dashed to the window. It was the most amazing thing. He saw PDF troops holding other PDF troops at gunpoint, the losers with their hands in the air, surrendering to the winners.

He didn't realize it at the time—in fact, the whole incident seemed minor, with maybe fifty rounds fired in total and no injuries that he could see—but he had just witnessed the heart of the coup, where Manuel Noriega's elite antiriot police, the so-called Dobermen, and a PDF infantry company had turned their weapons on what turned out to be precious few Noriega loyalists. Just like that, a government had been toppled.

For a few hours.

The next time Kurt was awakened, it was by the full-scale counterassault, and it came like thunder from hell. Gunfire erupted from all over, tearing at the humid air with a relentless cacophony of explosions. Again he darted to his window, and with a single glance, he knew that the Comandancia had been retaken. Armored personnel carriers surrounded the walled facility, and loyal soldiers swarmed to take their government back from the rebels.

As Kurt watched the bedlam unravel, a heavy machine gun opened up from just yards away to his left, spraying deadly cover fire over the heads of the invaders and into the grounds of the Comandancia. They had set the gun up in the window of the cell next to Kurt's, a perfect vantage point from which to accomplish its mission. Repelled by the deafening noise, Kurt dropped to the floor to take cover from the return fire that never materialized.

The counterassault was over in a matter of minutes and relative quiet returned, punctuated by the single gunshots that marked the initial executions that would ultimately consume every officer and noncom involved in the attempted coup. Within moments after the shooting stopped, the truckloads of new prisoners started to arrive.

Inside the walls of Modelo Prison, Kurt could hear the sounds of panic, men running and shouting. They were preparing for something, and just in case that something included a chance to get away, Kurt put on his shoes and socks and prepared to take advantage of any opportunity that might arise.

He heard the sound of doors opening and closing, and of many feet in the concrete hallways. Through his window, he could see a large portion of the prison population being loaded into trucks and driven out through the walls of Modelo, off to God knew where, but what he later learned was Coiba Prison, an island fortress off the coast of Panama.

They'd barely left when truckloads of new prisoners arrived to take their place. These, however, were prisoners in military uniforms, and they were bloodied and battered. At first, Kurt was reminded of the groups that arrived on the heels of the stolen elections, but there was a viciousness to the treatment of these new arrivals that made the post-election cruelty seem like schoolyard play. These men were beaten every step of the way as they were herded into the Modelo dungeons, and the screams commenced almost immediately.

At least one prisoner—a military officer of unknown rank—never made it that far. With his hands and feet shackled, he was still in the prison yard when a loyalist soldier knocked him to the ground, slipped a black plastic bag over his head, and fastened it at the prisoner's neck with a length of tape. The prisoner suffocated right there on the filthy concrete, flopping and writhing like a fish on a dock.

With the changeover of the prison population came a changeover in the guard staff as well. The somewhat bumbling, often laughable incompetents that Kurt had come to know were now replaced with regular soldiers who accepted the sadistic side of their job with a particular glee.

Over the course of just a couple of hours, Modelo Prison transformed from a common prison to a medieval torture chamber. Gone were the mere beatings with wire-reinforced rubber tubes. Now the beatings were meted out with fists, bats, and tire irons. This was no longer about instilling fear; it was about exacting punishment on soldiers who had taken up arms against their leaders. All too often, that punishment was death.

There simply weren't enough spaces for the torturers to work their craft. With the cells and dungeons filled with dissenters awaiting their turn, the beatings spilled out into the hallways and, ultimately, the officers' quarters, which were located across the hall from Kurt's cell. That brought the screaming and the pounding and the bleeding so close that Kurt could smell it. It was as if each blow somehow reverberated through the concrete.

Kurt watched, helpless, hopeless, and appalled, as one poor soul, bound to a chair, was dragged out into the hallway. He begged for mercy as PDF soldiers wrapped his head in a white T-shirt—white for the color of the opposition. They beat him with their fists for ten, fifteen minutes. They beat him long past unconsciousness, long past their own apparent exhaustion. They beat him until the white shirt had turned crimson, completely saturated and dripping with blood.

Kurt was certain that he had just witnessed a man's murder. He felt sick for the man and for his family, and ashamed of himself for not looking away; but it was like the cliché about not looking at a train wreck. Over the years, through the nightmares that would follow, Kurt would learn to find some solace in being the sole witness to what actually occurred there that night. He never learned the name of the murdered man, and he'll never know what the official record shows for his cause of death, but God knows the true cause, and so do Kurt and the men who pummeled him.

There is no sound on the planet, Kurt learned, that is as horrific as the sound of a man being tortured. The pleading screams of agony, the cries for mercy, were so pitiful, so awful, that they became a physical presence in the building, every bit as much a part of the architecture as the concrete and mortar that held it all together. It became a part of

Kurt, too, from that night on. The heavy wet sound of wood against skin, the snap of bones, the shrieks of pure pain. The look of satisfaction on the torturers' faces. All of it would remain with Kurt forever.

Witnessing such unspeakable suffering, it was impossible not to wonder, if only for a fleeting moment, whether Kurt was somehow responsible for the torment of these fractured and tortured revolutionaries. These soldiers and Dobermen had been his focus, after all. These were the very people whom La Voz de La Libertad had been hoping to reach through their broadcasts. From the earliest days of their illicit transmissions, La Voz had prompted and prodded these men to turn their backs on corruption and embrace the principles of their parents and their church. Over and over again, Kurt and his compatriots had begged men just like those who shook Modelo with their screams to rise up and do what was right.

Now, here they were, paying the ultimate price for their patriotism.

Kurt closed his eyes and tried to push the horrors away. This was not what he'd hoped for, not what he'd planned.

He forced himself to think of his successes, his goals. He forced himself to think about the day he saved the de facto president of Panama from certain arrest.

38

For a brief moment in time, in late 1988, Roderick Esquivel, a gynecologist from Panama City, was the de facto chief executive of a tiny republic caught in a spiral of corruption. Within hours of his ascendancy, he was marked for arrest. A soft spoken, dignified professional, Dr. Esquivel had been a long-time critic of President Eric Arturo DelValle, whose own rise to the presidency reeked of corruption of the worst kind.

On October 11, 1984, by a margin of fewer than two thousand votes, the world recognized the election of Nicolás Ardito-Barletta as the president of Panama, with DelValle and Esquivel installed as first and second vice presidents, respectively. A former officer of the World Bank, Barletta seemed well qualified on paper, but he was elected without a significant power base, and as such he appeared to Noriega—who had just appointed himself leader of the army and the national police—to be an easy pawn. He lasted only eleven months in office before he was forced to resign.

While conservative economic policy was the principal trigger for his resignation, many people—Kurt among them—believed that Noriega had forced him out for fear that he would reveal Noriega's role in the brutal murder and mutilation of Hugo Spadafora.

A prominent critic of the Panamanian military, Spadafora—a leader in the anti-Sandinista campaigns in Nicaragua—had announced that he had information linking Manuel Noriega to drug trafficking and illegal arms dealings. When last seen alive in the Costa Rican border areas, Spadafora had been in the custody of Panamanian security forces. On September 14, 1985, his castrated and beheaded body was discovered near the Panamanian border. That Noriega was responsible was never proven, but accepted by many as fact.

The coincidence that Barletta was pressured out of office within days of announcing his intention to investigate the army's involvement in Spadafora's murder was just too much for Kurt to accept.

With Barletta gone, Vice President DelValle became Panama's third president in less than four years.

The new president did not bring a sense of calm, however. Protests over Spadafora's murder only added to the already-growing protests over the economy. Barely a month after taking office, the DelValle government was forced to close all its schools for several days due to lack of funding.

As officials in the United States decried the ouster of Barletta, Del-Valle tried to quell the rising domestic discontent by reintroducing the populist policies reversed by the previous administration. Prices for milk and gasoline were lowered, and the new president promised that labor groups and the private sector would be involved in any future negotiations with the International Monetary Fund. He seemed willing to promise anything to anyone who would listen, but in the end, economic realities could not be denied. Soon, the austerity measures were reinstated, and the public uproar grew louder.

A general strike protesting the DelValle economic policies was averted only by the intercession of General Noriega and his troops, a move that was just the first of several that showed who was truly in charge of the government. Whatever doubt might have remained disappeared entirely in October 1986 when DelValle fired four cabinet ministers and installed Noriega's hand-picked candidates to replace them.

As Noriega built his power base, the Western world took note of the blatant corruption. The U.S. House of Representatives opened up hearings on the political shenanigans even as the columnist Seymour Hersh published a series of articles alleging high-level Panamanian involvement in drug trafficking, murder, and the smuggling of sensitive information to America's enemies in Cuba.

As the world protested, the Noriega regime, as led by his puppet

DelValle, continued to push the tiny nation in any direction the general wished it to go.

The end of it all began on June 1, 1987. On the heels of a years-long power struggle within the PDF, Noriega forced his chief of staff, Colonel Roberto Diaz Herrera, to resign. A week later, Herrera took to the airwaves and to the soapbox, publicly accusing Noriega of active involvement not only in the death of Hugo Spadafora—still a very raw wound for the Panamanian people—but also of the former president Omar Torrijos, whose death in a plane crash years before had always been the source of much mumbling. Furthermore, Herrera played on the closeness of the Barletta victory in 1984 to accuse Noriega and DelValle both of massive election fraud.

The response of the Panamanian people was both immediate and vocal. Businessmen (including Kurt and his coconspirators as representatives of the Panamanian Rotary Clubs) participated in the formation of the National Civic Crusade to demand changes in the government. Demonstrations spread like wildfire, prompting the president to declare a state of emergency, thus suspending constitutional rights and silencing all official avenues of dissent. But the National Civic Crusade would not be silenced. Protestors called for a national strike that paralyzed the nation for days. The government responded to these strikes with violence.

Protests and strikes raged throughout the summer and fall of 1987, crippling the economy and throwing the government into chaos. It was in the midst of all this that Kurt launched La Voz de la Libertad, stirring the revolutionary juices even as they successfully kept their own identities a carefully protected (and frantically sought) secret.

On February 4, 1988, a federal grand jury in Miami, Florida, indicted General Manuel Noriega on charges of drug trafficking.

To preserve his presidency—and his own ass—President DelValle took the only action available to him. He announced in a televised speech that he was relieving Noriega of command of the Panamanian Defense Forces.

Kurt was in the home of Pablo Martinez, discussing the strategy for their next radio broadcast, when DelValle dropped his political bomb. A soft-spoken man with an encyclopedic knowledge of Panamanian history and politics, Martinez had been the only "professional" politician among Kurt's coconspirators, and his job was to make sure that the points made during the broadcasts of La Voz de la Libertad were both coherent and consistent. Kurt's wont had always been to make the messages angry and vitriolic, while Pablo sat on them all to keep the messages calm and rational.

"Did you hear that?" Pablo asked Kurt, rising from his chair and moving to the near-muted television.

"Hear what?"

"DelValle just fired the Pineapple."

"*What?*" It would have been easier to believe that the earth had been knocked off its axis. Sure enough, there was the Panamanian president on television making the announcement that due to the recent controversy created by Colonel Herrera and the indictment from the American grand jury in Miami, the general was being relieved of his command.

"He's a dead man," Kurt said of the president. As the words passed his lips, he knew that what he'd intended as hyperbole was anything but. It was a prediction for the future.

Almost immediately after the announcement was made, the ever-present (and always-illegal) scanner on Pablo's desk jumped to life with radio traffic. A lot of it was chatter, idle gossip about the news that had just broken, but within a few moments, they heard an announcement that startled them both: orders were issued to arrest not only President DelValle but Vice President Roderick Esquivel as well.

Rod was an interesting duck. Never a supporter of the administration he served—certainly not in the years since Barletta had stepped down in favor of Noriega's marionette—he was officially first vice president now, but he'd months ago stopped doing any of the administration's work. Neither DelValle nor his master needed him any more than he could tolerate them, so he had busied himself with perpetuating the medical practice he had built over a lifetime. He was, in fact, the man who had brought both Kimberly and Erik into the world. He was also a Rotary brother.

"If they get him, they'll kill him," Kurt said to Pablo.

Martinez shook his head. He didn't believe that for a moment. But they would certainly arrest him and put him in a place where a man as fine as he did not belong. "We should warn him."

"Surely he knows."

"About the firing, perhaps, but how could he know the rest?"

Fair enough. The orders weren't yet five minutes old. But once warned, what was next? He needed a place to go, a place to hide.

"Do you have his phone number?" Kurt asked.

Pablo shrugged. "I have it here somewhere, I'm sure."

"Then call him. Tell him I'm coming to get him."

Martinez looked stunned. "Coming to get him? Then what?"

"I don't know. But we have to do something."

"You're not Rambo."

There wasn't time for this. "For two years we've talked the talk, and we've said all the things about rising up against the Pineapple, and now it's time to walk the walk. I can't leave Rod out there to twist in the wind."

Pablo knew Kurt was right. But he also knew it was a foolish thing to do. In just seven more months it would be time for the elections, and they had all promised each other to keep a low profile. To be detected was to be defeated. It was one thing to make a phone call, but something else entirely to actually harbor the target of an active coup. Suddenly, the stakes had risen through the roof, and all the conspirators' profiles rose with them. Pablo didn't worry about himself—none of the team worried about themselves. But he did worry about his son, Antonio, whose hot-headedness gave him too high a profile as it was.

But there really was no choice. Rod Esquivel was a friend. A brother. And they shared a common enemy.

"What do you want me to tell him?" Pablo asked.

"Tell him to drop what he's doing and wait by the door. I can be there in five minutes."

Pablo cast a glance back toward the scanner, where the radio traffic was growing exponentially. "Better make it three."

Kurt split the difference, arriving in four minutes at the entrance to Rod Esquivel's medical office, where the vice president was waiting for him at the door. Offering up a silent prayer of thanks that he'd driven the Cherokee today instead of his usual Volvo, Kurt threw the transmission into park and ran around to the passenger side back door. "Climb in here on the floor," Kurt said, opening the door.

Rod moved with a deliberate speed and professional grace that both impressed and infuriated Kurt. If someone were watching, Rod didn't want to give them the satisfaction of seeing him ruffled. Kurt saw it a little differently. PDF officials were on their way, and if they were close, he'd just as soon get the hell out of here. Rod climbed into the back and sat on the seat, as if he were any other passenger.

"On the floor, Rod," Kurt said, pointing to the crap that littered the floor of the backseat.

The vice president hesitated.

"You can't afford to be seen," Kurt explained. "I don't know what Pablo told you, but DelValle just fired Noriega, and Noriega has dispatched his goons to take you to prison. If you could hurry a little, that would be really good."

The Cherokee was the vehicle they used to transport the kids from one event to the next, and like kid-mobiles all over the world, this one was a mess on the inside. On a different day, Kurt might have been embarrassed. As it was, he was relieved to be able to cover Rod with the blanket they normally used to sit on the grass at soccer tournaments.

"Stay down, be still, and hope we don't hit any road blocks," Kurt said, tucking the blanket in around his passenger then hurrying back to the driver's seat.

The road block was the nightmare scenario. Ever since the National Civic Crusade had begun wreaking havoc, road blocks had become a way of life in Panama. Kurt never got the sense that the soldiers were ever actually looking for anything; rather they were just rousting people as a way of flexing their muscle—rousting people because they could. A little rousting would go a long way on this particular afternoon.

As Kurt pulled away from the curb, Rod asked from the back, "What about the president? Who's taking care of him?"

Kurt had no idea, but in deference to the high office held by his passenger, he refrained from saying what was really on his mind: "I could care less what happens to that pussy."

"Where are you taking me?" Rod asked.

Another very good question. This entire operation was way beyond the scope of anything they had planned for. This was improvisation in its most deadly form, but he hesitated to confess as much for fear of seeming less . . . *noble* in the mind of the vice president.

"We'll go to my house," Kurt said, trying his best to make it sound like a well-considered decision. "Once we're safe inside, we can figure out the next step."

"I need to get word to my family."

"I think Pablo is already doing that, but once we get to the house, my home is your home." In a country where virtually every phone was tapped, Kurt wondered if his bravado sounded bold or merely stupid. If Pablo had, in fact, called Jean Esquivel to warn her of the family's impending arrest, then the PDF would know more about the conspirators' operation than any of them had ever imagined. Surely, he would not have done that, Kurt told himself, and as the words formed in his head, he knew instinctively that he was right. Never once in the two-plus years of Radio Constitucional, and more recently, La Voz de la Libertad, had any of the team made so foolish an error as to use the telephone as a means for conducting their business. They had their radios for secure communications.

But this was a palace coup, for God's sake, and the key players had no radios. What choice would Pablo have had *but* to use the telephone?

That's when Kurt's mind grasped the reality that Rod must have known from the beginning. It was he who was the vice president of the country, not his wife. It was he who must be whisked to safety. To include his wife in the evacuation would be merely a gift, a courtesy. A wonderful bit of news. If she could not join him, then Rod would face the worst choice that patriots the world over have ever been forced to make: to stay true to his cause and principles even as his loved ones are tortured.

It was only a few miles back to the house, and as Kurt negotiated the route in the Cherokee, he tried not to think about these things, even as he grappled with the reality of what he, Tomás, and the others had been playing with all these months. You can talk about toppling a government, and you can talk about taking on a murderous dictator single-handedly, but until you see a wanted man—a man who exuded dignity and political savvy—sprawled like a bag of grain on the backseat of a car enduring fears that no man should ever face, you really don't understand the consequences of your political actions.

At this very moment, as they had been for many weeks, the streets were filled with special listening trucks manned with Cuban audio technicians scanning the air twenty-four–seven, with the single goal of putting Kurt and his pals out of business. In the game Kurt had chosen to play, the penalty for losing was a lingering, unspeakable death;

not just for the individual perpetrators, but in all likelihood for their extended families as well. Just who the hell did he think he was to bring this kind of danger down on the shoulders of his family, merely in pursuit of principle? And of all the people in the country with cause to hate Noriega, who the hell was Kurt Muse, the towering blond-haired gringo who could leave the country in an instant and cash in on his American citizenship, to be leading the fight?

He pushed these thoughts out of his mind. They didn't matter anymore. What was done was done.

Today wasn't about La Voz, and it wasn't about Kurt. Today was about Rod Esquivel and the preservation of the rule of law in Panama. There'd be plenty of time to worry about all the rest later.

Unless Pablo had used the phone.

Without a garage to cover their actions, they had to risk detection by prying eyes as Kurt whisked the vice president of Panama into the house through the front door.

To watch Rod, who stood tall and walked with graceful dignity up the walk, you never would have known the danger he was in. If Kurt had had the power, he would have whisked the man to the door as if they were under fire. He hated being exposed like this. In El Avance, the upscale neighborhood where the Muses lived, they were surrounded not just by the successful business people one would expect, but also by senior PDF commanders whose second and third incomes from graft and outright theft allowed them to afford their mortgages. As the politics became progressively more bitter, and the protests were put down more violently, it only made sense that the PDF goons would be watching their neighbors even more closely than they'd been watching before.

Finally, they were at the threshold, and as Kurt reached for his key, his heart stopped for an instant as he realized that the door was already unlocked. *Is it even possible?* he thought as his mind jumped ahead to a trap having been laid in his house.

The ridiculousness of the thought became apparent as he pushed the door open and he heard Kimberly call from upstairs, "Hi, Daddy!"

Overhead, he could hear her bounding footsteps as she came from her bedroom to greet him. She was halfway down the steps when she saw Rod, and she froze. Her face was a mask of confusion.

"Hi, honey," Kurt said. "You remember Dr. Esquivel." Turning to their visitor, he added, "Rod, this is my daughter Kimberly."

Esquivel smiled and offered a courteous nod. "Nice to see you again."

Kimberly's scowl deepened. "Hi." To her father: "Is everything all right?"

"Everything's fine," Kurt said. He marveled at his daughter's intuitive powers sometimes.

"Have you heard the news about the Pine—" she cut herself off in deference to the vice president. "You've heard about General Noriega?"

Kurt knew that she was putting the details together in her head, and he didn't want her to go there. "We've heard, but that's nothing for you to worry about. Go on upstairs and finish your homework."

She didn't want to go. He could tell from her posture alone that she expected some answers.

"Please, Kimberly," he urged one more time. "Really, everything is fine. Dr. Esquivel and I just need to discuss some things."

Her eyes moved from her father to his guest and back again. She wanted to discuss some things, too, but she didn't push the point. "Well," she said, "nice seeing you, sir. Welcome to the house."

Another courteous nod from Rod, and then Kurt ushered the man upstairs into the master sitting room and offered him a seat.

"Your daughter looks confused," Rod said.

Inexplicably, Kurt found himself defending her. "Oh, she'll be fine. She just—"

Rod interrupted with a flick of his hand. "I understand perfectly. It's not every day that a young girl finds an exiled vice president taking refuge in her house. Were I her, I think I might look a little stunned myself."

Kurt smiled. He appreciated Rod's understanding, even as he dreaded Kimberly's future questions. Annie knew everything about what Kurt and the others were doing, but they deliberately kept the children on the outside of that facet of their politics. The questions raised today, though, would likely end whatever reign innocence held over his daughter.

Kurt ushered the vice president to a chair in the living room and asked, "Can I get you something?"

Rod waved off the gesture. "I don't need you to get me anything," he said. "But I do need you to carry something for me."

Kurt felt his stomach tighten.

"A message," Rod clarified. "To Jean. By now, she should be at the U.S. ambassador's residence. I spoke to her after your initial phone call to me, and that's where she said she was going to go."

Kurt found himself nodding his agreement to visit the residence before he even had a chance to think through the consequences. For a man who had valued stealth and low profiles for so many months, he sure as hell was playing fast and loose with his profile now. He listened to the message and committed it to memory, understanding right away why it had to be delivered in person.

"Can you do that for me?" Rod asked. "Are you willing to do that for me?"

"It would be an honor, sir," Kurt said. He found himself swelling with pride as he considered the mission that lay ahead.

"Thank you, Kurt," the vice president said. "And while you're on U.S. sovereign ground, there's one more favor I'd like to ask of you."

39

The home of U.S. Ambassador Arthur Davis quite literally occupied the high ground in Panama City, perched atop an area known as La Cresta—the high ground. Kurt had been here several times in the past for official receptions and the occasional cocktail party—nothing unusual for any American ex-pat in the relatively closed community of Canal Zone employees and military officials—but never before had he been so aware of the houses across the street from the elaborate security gates, where he knew for a fact that Noriega henchmen carefully noted the comings and goings of visitors. For an American to show up on a day as politically crazy as this one would not necessarily be cause for concern in and of itself, but this business of playing fast and loose with all of La Voz's long-standing obsessions with anonymity were beginning to wear on Kurt.

"American citizen Kurt Muse to see Ambassador Davis, please," he said to the young embassy guard at the guard house. "I bring a very important message."

It wasn't until the guard started to speak that Kurt noticed the M-16 slung on his shoulder. Clearly, security had been ramped up considerably since President DelValle's announcement. "I'm sorry, sir, but the residence is closed to visitors this afternoon."

Kurt shook his head. "But it's important," he said, recognizing as they left his lips that these were words that the kid with the gun had heard a dozen times every day.

"Sir, I'm going to have to ask you to turn around and try again another day."

Damn. There was no other way but to spill the beans and hope that the goons across the street didn't have state-of-the-art listening devices. "Look," Kurt said, leaning closer through the open window, even as the guard leaned cautiously away from him. "I need to speak to *someone* in an official capacity. I have a message from Vice President Esquivel, and he asked me to deliver it personally."

The security guard's eyes narrowed as he considered the ridiculousness of the claim. But there was a spark of belief buried just under the surface of his suspicion. "Pull over to the side there and wait, please." He gestured to a parking slot off to the side of the gate that seemed designed precisely for the purpose he described.

As Kurt moved the car, the guard made a phone call. A moment later, the guard emerged from his hut and gestured for Kurt to leave his car where it was and walk closer. He did exactly that. Off to the right, beyond the gate and ahead near the house, Kurt saw Susan Davis, the ambassador's daughter, approaching him from the residence. The personnel gate to the side of the vehicle gate buzzed, and Kurt confirmed with a glance back to the guard that it was all right for him to pass.

Susan Davis was the reason why Kurt and Annie had been invited to the embassy events that they had attended. In her thirties, they were more or less the same age and frequently ran into each other on the social circuit. As he neared, he noted an air of tiredness about her this afternoon. They were still in plain sight of any and all prying eyes from outside the compound.

"Hello, Susan," Kurt said when they were within easy earshot of each other. "I need you to do me a favor and give me a big hug, as if I were your best friend back from a long trip."

Sensing the need for high drama, Susan's face broadened to a bright smile. As they embraced, Kurt whispered, "I've got Rod Esquivel hiding in my living room. I have a message from him for your father."

"How nice to see you again," she said, for the benefit of long-range microphones. "Please come on inside and have something to eat."

"Is your father here?" Kurt said in a barely audible voice.

"Let's go in and get something to eat," Susan said again. Neither one of them believed that the PDF had listening equipment sharp enough to hear them, but it made no sense to take the risk when a completely shielded residence lay just a few yards ahead.

The ambassador's residence was palatial in both size and grandeur, befitting the nation that brought Panama into the twentieth century. The last time Kurt was here, the ornate marble foyer was filled with visitors, all of them having a marvelous time. Today, on this afternoon, the tension in the house took on a physical weight.

When they were inside and the door was closed, Susan said, "My father is not here. He's at the embassy, but I can take you there. Come with me."

She led the way through the center of the house, through an official reception area. It was there that Kurt stopped dead in his tracks, stunned at what he was seeing. On the left hand side of the room, the entire DelValle family—minus the president—sat scattered among the various pieces of lush antique furniture. They spoke in hushed tones, and when they noticed the towering blond-haired gringo staring at them, all conversation stopped.

"Buenos dias," Kurt said politely, even as his mind put the awful pieces together. President DelValle had set Rod up. The son of a bitch had already arranged for asylum for himself and his family *before* he made his speech firing Noriega. The weasely bastard finally had made his first and only decision to stand up against the man who so plainly and publicly manipulated his strings, but only after seeking safety for his own family, and without so much as a nod of warning to the rest of his administration.

Disgusted, Kurt turned away from the DelValle family and was even more startled to see Jean Esquivel huddled with her two children in the far corner of the room, frightened and clearly ostracized from the DelValle clan. "Wait a second, Susan," he said to his escort. Before she could respond, he peeled off the prescribed path and walked over to Jean.

"Rod is safe," he said, approaching Jean. He wrapped her hand in both of his and leaned forward to kiss her cheek.

Jean nodded. "I know," she said. "He called me from the office before he left. I was wondering who would endanger themselves so by coming to whisk him away. I'm sorry it had to be you, Kurt."

He smiled. "I wouldn't have it any other way."

"I won't ask how you knew to come get him," Jean said, opening the opportunity for an explanation.

Kurt smiled and nodded. "I appreciate that."

"Have you endangered your family?"

His smile turned wry. "I suppose we'll all know that in the next couple of days, won't we?" He saw that he was making things worse for a worried wife and mother. "I'm sure we'll be fine. Rod gave me a message to funnel through Ambassador Davis to you. I guess I can give it to you myself. He—"

"He wants us to leave the country," Jean said, finishing the thought for him. "That's why we're here. That's why we're all here, I believe." A mask of disgust invaded her countenance as she cast a sneering glare toward the DelValle family. "What about Rod? Did he tell you his plans?"

Kurt grew visibly uncomfortable as she asked the question. He did, in fact, know, but it was not part of the message he'd been told to deliver to Jean. Given the way they clearly loved each other, he supposed there was no harm in sharing the details with her, but still—

"That's all right," Jean said, letting him off the hook. "These are secretive times."

Kurt felt a warm sense of relief wash over him. "Thank you, Jean. And good luck to you." With that, there was nothing more to be said. He kissed her again on the cheek, and then it was time to go.

"Will they be safe?" Kurt asked Susan, as she resumed leading the way through the house.

The look she gave him could only come from a diplomat's daughter, a practiced indifferent optimism.

Kurt changed the subject. "Where are we going?" he asked.

"To see my father, just as you asked." As she spoke, she led him through the kitchen to a door that could only lead to the basement.

"You keep your father in the cellar?"

Susan laughed. "Sometimes I wish. But no, we need to get you to the embassy, and I'm sure you'd prefer not to be seen while we do it."

She led the way to an underground garage. Nothing fancy; in fact just the opposite. Built of indigenous clay bricks, the garage had the feel and dampness of a cave. And there, waiting for him, was a black

Cadillac with tinted windows and an armed driver. "I'll leave you in the capable hands of Joseph," Susan said.

As if on cue, the driver seemed to come to life. He had the posture and demeanor of a soldier, with the haircut of an American college student. "This way, sir," Joseph said, opening the back door.

Kurt climbed in and took a seat.

"I think it would be best for you to lie on the floor," Joseph instructed. "I know the windows are tinted, but this is a tense day, and you can't be too careful sometimes."

Never had Kurt heard the order "Shut up and stay low" delivered with greater diplomacy.

The short ride to the embassy couldn't have lasted ten minutes. Every second of it, however, was extended to its maximum extreme as Joseph obeyed every traffic ordinance. Kurt thought it was interesting that a professional such as this driver would have the very same concerns that he'd had as he was spiriting Rod away from his office.

The reception at the front gate of the embassy was one of ambivalent free passage. Joseph didn't even roll the window down as they passed through onto the compound itself.

"We're on the grounds," Joseph announced, "but I'm going to ask you to stay down for just a moment more, sir."

Kurt understood fully. It was a point of simultaneous strength and weakness that Panamanian citizens worked side by side, shoulder to shoulder with American workers wherever the U.S. government or its prime possession—the Canal—did business. The strength was derived from the loyalty that was naturally spawned from such close working conditions, and one could only pray that that ultimately trumped the weakness born of the fact that every third worker was possibly a paid informant to Noriega.

There were no Panamanians, however, at the rear of the embassy when the Cadillac discharged its passenger. No one would report seeing Kurt Muse climb out of the backseat and get hustled up to the second-floor reception area.

Joseph handed him off to a diplomatic liaison of some sort, who was overly officious in his offers of seating, food, and drink.

An hour passed.

Ambassador Davis was allegedly behind closed doors, dealing with a very important matter, and Kurt could only imagine that it had something to do with that coward DelValle begging for his asylum. It was only there, in the grand reception area of the embassy, that Kurt understood the final piece of the DelValle puzzle: that the president had fired his thuggish military commander from the safety of U.S. soil. Not only had he sought to protect his family before he took a stance but he'd also run to hide behind the American house dress before he opened his mouth.

The more Kurt thought about it, the angrier he became. He thought back to the picture of the two families in the residence: the DelValles all abuzz about their new adventure in an all-expenses-paid exile juxtaposed against the Esquivels, who knew that their patriarch would stay behind and stand tall against the best of what Noriega had to throw at him.

The anger settled deeper still as he realized that President DelValle was in all likelihood just yards away, on the other side of the paneled door where Ambassador Davis was allegedly working hard to alter his schedule to give Kurt an audience. Try as he might, though, the ambassador somehow couldn't quite bring himself to follow through on the promise.

Twice, Kurt came *this close* to just walking out. Here he was, risking his life to deliver a message from the only remaining patriot in the official government of Panama, and no one could find the time to come out and hear what he had to say. Who the hell did these people think they were? Forever a loyal patriot to the United States, Kurt nonetheless remained completely baffled and unspeakably angry at the conflicting messages that the American government gave to the people of Panama. On the one hand, the United States insisted that the nation hold free elections; yet on the other, when the results of the election showed that it was clearly stolen, as they had in 1984 when Barletta and DelValle came to power, there was the United States standing first in line to recognize the new regime.

During the drug wars of the Reagan administration, the CIA had heaped praise on General Noriega because of the information he passed about the Colombians and later the Sandinistas, even as they ignored the world's worst-kept secret that the Pineapple was funneling drug money to fill his own pockets. Now, though, with the murder of Hugo Spadafora and the pressure brought to bear by a few inquisitive congressmen, Noriega was persona non grata in Washington. Caught in the middle of all the political ping-pong were the people of Panama, who by and large wanted nothing more complicated than enough money to feed their families and enough freedom to keep them from being molested by troops at every intersection.

Finally, to make it all as bad as it could be, on the day of the palace coup, Kurt was here, sitting alone and ignored. And he was getting truly pissed about it.

At long last, a middle-aged political advisor wandered into the reception area and offered her hand. "Mr. Muse," she said, her face alight with a beaming smile. "I'm so sorry to have kept you waiting this long. As I'm sure you know, it's been a busy day, and—"

"You're sure I know?" Kurt said, his tone betraying his contempt. "You're damned straight I know. I've got the vice president of Panama in my living room, for God's sake. You'd think that might give me an inkling."

The smile on the diplomat's face never faded. "Indeed. I guess it's been a long day for you, as well. Unfortunately, Ambassador Davis will not be able to see you this afternoon as we had hoped. He asked me to meet with you on his behalf and to tell you that we have found several countries that would be more than happy to accept Doctor Esquivel and his family in exile."

Kurt was stunned. "You think *that's* what this is about? You think Rod and Jean Esquivel are here to beg for asylum? Jean's an American citizen for crying out loud. She doesn't need asylum from anyone."

Finally, the political advisor's calm façade showed the first sign of cracking. "But the vice president is not an American citizen. We only assumed—"

"Well, you were wrong," Kurt said. "In fact, that is the very substance of my message from the vice president. He wanted Ambassador Davis to know that he will be joining active elements of the opposition against Noriega. He'll be going underground and continuing the fight for freedom in his homeland."

The diplomat scowled and cocked her head. Clearly, this was not what she'd been expecting to hear. "Very well, then," she said. "I'll pass that along to the ambassador. Thank you so much for coming."

Kurt accepted the diplomat's hand and successfully fought off the urge to break it. "On a personal level, I'd appreciate it if you could make sure that President DelValle finds out what Rod is doing so that he can take a quick glimpse of what honor looks like."

The diplomat didn't respond and Kurt hadn't expected her to.

In the ensuing weeks, Rod Esquivel disappeared from view, joining a band of underground patriots whose mission it was to restore Panama to its citizens. While in his self-imposed exile, the deposed vice president recorded several of the radio messages that Kurt would broadcast through La Voz de la Libertad. Over time, he cautiously reappeared in public view, testing the safety of his presence, and finally reestablishing his medical practice.

For his part, President DelValle was likewise active in the cause of freedom. When Kurt and his coconspirators found themselves short on funds for the apartment leases they needed to hide their transmitters, DelValle forwarded, through an intermediary, the paltry sum of $2,000. Here he was, living in the most opulent exile the world had ever seen, safe with his millions, and he had the audacity to offer a mere two grand.

The exchange of cash happened at night, in the parking lot of a supermarket. When Kurt opened the envelope and counted the bills, he looked up at the messenger and said. "Okay, listen to me, because I want to make sure you get this exactly right. You need to quote me verbatim for President DelValle. Are you ready?"

The messenger nodded.

"Good. Tell him he should be ashamed of himself. It's his country too." He slapped the envelope into the messenger's chest. "I don't want his money. Give it back to him and tell him to shove it where the sun never shines. And we will never broadcast anything from him again."

40

Ever since the coup, Modelo Prison had become a warehouse for political prisoners. Gone were many of the rapists, murderers, and common criminals; they'd been shipped off for internment elsewhere. In their places came the dissidents and coup followers—the organizers were mostly dead—sent to this godforsaken hole to await whatever the Pineapple could dream up for them.

Also gone were the guards who had patrolled the corridors and harassed the prisoners. Their roles had been absorbed by regular PDF soldiers who carried about them an air of military professionalism that their predecessors could never project.

Early one morning, just a few days after the coup, one of these new guards came to Kurt's cell and peered at him through the bars, presumably to verify that he had neither escaped nor died during the night. He greeted Kurt cordially and introduced himself as the sergeant in charge of Kurt's section of the prison. He seemed intent on reassuring his prisoner that there was nothing to be concerned about. "I want you to know," the sergeant said, "that prison operations will remain unchanged."

"Thank you," Kurt said. "I appreciate that."

With a courteous nod, the sergeant started to leave, and then Kurt was overcome with a sense of unique opportunity. He stepped to the bars and caught the guard's attention just as he was about to disappear into the officers' quarters across the hall. "Excuse me, Sergeant?"

The guard turned.

"Don't forget my coffee," Kurt said.

The sergeant's jaw dropped. "What?"

"My coffee," Kurt said, as nonchalantly as he could manage. "I get coffee every morning. I consider it an important part of my day."

"Coffee." The sergeant seemed stunned.

"First thing," Kurt said. "Thanks so much." He turned and went about his day.

The next morning, Kurt nearly fell over from shock when the sergeant obediently delivered a yellow-and-black-striped paper cup of Café Duran. Containing his disbelief that the ruse had worked, Kurt accepted the coffee with a polite smile and a nod, and then sipped the nectar of the gods.

Every morning, for the remainder of his captivity, Kurt was served hot coffee by the guard staff.

Outside the walls of Modelo Prison, relations between Panama and the United States were coming unhinged. Noriega had become progressively more paranoid since the coup and had decided that the whole effort had been instigated by the American government as a ploy to have him removed from power. In retaliation, he redoubled his harassment of American troops and civilians and greatly increased his anti-American rhetoric.

The Pentagon, the State Department, the CIA, and the White House had finally converged on the same conclusion: Noriega had to go. They'd tried to let the electoral process make the change, but the Pineapple had quelled democracy with violence. The people of Panama had tried rising in rebellion, and that, too, had been crushed, surprisingly peacefully, with the real violence following in its wake.

For many months, Operation Blue Spoon—a plan for the forcible removal of Manuel Noriega from power—had been in the can, waiting for somebody to pull the trigger. The mission's time had come.

And the right man was in command.

41

Jim Ruffer was at the meeting in the Tunnel when General Woerner wept during his announcement that he would be retiring in thirty days. He had never been a supporter of Blue Spoon, having always thought that it would bring more harm than good. Woerner seemed to believe that as a sovereign nation, Panama had a right to the government that its people inflicted on themselves. Whatever we did to interfere, he said, would only make the United States look like meddlers.

He was not the first, nor would he be the last, to express these thoughts, but generals are the enforcers of national policy, not the makers of it, so it surprised few when he was ultimately relieved of command.

In Woerner's place came General Maxwell "Mad Max" Thurman, who told his senior staffers during the change of command ceremony, "Ladies and gentlemen, from now on the uniform of the day will be battlefield utilities. We are at war. Dismissed."

American military activity increased dramatically following the change of command. Partly to bring troops into battle-readiness, but also to desensitize the Panamanians to the rhythms and noises of invasion, Thurman ordered regular nighttime mobilization exercises in which tanks, trucks, and aircraft would go through the motions of war, without ever actually firing a shot.

One night, from the window of his cell, Kurt watched in stunned amazement as fighter jets and attack helicopters carried out a full-scale mock bombardment of the PDF Special Forces barracks on Flamenco Island.

The exercises, of course, infuriated Noriega, who saw the saber-rattling as an act of war. Like so many doomed dictators before him, he made blustering speeches to his people about the blood-letting that would follow any attempt to topple the duly elected government of Panama. Didn't the world remember what happened to the last American-led coup just months before? Those traitors were still in prison, where they would remain for a long, long time, forever in some cases.

Apparently accustomed to seeing the Americans back down under his rhetorical pressure, Noriega seemed to have difficulty dealing with an American general whose response to his threats was largely one of indifference.

In a move reflective of his growing panic, Noriega officially changed the status of Kurt Muse from that of political prisoner to that of hostage. That was the word he used: Hostage. Furthermore, he announced to the world that if any attempt was made to topple his government, the first bullet fired in the resistance would be aimed at Kurt's head.

It was a standing execution order, and to add credence to the threat, Kurt's patrolling guard was replaced by a stationary one, whose job it was to sit in a chair, all day long, waiting for the order to shoot.

Back at home, in their tiny townhouse in Burke, Virginia, news of the death threat to Kurt felt like a knife in the heart. After hundreds of phone calls and dozens of letters to everyone from the president on down to midlevel staffers who helped put her through to high-level decision makers, Annie was beginning to feel helpless.

The extended family had begun to reestablish contact after months of dismal silence, but Kimberly and Erik, while putting up a good front and a good fight, were clearly beginning to sag under the strain of being so horribly displaced from everything they had come to know as normal. Erik, in particular, was having a hard time, and his difficulties were reflected in his report card.

Annie had pulled every string she could find, and now she found herself hounding those who were cooperating to the point that she feared driving them off. But what else was there to do? She couldn't stop pushing. Not now. Not on the heels of the coup and the impending death threat to her husband. Kurt needed her to be strong and active now more than ever before.

It was so easy to feel as if no one was listening. The government apparatus was so huge and so complicated, fraught with so many conflicting priorities, that she wondered sometimes if it was even reasonable to expect powerful people to pay close attention to one man's plight.

Then, one day in early November, she found a letter in the mail that reaffirmed her belief in God and the government and in the goodness of people, no matter how lofty their station in life:

The White House
Washington, DC

October 30, 1989

Dear Mrs. Muse:

Your letter of September 13, 1989, and the accompanying letter from your husband are poignant reminders of the sacrifice your family has made for democracy in Panama.

We are doing everything we can to bring about an end to this crisis and the release of your husband. I know this is a very difficult time for all of you.

Your husband is a brave man; his courage and conviction have my respect and admiration. I also recognize the burden you and the rest of your family bear. You, too, have earned my respect and gratitude.

Once this crisis is over and your husband is free, I hope you, and he, and Kimberly will visit the White House so that I can thank you all in person.

God bless all of you.

Sincerely,
George Bush

Annie read the letter over and over, to herself and to her children. Respect. Admiration. Gratitude. These things did matter. They mattered to her, to her children, and to the president of the United States. Kurt *was* a brave man, and it was important that he be recognized as such. But more than that, Annie saw in the letter a subliminal message that she should take heart, have faith that her suffering and that of her family would not go on forever.

"Once this crisis is over and your husband is free . . ."

Not "if" this crisis ends, but "once this crisis is over." That was a sign, wasn't it? The president of the United States of America isn't glib or careless in his wording of correspondence. No, he's precise in all such things, and for her, the message was clear. Kurt's ordeal would end. Soon.

Visits with Kurt Muse had become Jim Ruffer's primary responsibility. Before each meeting, he would convene in the Tunnel with Colonel Green—a Delta operator whose name was clearly not Green, and who, for all Ruffer knew, may not even have been a colonel. The man never even wore a uniform. They'd meet for at least ninety minutes before each meeting at Modelo, and then again for at least four hours after the visit was completed. They had Jim drawing pictures and locating equipment with a level of precision that was far and away more demanding than counting steps from here to there and the other things they had him looking for after the elections.

Last week, they'd been so intent on knowing specifically what kind of lock Kurt's cell had that he'd raced ahead of the escorting guard just to get a look. It was a stupid thing to do, he realized, not just because it could have gotten him shot but also because it potentially showed their hand, but how the hell else was he supposed to get that kind of information?

In the eight months that Ruffer had been making these treks to Modelo, he'd come to develop a level of respect for Kurt Muse that frankly inspired him. Here was a man who had lost everything, yet despite the occasional ups and downs, the occasional paranoia and fear, he kept an outlook on life that was first and foremost optimistic. Surrounded by misery and subjected to unspeakable hardship and degradation, Kurt had somehow kept an air of humor about him that Ruffer didn't know that he could maintain in a similar circumstance.

There was a pervasive innocence about Kurt's worldview—a profound disbelief that the kind of cruelty he witnessed could actually exist in the world—that Jim Ruffer found instructive and refreshing in his own life.

He'd come to look forward to his visits with Kurt, come to see them as visits with an old friend. He prayed that whatever lofty plans the Delta dogs had in store would somehow liberate this fine man from his cell; but after countless trips to this fortress, he honestly didn't see how it was possible.

42

Dear Anne, Kimberly and Erik

Thank you so much for your wonderful cards to me. You are so thoughtful. I feel now that it should have been me that wrote to you. After all, I have visited with Kurt so frequently and truly have some marvelous impressions of him that could have been shared with you over the months. Because he is so special, I believe that I have received much more than I have given: To be with Kurt is to receive! He too is very thoughtful and once he stopped me at the end of a visit and apologized so solemnly for not having thanked me at an earlier visit for having brought him something. Under the circumstances, I didn't even think of being thanked. Kurt is very thoughtful of those around him. I have come to love the man and our visits are a big part of my life. But I have never mentioned it to him. A lot about our relationship goes unsaid. It is kind of ex-traordinary. When I am with Kurt, Marcos and usually a prison guard or medic are always there. Kurt and I act somewhat formal. I have tried to preserve the formality so that the whole event has a down-to-business officialism about it. My hope, each visit, is to be with him, cheer him and remind him of the real world that we both know—the physical exam just being a medium for the con-tact that I felt I must protect.

Kurt is a wonderful fellow. He has a beautiful sense of humor that is at no one's expense. He seems happy to me though I know that to some extent he tries extra hard to seem well to please us. He also can be very honest and open about his feelings. This is good too and keeps him emotionally healthy.

Marcos Ostrander has a great respect for Kurt and an extreme sense of devotion to his welfare. Kurt couldn't have had a better man than Marcos. I've never been there when the two of them talk. I try to engage Dominguez and the others in conversation to lengthen the time of their visitation. Once I put Dominguez to sleep right in his chair while I rambled on and on about English history and poisonous spiders. Another time I talked so well that Marcos and Kurt must have gotten tired of waiting and came back in to break it up. By the way, when I get back to my office I write up the entire visit in as much detail as I can remember. I'll turn these over to Kurt when we finally all go home together— soon I hope.

Well, I had better end this letter here. But I have enjoyed writing these things to you immensely. Kurt speaks so highly of you, Anne. He is certainly your greatest admirer. He is very, very proud of you. And, I might say, that you can all be very proud of him. He is a true and brave man. I have the greatest respect and admiration for him. And because all aspects of life can be a blessing for us, you will get him back better than ever because he has chosen to make it that way.

God bless you all. I send you the heartfelt love and respect from the Ruffers.

Sincerely,
Jim Ruffer

43

Kurt knew this would be the day he would die.

It was late in the morning, one day in November when something had clearly gone terribly wrong. The corridors of Modelo Prison reverberated with the sound of booted feet, not running, exactly, but moving quickly, the staccato beat of foot falls punctuated by shouted orders and the distinctive *clack* of weapons being charged and the unmistakable rattle of belted ammunition.

The first bullet fired will be aimed at the head of Kurt Muse . . .

Kurt jumped to his feet and put on his shoes; this was part of a ritual he'd practiced more than a few times, whenever he sensed that the goons were coming to harass him or toss his cell. In this environment, shoes were essential. Without them, he felt one tick too vulnerable, one inch too far from the possibility of making a break if the occasion arose. Watching those poor souls in the prison yard, roaming in rags that left them nearly naked, he realized that clothes were an issue of dignity as well as practicality. Thus, another of his rules was to never be naked in the presence of the guards. The fact of his tiny bathroom, located at a right angle to the rest of his cell, made a certain degree of modesty possible, and Kurt capitalized on it by taking his showers only at night. He kept his clothes as clean as possible by washing them regularly in the shower, and he hung them to dry by pressing bunches of the garments through the expanded metal grates that served as bars on his windows to the prison yard.

In recent weeks, since the aborted coup, they'd been rotating him between this cell on the third floor and a nearly identical one on the fourth. He didn't understand the logic, and never bothered to ask, but he figured it had something to do with either messing with his head, or with confounding any rescue attempt that might be mounted by the U.S. government. The reality probably lay somewhere in the middle of those options, though to Kurt the notion of an organized rescue was absurd at both the political level and the practical one. This was a fortress, for God's sake. No one could possibly lead a breakout without killing huge numbers of people.

For Kurt, that meant that he had to make his own escape opportunities. In his wildest daydreams, he fantasized about grabbing one of the guards' M-16s and shooting his way out of the building, but as intriguing as that was, the fantasy always ended with the inevitability of Kurt's bullet-riddled body dropping like a sack about three feet beyond the first door.

More recently, just before the coup and Lieutenant Dominguez's removal from duty, he had devised a plan that he thought might actually have worked: a good old-fashioned bribe. Dominguez frequently complained about how woefully small his pension would be following his retirement in a few years. Kurt figured that $20,000 in cash would be enough to convince Dominguez to look the other way one night while Kurt walked out the front door to a waiting car. There might have to be some pretense to make the plan workable, but Kurt was certain that Marcos Ostrander would be more than capable of stitching something like that together. It was a high-risk plan, no doubt, but if the alternative was a lifetime of confinement in a concrete cage, then a little risk would be just fine with him.

He'd been on the edge of suggesting the plan to Ostrander when the coup went down and Dominguez went away. It would take months to cultivate with these regular army types the kind of friendly relationship he'd developed with Dominguez. Lesson learned: think less, act faster.

On this morning, as the prison teemed with heavily armed soldiers, Kurt sensed that something unique and terrifying was in progress. Clearly, they were expecting the impossible, some kind of storming of the prison. Kurt felt his heart beginning to race. If that was the plan, then someone was botching the hell out of the element of surprise.

He watched in stunned horror as a PDF soldier set up a 5.56mm

SAW—Squad Automatic Weapon—mounted on a bipod. The weapon required the gunner to sit on the floor and was fed by a side-mounted box of linked ammunition. The gunner set up his weapon directly in front of Kurt's cell, a spot from which he could protect the entire hallway with a fusillade of withering fire. Or, by simply pivoting the weapon, he could shred Kurt Muse with a single short burst.

Kurt didn't know how, and he didn't understand why, but in an instant he convinced himself that these were his final moments on the planet. He started to sweat profusely as his heart rate tripled. In moments, his T-shirt was soaked with flop sweat. He was *shaking* for God's sake, uncontrollable quivers in his hands and legs, his whole body quaking in a way he had never experienced. So, this was what abject terror felt like. This was what panic was all about.

The crash dive in his emotions happened with frightening speed, overcoming him in seconds, and even as he told himself that he had to calm down, his body refused to cooperate.

It didn't help at all that the soldier in the corridor was so thoroughly enjoying his terror. The soldier watched Kurt's meltdown with a smug smile, ostentatiously fingering the cartridges in the box. "These are for you, no?" the man said in fractured English.

Those are for me, yes, Kurt thought.

His mind reacted to the panic by instantly jumping to places he didn't want to go. He thought yet again of the anxiety and the hardship he'd brought down on his family. He thought of his children and of Annie, his wonderful, beautiful Annie, and of the terrible grief and anger she would feel when he was gone. He thought of the apology he would never have the chance to utter to his father and mother.

He thought with crushing bitterness of the fact that the Pineapple had won. He would have the body of an "American spy" to drag in front of the cameras as a warning to any others who tried to rise against him.

Then he thought of the Kingdom of Heaven, of the reward that he prayed awaited him on the other side of this life. They say there are no atheists in foxholes, and Kurt figured there had to be an impending execution corollary. His faith had never come close to the relationship that Annie enjoyed with her Creator, but in that moment it occurred to Kurt with perfect clarity that death was not an event to be feared. Rather, it was the necessary next step in life, and as such it should be embraced as the natural order of things. God would not have put him here in this spot if this were not the spot where he belonged.

The realization brought a sense of peace and relief almost instantly. In the clarity of that moment, he felt angry with himself for having given the guard in the hallway such a show. For Noriega and his henchmen, people responsible for so many murders over the years, the sense of victory would not come so much from the fact of his death, but from the stories of his panic and emotional meltdown. The very thought of being the subject of that conversation pissed Kurt off.

Okay, he thought, that show is over. Right by-God now. If they have to shoot me, let the bullets fly. Just please, God, give me the strength to stand tall when it starts.

Before those shots were fired, however, he had one last detail to take care of. He lifted his Bible from where he'd left it next to his cot and retreated into his bathroom. There he jotted his good-bye to his family on the onion skin paper. Just a quick note, "Annie, Erik, Kimberly, I love you so much. I will miss you terribly. Love, Dad."

That done, he tore the page out of the Bible, folded it into the tiniest possible ball, and stuffed it deeply into the seam of his pants pocket. When the Americans took custody of his body, they would search his clothing carefully, and he hoped they would find the note and deliver it.

That done, he returned to his cot and lay down. Kurt watched the guard watching him for a while, and then he fell asleep.

When he awoke, the crisis had apparently passed, and the guard was gone.

44

Dear Kurt,

There are so many things that happen that I wish I could remember to tell you.

Like: The many nights I sit up with Kimberly talking about how wonderful you are. She wants to marry someone just like you. Then we spend some time talking about your qualities. We've decided that you have no bad points. Tonight she said what's that saying about being away from each other and love. I said, absence makes the heart grow fonder. "Yes it does."

We spend hours talking about our hopes, our doubts. We support one another.

Another beautiful thing is that K & E are getting along so beautifully. K talks to E, compliments his clothes, his sense of humor. She's so thankful that he's not obnoxious, in love with himself or insensitive. Erik is such a gentle soul. Last Fri. K & E played electronic Battleship. They also spent 2 hours talking to one another & looking at old pictures. There's a growing bond between them.

We spend so much of our time talking about you. We've started the Advent wreath. We say our prayer before dinner, eat and then light a candle and read the reading for the day.

*I've always wanted to spend some of our time in prayer and we
are.*

I adore you,
Annie

Annie sat quietly at the dining room table—her command center in
Burke, Virginia—as Father Frank sipped his coffee and ticked off one
element of bad news after another. Intellectually, she understood how
grateful she should be for Father Frank's unflinching candor in his
presentation of the facts and in his faithful relaying of information
from, to, for, and about Kurt, but on an emotional level, a part of her
craved some sliver of happy news, even if it was a lie.

She knew now, through Marcos Ostrander, of the machine gun in
the corridor and of Kurt's epiphanal acceptance of his impending
death, just as she knew that the encouragement and sense of hope that
had been triggered by President Bush's letter was short lived, replaced
by endless weeks of more of the same. Now that the holidays were approaching, it was hard to fight off the crushing sense of sadness, the
thought that one day she might have to face the reality of a future
without Kurt. The thought was too much to bear, and she forced it out
of her mind. Again.

When Father Frank was done with this latest update, the two of
them sat in silence, sipping their coffee. This was Annie's opportunity
to say something; to make a speech, to vent her frustration, or to ask
a series of questions, all of which she had done uncountable times in
the past. Today, though, she felt as though she had nothing left.

"I'm sorry that the news isn't better," Father Frank said.

Annie shrugged, hoping it was a gesture of bravery, not resignation.
"The news is what it is."

Father Frank shifted in his chair and cleared his throat, seeming
suddenly uncomfortable. "There is one thing we haven't yet tried," he
said. "We at the Agency think that the approach of Christmas gives us
a unique opportunity for a personal appeal."

Annie scowled. "What kind of personal appeal?"

"One directly from you to General Noriega."

"Absolutely not."

Father Frank raised his palm in rhetorical defense. "Don't be so fast. Think this through, and keep your eye on the ultimate goal here, which is to get Kurt out of prison. Politically, things haven't been going so well for Noriega. The whole world is beginning to see him as a bully, and even he knows how difficult it is to counter that kind of press while you're still trying to run a dictatorship. If you made a personal appeal for Kurt's release, it would give him the opportunity to do something genuinely good during the Christmas season. It's great PR for him, and you get your husband back. It could be a win for everyone."

Annie was stunned. "What does Marcos think about this?"

"He agrees that it could work."

"Does he agree with it as a plan?"

"He agrees that it could work." She recognized spook-speak for, "You'll have to ask him yourself." If there was anyone on the planet who hated the Pineapple more than she, it was Marcos Ostrander; for him to even obliquely oblige a public relations coup for Noriega must mean that the options were dwindling to nothing. "How would it work?" Annie asked. "What would I do?"

Father Frank explained the strategy in a way that made it sound like nothing at all. "You'd write a letter to Noriega. You'd describe your life as a single mother, and how important Kurt is in not only your life but in the lives of Kimberly and Erik. You'd say that you know that he is a father as well, and that surely he must understand the difficulty of this kind of separation during the holidays, and you'd appeal for his mercy."

Annie stared, her mouth dry. "He would make that letter public."

Father Frank nodded. "Undoubtedly."

The very thought of groveling at the feet of the Pineapple made her stomach churn. But wasn't that a better alternative to letting Kurt continue to rot in prison? Didn't she owe him and her children—heck, didn't she owe *herself*—at least that much of an opportunity?

"And you think it will work."

"We all think so. Fact is, Noriega desperately needs some good press right now, and we think this is a unique opportunity."

Annie still couldn't quite wrap her arms around the concept. "What does Kurt think about the idea?"

"No one has mentioned it to him yet. Marcos wanted to get your reaction before mentioning it to him." They'd already established that

Marcos's plans to attend this particular meeting had been superseded by conflicting events.

She called Marcos on the telephone. "What do *you* think?"

Marcos took a moment to answer, clearing his throat first. "He's not my husband, and I'm not in jail. I don't get a vote."

Images flooded Annie's mind of a reunion with Kurt. She saw him walking through the door, saw him at the Christmas tree, watching the kids open presents. She felt his warmth pressed against her, smelled his aftershave, heard his laugh. It was everything she'd dreamed of, everything she'd been fighting for all these months. And she could make it all happen by writing one letter?

So what if she had to grovel? So what if she gave the Pineapple the bragging rights that he'd prevailed in the battle? Kurt's battle.

Sure, they were all in it together, but it was Kurt who led the team to cobble the Voice of Liberty out of the ether, and it was he alone who was paying the price. He needed a say in what the price of freedom would be.

"I'll do it," Annie said, "but only if Kurt says it's all right."

"No." Kurt's answer came quickly and emphatically. And, frankly, a little too loudly.

Marcos shot a quick look over his shoulder, but saw that Jim Ruffer still had the guard distracted by some mind-numbing discussion of anatomy or politics. He leaned in closer. "Keep your voice down," he admonished, "and think for a second before you reject it out of hand. This has a real chance of working."

"I don't care," Kurt hissed. "I am not sucking up to that asshole just to get out of here. I'll stay here for fifty more years before I give him that kind of satisfaction."

Marcos squirmed a little in his seat. "Well, technically, you wouldn't be the one sucking up."

Kurt shook his head. "I'm the one in prison, I'm the one who would be released."

"Annie won't write anything without your permission."

"Okay, then. She doesn't have it."

Marcos sighed, trying to find another angle. "I just wish—"

"We're not discussing this anymore, Marcos."

Ostrander stared at Kurt for a long moment, and Kurt stared right back. All the arguments were on the table, and all of them had been killed as quickly as they'd been posed. With nothing more to be said, it was time for this meeting to end. Marcos rose from his seat, and Kurt stood with him. As they shook hands, a tiny smile blossomed on Marcos's face and he winked.

He could see that the expression confused Kurt, but that was all right. Marcos knew what Kurt never could: that the Muse family had just taken a test and they'd passed with flying colors.

An hour from now, Marcos would sit with Colonel Green in the Tunnel and report the results verbatim. Clearly, Kurt Muse had the emotional stability and the willful commitment to carry out his end of what was coming his way.

45

Kurt,

The children haven't had school for the 2nd day now—Snow!

I'm sitting at the kitchen table (the glass and sawhorse one) with a cup of coffee peering through the windows. The pine trees are weighted down with snow. The bare trees have snow balancing on their spindly branches—a red cardinal is playing with the clumps of snow that lose their balance and plunge to the ground.

Erik is outside (10:00 a.m.) arranging a football game—he loves it. He wears sneakers (with traction as he says) and can beat the others receiving the pass because the others are in boots.

He is also cleaning my car and shoveling the walkway—he has done that for me every time I have asked. You'd be very proud of him. He is growing up.

I'm really working hard to keep our spirits up for Christmas— the Pollyanna factory is doing double-time. I'm thinking of you constantly, wondering what it must be like—praying for your peace of mind and strength for all of us.

I'm going to try for more pictures today. I'm looking around town for the best pair of red boots. I think it's about time. It seems to me we're snowed under, maybe the boots will help.

I adore you,
Annie

Annie sat with the children in the living room of their little rented townhouse, the three of them admiring the job they'd done preparing the place for Christmas. They all played their parts well, manufacturing the joys of the season as they hung brand new decorations on the tree and hung stockings they'd never seen before from a mantle that wasn't theirs. The tape deck played carols from a Christmas collection that Annie had picked up from the store, while cookies baked in the oven.

Peace on Earth, good will toward men.

The whole scene was like something from a play or movie, touching on the outside, but with roles played by actors who didn't fully believe in their character's motivation. At a time of year defined by traditions and rituals, the Muse family was entirely divorced from all of that. There were no friends to invite over, no precious ornaments from days gone by, no links to anything that was precious or even normal. Annie imagined that this must be how people feel when they are burned out of their home or when tragedy strikes. As a parent, you go through the motions, because you want to shield the children from the seemingly hopeless reality. As a child, you pretend not to notice the charade because you don't want to upset your mom.

This should have been a special Christmas, when you thought about it. It was the first time the children had ever seen snow; it was the first time to witness the distinctly American traditions involved in selecting the Christmas tree from the lot, and tying it on the roof of the car, all the while dancing to keep warm. They were moments that Kurt would have enjoyed. Those tree-related chores were a father's job, after all, and the fact that Annie was doing them alone with the kids somehow emphasized even more the fact that their family was no longer whole.

It was a terrible way to think, but at one level, a death of a loved one is better than this hellish kind of perpetual limbo. At least death is final; it allows you to grieve and move on. The Muse family was trapped in the netherworld of waiting and worrying, unsure if the time would ever come either to grieve or celebrate.

With the decorations done, the three of them sat on the sofa, basking in the beauty of their handiwork. Even under these circumstances, there was no denying the charm and beauty that holiday decorations brought to a home. Charade or no charade, they'd done a pretty good job of it.

Kimberly was the first to say it: "I wish Daddy were here. He'd like this."

Annie nodded, not trusting her voice.

"It could happen," Erik said. "Christmas miracles happen all the time." He turned to Annie. "Don't they, Mom?"

Something about the question took Annie by surprise, the purity of twelve-year-old innocence. She felt her throat thicken as her vision blurred. She spread her arms like giant wings and pulled her children close to her. "How many stockings do you see on that mantle?" she asked.

"Four."

"Well, there's your answer," she said. "Christmas miracles happen all the time."

46

Dear Kurt:

The temperatures have dropped here. The wind is rising, the sky is clear and there is snow in the mountains. Our Christmas tree is up and we've had guests for a drink and a bite. We're trying to make it seem like Christmas, but, at best, it's a wooden legged one. We can move about but there is no run or jump in it. You and your family were the leg we are just simulating. We hope we can soon find a way to graft it back so we can be a complete family again.

Love,
Dad

December 18, 1989

Dear Kurt:

Seems that my last letters to you may have gone astray which makes finding where to begin difficult. So I'll dispense with all the bullshit and get down to what I've wanted to say all along but wouldn't.

Whatever were our differences have long since been blocked from my memory by feelings for your suffering and by my pride *in your having been able to bear it so long. You can't "tapar el sol con la mano" nor can a stupid argument between two bull-headed idiots erase from a man's life the good times we had together in Panama for so many years.*

My Christmas wish is that you and I can become the loving and caring team we once were and that Panama will become again the beautiful place to live and raise a family as it was when I chose to live there 35 years ago. You had no choice in that decision. You were just a "novato en mi Escuelita," but you grew to love the country as I did.

I trust that God will see what is truly good for you and me and that He will lend His blessing to our achieving it, just as I have faith that He will know what is truly good for Panama and will bless any effort by either side capable of restoring our adopted country to its proper and respected place in the community of nations.

I told a friend to remind you that I make the world's best martinis and that I will brew two of the finest when we next meet. Your mother, of course, will protest that two are enough, but I will say to her, as Rhett Butler to Scarlet, "frankly my dear, I don't give a damn," and we will laugh and it will seem like old times.

Love,
Dad

Dear Daddy
I really love you. Merry Christmas. Ho . . . Ho . . . Ho . . . I wish you were here for Christmas to celebrate with us. We think we're going to have a white Christmas. I hope so. Our tree is splendid. I hope you like the shirt we're sending you. Today we went to the mall. Mom got me a few things. But I couldn't see them.
Miss you.
XXX
OXX
OO
Merry Christmas

Love
Erik Muse

December 18, 1989

Hello my Dearest Daddy,

Christmas is only a few days away and you're not here, but guess what I'm holding up very well and I hope you are too. Daddy I think you'd be proud of us, we are all supporting each other and in return we haven't only gotten closer but we're like friends. Especially between mommy and I. We have chats almost every day.

I've decided not to send you a present physically just yet because you know that if I could I'd give you the world and get you out of there. But I am trying to send a mental present, that is for God to walk where you walk and keep you going the way you have been.

Daddy, I hope our letters and prayers are enough because I don't know what else to do. I'm trying to do everything just right so you'd be proud and I'm always thinking of you.

You know Dad, I think that things will be getting better soon. I have a feeling that they just might. Daddy it's dumb to say have a merry Christmas under the circumstances, but when you come back to us that moment will make you forget the hard times. Daddy, I do want you to have a very spiritually filled Christmas though. Think a lot about God, talk to him, and think of all our good times past and the ones ahead of us. Daddy I'm warning you now when I see you I'm going to squish you tightly and never let go. I love you even more than before, which was a ton I garantee it, and I think you are the best and greatest, most caring, loving, generous and of course the funniest Daddy a girl could have. I do thank God for you!

Bless you my Daddy,
Kimberly

P.S. Our Christmas tree is perfect.

47

On December 15, 1989, the Panamanian Assembly named Manuel Noriega "Maximum Leader" and declared that a state of war existed between Panama and the United States of America.

The next day, Marine Corps Lieutenant Robert Paz was shot to death by PDF soldiers at a road block in the streets of Chorrillo; this on the heels of another traffic stop in which a U.S. Navy lieutenant and his wife were savagely beaten after similarly being stopped at a PDF road block.

In Washington, D.C., President Bush had had enough. If Noriega wanted war, he would get it.

48

The rhythms of Modelo Prison had changed dramatically since the news of Lieutenant Paz's murder had broken. Gone was the quiet routine of prisoners and guards going about their chores as part of a daily routine. Now, every order had an edge to it, every comment bore an unstated threat of violence. To Kurt, it felt reminiscent of the days that immediately followed the October coup attempt, but perhaps without a touch of the urgency.

People here seemed to be anticipating something, and the more nervous they got, the more he found himself watching the corporal out in the hallway with his M-16. Despite the guard's willingness to follow any orders he received, Kurt wondered if he'd actually be able to pull the trigger to kill in cold blood. Had it been Cáceres himself, there would be no doubt, but to date, the corporal had shown no overt animosity for Kurt.

Three days ago, Kurt had decided to be bold and ask the question. "Corporal," he called, attracting the guard's attention. "Would you really shoot me?"

The corporal's expression never changed from its constant, practiced indifference. "Sí señor." Then he turned and walked away.

It was almost amusing now. Ever since the morning of his encounter with the machine gunner, Kurt had become almost philosophical about his impending death. He mourned all that he would never see—his kids' graduations, their weddings and his grandchildren; and most of all the warmth and comfort of Annie as an old lady pressed against him as an old man—but that loss was just a small price compared to what the world would see because of him. Namely, future grandchildren in the likeness of his perfect children. Annie would miss him, but she would survive, knowing full well that he was in Heaven waiting for her, a special seat reserved in Paradise.

What he found himself wishing for more than anything was the courage to accept with dignity and resolve whatever fate awaited him.

The war games had had their impact. Across the street, activity had been increasing exponentially in the Comandancia, as well. Most recently, they'd installed what appeared to be an antique World War II–era antiaircraft gun emplacement, similar to the quad-fifties he'd seen in so many vintage war movies, but with that distinctly Russian touch that transformed a sleek piece of lethal hardware into something that looked like the mechanical equivalent of a gangly teenager. The wheels seemed too big, and the gun barrels too long. But that probably meant very little to the poor flyboy who found himself in the crosshairs of such a weapon.

On the morning of December 19, 1989, Kurt was thinking about these things while lying on his cot, half-in and half-out of an early morning doze. Since the tensions began to rise, he'd found sleep to be an elusive commodity, and as such, he found himself to be groggy and listless more hours of the day. At one point, he'd revisited the notion that maybe they were trying to poison him, but then rejected the notion as paranoia. He wasn't exactly a difficult target, after all, and they had a damn guard posted mere feet away to blast him into the next dimension if the whim had struck them.

He was thinking of all these things when he became vaguely aware of a new breed of commotion surrounding him. He must truly have been asleep, because he was having genuine difficulty putting the sound cues together in his head. There were the shouts and the quick staccato of running feet, and beneath it all what sounded like the steady thrum of helicopter rotors beating at the midmorning air.

It was the thought of the chopper that snapped Kurt to wakefulness. What the hell was a chopper doing in so close to the prison? Rolling off his cot, he hurried to the window for a look.

Sure enough, a Cobra gunship hovered in the air at an altitude of maybe a hundred feet, just hanging there over the prison wall. On the ground below, prisoners and guards alike scurried for cover, even as the guards in the towers made threatening movements with their rifles without making the fatal mistake of actually pointing them in the direction of the menacing bird.

It was an odd sight, and it was one that brought a sense of pride to Kurt's soul. Those young men at the controls—he could make out the features of their faces from here—were his countrymen, and no matter how the Pineapple blustered and blew, nothing the Maximum Leader did or said could begin to touch the firepower of the U.S. Army.

While Kurt watched, the Cobra's gunner—sitting in the chopper's front seat—made eye contact and pointed. Instantly, the aircraft started drifting closer. A punishing dust storm bloomed in the rotor wash as all manner of trash and prison yard debris was hurled in all directions. As the Cobra moved closer and closer, it continually lost altitude until the nose of the chopper was level with Kurt's third-floor window. For a moment, he thought the pilot might land the Cobra right there in the yard.

But they weren't interested in landing; it seemed that they were interested only in looking at Kurt through his window. As ridiculous as that sounded, it was the only theory that made sense. The chopper crew knew that their presence at the wall would raise a ruckus, and they certainly knew that it would draw every face to every window in the prison. It couldn't be a coincidence that this airborne ballet only began when Kurt's face joined the others.

The Cobra was so close now that Kurt feared that the rotor disk would start digging a trench in the concrete wall. So close that he could count the front-seater's teeth. In addition, Kurt could swear he saw a thumbs-up. They held there for a couple of seconds, staring each other in the eye, and when a huge grin bloomed on the crewman's face, Kurt couldn't help but return it.

They had just come by to say hello, and there'd no doubt be hell to pay when word of what they did got back to their commanding officer. For the first time in God knew how long, Kurt felt emotion pressing behind his eyes. This time, though, it wasn't sadness or self-pity; this time it was that intense pride and emotional lift that comes from witnessing a simple act of kindness. Clearly, Ostrander and Ruffer had passed along Kurt's love of helicopters to the people who had the

264 • Kurt Muse and John Gilstrap

power to alter the flight routes of the choppers at Quarry Heights, and clearly that word had gotten back to these two yahoos in the Cobra. He'd never met them, and probably never would, but he loved those two pilots right at that moment as intensely as he'd ever loved anyone but Annie and the kids.

As the Cobra pivoted and pulled away with a full-throttle roar, Kurt knew how foolish he'd been to think that he might have been forgotten by his government. He found himself grinning like a kid on Christmas as he watched the departing chopper grow smaller with distance and finally disappear from view. He was still smiling when he turned back into his cell.

The smile disappeared in the space of a heartbeat when he saw that the corporal had brought his M-16 to his shoulder and that the muzzle was leveled at Kurt's chest.

For what felt like a long time—maybe as long as five or ten seconds— the jailer and his prisoner just stared at each other. For the first time, Kurt saw the anger in the other man's eyes. He was a soldier, after all, relative competence notwithstanding, and he'd just been humiliated with a demonstration of the PDF's emasculation. At most, they could pretend to be a military force. At most, they could intimidate the weak, but even then, it was only the weak who had no powerful friends.

What better way to jam a thumb into Uncle Sam's eye than to shoot the man who had brought about so much of the current troubles?

But he didn't shoot, and as reasonableness displaced the anger, the corporal became a professional soldier again. He lowered his gun and settled himself back into his seat, where he would await his orders.

In prison, the smallest excitement—the slightest departure from endless routine—kept the blood pumping for a long time, and the visit by the helicopter gunship kept the place alive for hours, but sooner or later, the excitement passed, and normalcy returned. For Kurt, this meant that it was time for him to exercise. After that, he would pray and maybe work on another letter to Annie. The helicopter would give him something to go on about, even though mentioning the morning's events would guarantee that the letter never cleared the censors.

His knee was bothering him more and more as he ran his short course, and unlike times in the past, reversing direction did nothing to relieve the discomfort. Both knees were hurting now. Add to that the fact that his arms were growing too short for his rapidly progressing myopia, and there was no choice but to finally conclude that he was getting too damn old for this shit.

Cáceres came for him around eleven in the morning, when Kurt was lying on his cot, thinking about anything except his current situation. "Muse!" the lieutenant barked in Spanish. "Get up. You have visitors."

Kurt was on his feet in an instant. He needed this. This was a good day for visitors. "Who is it?"

The corporal fumbled with the lock, slipping it from the hasp. "Come," Cáceres commanded.

The corporal fell in behind with his M-16 at the ready as the lieutenant led the three-man parade down to the main level, where an American Army lieutenant colonel sat ramrod straight in a wooden chair. The lieutenant colonel looked vaguely familiar, but Kurt couldn't place the face. The army officer stood as Kurt entered the tiny interview room and offered his hand.

"Hello, Mr. Muse, I'm Robert Perry, the Treaty Affairs officer here in Panama. How are you, sir?"

Kurt shook the hand gratefully. Of course. It had been nine months, but this was the first American Kurt had encountered after his arrest—the man who brought Jim Ruffer to DENI headquarters. They were meeting in a room Kurt hadn't seen in months, and they were surrounded by a throng of prison guards. If he hadn't known better, Kurt would have bet there was a craps game being tossed in the middle of the crowd somewhere.

"You look confused, Mr. Muse," Perry said, gesturing to the unoccupied seat with an open palm. "Please have a seat and I'll try to explain."

Kurt sat, but he didn't like the feel of any of this. Certainly, there would be no relaxing.

"In my official capacity, I have certain rights and obligations, and as an American citizen, you likewise have certain rights and obligations. I've asked the prison staff to gather so I could review some things." He gave a nervous little smile when he was done with this preamble, as if to give Kurt a chance to acknowledge the words or ask for an explanation.

Kurt nodded. So far, he hadn't heard anything that was too difficult to understand. He did get the impression, though, that Perry had rehearsed his words.

The lieutenant colonel continued, "You're aware, are you not, that General Noriega has threatened to kill you if things don't go his way in the ongoing discussions between our governments."

Kurt cast a sidewards glance toward the corporal and his rifle. "I've heard the rumor, yes." In the background, he became aware of another break in routine as commotion within the prison walls seemed to peak in intensity. The guards were aware of it, too. They started shifting their weight uneasily as the sound of approaching helicopters again cut the calm of the warm afternoon. Only this time, there was more than one chopper, and they seemed to be circling the prison. Everyone, in fact, seemed unnerved by it all. Only Perry seemed nonplussed.

Perry raised his voice to keep ownership of the moment. As he spoke, his eyes never left their lock on Kurt's even though his message was clearly meant for the others in the room. A big Puerto Rican U.S. Army sergeant in the corner—Perry's driver, Kurt figured—had grown pale and was visibly trembling, sweat pouring off of him.

Perry looked as crisp and as cool as if he were in an air conditioned room. "Kurt," he said, "you have undoubtedly heard that General Noriega has announced that any armed conflict between our two great countries will result in reprisals against American citizens, and that you will be the first to die."

Kurt swallowed hard, wondering where this was going. "Yes, sir."

"Well, I want you to know that if anything happens to you no one will walk out of this prison alive."

The stenographer froze. Somebody gasped.

"Do you understand what I'm telling you, Kurt?"

An official of the U.S. government had just threatened to execute his would-be murderers. What does one say to such a thing? Vaguely aware that his mouth was agape, Kurt nodded.

Perry smiled and stood, again extending his hand. Kurt returned the gesture, and as the visitor left, there was a dizzying sense of finality to all of this. His stomach churned, not with a sense of dread, but with a sense of hope and empowerment.

Cáceres moved quickly to roust Kurt back up the stairs to his cell, ordering the guards to return him there at once. The guards in turn barked the appropriate orders, and Kurt complied, but this time, there was none of the regular taunting or pushing. Maybe it was just the lingering euphoria of Perry's little speech, but Kurt could have sworn that they now seemed a little nervous in his presence.

As he climbed the concrete steps, he thought about how he was going to word all of this in his letter to Annie.

PART 3

Acid Gambit

49

It was nearly midnight—twenty minutes till tomorrow—and Staff Sergeant Jim Nelson and his crew were finally airborne, ready to execute the mission they'd been planning since May and practicing since July. This guy Muse—Parker Sturbridge called him Moose because of his size and because it was Parker's job to carry him if he couldn't or wouldn't walk—was one hell of a guy. Jim and the rest of the Delta operators knew all about their precious cargo's refusal to accept an easy out through that letter from his wife, and anyone with balls that size deserved to be snatched back into the world.

Jim's job was to be in on the explosive entry, unless that didn't work for some reason, in which case his job was to rappel down the side of the prison and cut through the bars with a cutting torch. That explained the big bomb on his back. Nothing like having a few dozen pounds of oxygen and acetylene strapped to your spine when you're planning to fly into a wall of tracer fire. Jim was sitting in the forward-most spot on the portside outboard bench of the MH-6 Little Bird chopper, facing the direction of flight because the oxygen and acetylene tanks wouldn't let him face out to the side like the other five members of his team. He kept his ankles crossed between the bottom of the bench and the top of the landing skid, keenly aware that a flimsy nylon strap was all that kept him from tumbling into the night. Yee-flippin'-ha.

They'd been waiting for weeks in Hangar Three at Howard Air

Force Base for the balloon to go up at midnight. For the time being, they were slicing through the darkness, awaiting the arrival of H hour at midnight, when the peaceful night would be torn open like nothing the Panamanian people had ever seen. The targets were selected and clear, and the rules of engagement were even clearer. Operation Just Cause, which had been the nation's greatest secret for weeks and was soon to be known as anything but, was a war against Noriega and the PDF. It was a war of liberation, not of conquest, and America's elite special forces teams had been entrusted with the two highest-priority objectives. Delta was tasked with these priorities: Objective One, the capture of Manuel Noriega, and Objective One Prime, the liberation of Kurt Frederick Muse.

The stakes could not have been higher. Delta's previous high-profile mission at Desert One in Iran had been such a royal disaster that anything less than unbridled success here in Panama would be vilified as a failure. A lot of good men had died that night, and a lot of careers had been needlessly ruined because of politicians' (and command officers') unspeakable ineptitude. Not that they caught the blame, of course—unless you count Jimmy Carter, who arguably lost the White House because of it. Rear-echelon types with their paneled offices and stars on their collars reserved only credit for themselves. When it came time for blame, there were plenty of company officers and noncoms to pad the list.

They had discussed these things among themselves from time to time as D day and H hour approached, but none of these things were of any concern to Jim Nelson tonight. Starting in the next fifteen or twenty minutes, and carrying on through the night, and perhaps into the days to follow, all that would matter was the mission, and that was about all there was room for in his head right now.

This tiny piece of the overall operational plan for the invasion of Panama, this Objective One Prime, was listed on the chart as Operation Acid Gambit, named as most such covert ops are by two words randomly generated by a computer. Jim didn't begin to think that he knew all the details, but what he did know impressed the hell out of him. When the balloon finally went up on this op, dozens of the most lethal warriors on the planet would swoop into action, backed up by some of the most lethal machinery ever devised by man.

Jim's was one of four Little Birds from the 160th Special Operations Air Regiment with orders to set down on the roof of Modelo Prison, where twenty-three Delta operators would disembark to do their jobs. Meanwhile, somewhere out there in the night, two AC-130 Specter Gunships were circling in the darkness waiting for their signal to turn the Comandancia into pea gravel, while the whole operation was supported with God only knew how many helicopter gunships. Elsewhere in the country, madness was going to rain down from every direction once Just Cause got under way, but for the time being, all those other ops were simply someone else's business.

Orbiting in the night as they were, Jim turned all the details of Acid Gambit over in his mind. They'd rehearsed this thing dozens of times since the summer, even going so far as to construct an exact three-quarter-scale replica of the prison in the wilds of Hurlburt Field, Florida. The level of detail was both amazing and frustrating, drawn largely from interviews of former prisoners, most of whom had never seen the prison in its entirety, but only their little sections of it. The path from the roof to the cellblocks was the biggest question. They'd been able to get their hands on some architectural drawings, and they'd been gathering intel data since the week after Kurt had been arrested, but significant holes still remained in their knowledge base, and those holes had been filled with educated best guesses, which in Jim Nelson's mind was the same damn thing as a wild-ass guess.

But what the hell? With as much firepower as they were bringing along, even the most outrageously wrong guess could be turned right again. If doors turned out not to be where they'd thought, they could always make a new one on their own.

Early on, Acid Gambit had just been one more planning mission, so similar to the countless dozens of similar planning missions that Delta took on. The vast majority never came to fruition for any number of reasons: in some cases Uncle Sam lost his nerve, and in a few others, the bad guys just got lucky; but mostly, when 0300 missions got scrubbed it had something to do with unreliable intel. For a while, it had been looking as if the precious cargo for Acid Gambit was going to get whacked in his cell, rendering the whole plan moot. Jim Nelson had really come to respect the guy. He showed a lot of guts. Jim was happy as hell that his Aztec Cycle rotation allowed his team—G Team—to be on the op now that the trigger had been pulled.

They'd thought they were close twice before, first pretty early on, and then again immediately after the coup, but on both of those occasions, the hammer was released gently, and they were forced to stand down. Jim didn't know how he'd respond if that happened again tonight. He was ready to go, dammit.

Of course, all the planning, and all the rehearsal—they'd been mounting weekly midnight raids on the roof of the Department of Defense's elementary school (ironically, a school that Annie Muse had visited often before being evacuated to exile) ever since they'd arrived in-country all those weeks before—would mean nothing once the shooting started. Wild-ass guesses could quickly become death sentences when the operation went hot. It was the part of Jim Nelson's job that he found most enthralling and most frightening. You can plan and rehearse down to the smallest detail, but at the end of the day, every plan assumes a certain reaction on the part of the bad guys, and if that reaction doesn't materialize, then everything flowing downstream from it will be entirely different than any scenario they'd thought of. After two or three iterations, the plan might as well never have existed.

Of all the variables, the one that weighed heaviest on the rescue mission was the one solitary soldier outside Moose's cell. Apparently, some Treaty Affairs officer had made a pretty good speech that was supposed to build hesitation into the guard's trigger finger, but you never knew how seriously some people took their sense of duty. One way or another, Kurt Muse was going home tonight, but it would be a hell of a lot better for all if he could cross the threshold alive.

On the second Little Bird, Staff Sergeant Peter Jacobs had the assignment to rappel from the roof of Modelo Prison, dangle in midair outside Muse's cell window, and take out the executioner before he had a chance to react. It was the one segment of this op that Jim was happiest he hadn't drawn. There was something unsettling about the thought of dangling without cover as the entire world tried to kill you, and yet staying composed enough to hit your target with one shot. Of course, the others on the roof planned to rain enough lead down on any potential sharpshooter that the bad guys would be too busy burrowing through the concrete to take decent aim.

Once the hallway executioner was neutralized, the rest should be easy—a standard shoot and swoop. As of eleven o'clock this morning, they knew exactly which cell the precious cargo was in—verified by an airborne eyewitness—and thanks to information leaked by an Army lawyer-doctor team, they knew virtually every detail of the cellblock level where Muse was being held. They even knew what kind of lock was on the door to Muse's cell. All the prisoner had to do was stay alive long enough to be rescued, and they'd be able to bring a happy ending to his story.

All of it, the whole dance, would begin straight up at midnight when a Delta sniper team on Quarry Heights would open up from a quarter mile away with M-60 machine guns to take out the ZPU-4 antiaircraft battery Noriega had recently installed in the Comandancia compound. Simultaneously, the snipers would take out the main power supply and the backup generators, plus any other targets of opportunity they could find.

There was a certain irony, Jim thought, to an entire invasion beginning with a single burst of 7.62mm bullets.

50

It was 23:50 hours, ten minutes before H hour, when a regular Army machine gun team mounted in an M113 armored personnel carrier in Fort Amador saw the school bus approaching. It was running hot and fast, and it was full of PDF soldiers who'd been rousted from their barracks.

If there was one point that was made perfectly clear during the final briefing on this mission, it was that no civilian vehicle was to be fired on without specific orders, and certainly not before kickoff at midnight.

But this was war, and in war, no standing order stands for long. Command had notified the team of this bus two minutes ago, and now here it was, racing straight for them.

It only took about twenty rounds of .50 caliber ammunition to reduce the bus to scrap metal.

Thirty seconds into the war, they were already ten minutes ahead of schedule.

51

Kurt had been sleeping only fitfully. The events of the morning and afternoon had left him feeling intellectually dizzy. Haunted by dozens of questions and possessing no answers, his mind whirled a million miles per hour. When he wasn't dozing, he found himself thinking about the trauma of his family's first Christmas without him, and his first without them. When he pictured the holidays, his mind conjured images all focused on his old house, the house of his kids' childhood. It occurred to him now that those images were all wrong. The faces were the same, he thought, but then he had to cancel that in his mind, as well. The Christmastime faces of the past were happy ones; he had no idea what they looked like anymore. He had no idea what terrible impact he might have had on the happiness of his children. Come to think of it, he knew virtually nothing anymore about what was important to him.

His family's lives were moving on, just as they were supposed to, in as normal or awkward a manner as circumstances would allow, and he was no longer a part of it. All the day-to-day activities, all the things that defined the very essence of family life no longer reflected his touch. It was a terrible thing to consider. It was a terrible thing to live—

What was that?

In the distance, he thought he'd heard the brissant thudding of a heavy machine gun. There was a rhythm and timbre to a .50 caliber machine gun that was unique to itself; once you heard it, you'd never mistake it for anything else. But in this case, it was far enough away that Kurt wondered if maybe it hadn't been something more benign— say, the beat of rotor blades, filtered through a dream he hadn't realized he'd been having.

He lifted his head from the pillow to glance out in the hallway, and when he saw the curious expression on the corporal's face, he knew that it had been real.

The next burst of gunfire was extended, and from much closer.

Still bathed in total darkness, Jim Nelson felt his Little Bird bank hard to the right and swoop into a steep, deep dive. His first thought was, these guys are going in too early! What the hell are they thinking? Then he realized that the pilots from the 160th were way too good to move without orders, so H hour had clearly been moved up.

They came in fast, and as they moved through the center of the city and beyond, Jim could see Modelo Prison clearly among the assorted tenements. Its flat cement roof was the clearest giveaway, and next to it sat the Comandancia with its antiaircraft emplacement, which frankly looked to be up and running just fine, even if its crew didn't yet know that the sky was full of targets for them to shoot at. Jim was watching, in fact, when the tracers streamed in from the high ground and killed both the gun and its crew.

This was it. They were on their way.

For a very brief instant, Kurt and the corporal just stared at each other, mouths agape, knowing that something earth-shattering was underway, but neither of them knowing exactly what to do about it. The close-in machine gun fire spurred Kurt into action. He rolled out of his cot and crawled into the bathroom for cover while his executioner was still weighing his options.

Kurt reasoned his way through the problem in an instant. Clearly, this was no repeat of the coup attempt. First of all, the rebels didn't have access to the kind of firepower he'd heard on the outside; second, most of the rebels of influence or importance were already dead or in prison. No, this was an American military action, and if the American military was involved, that meant that Noriega was finally going down.

It was time to get dressed. He quickly, frantically, changed from his orange surfer shorts into some underwear, and from there quick-stepped into a pair of blue Docker slacks, a green Polo shirt, and his running shoes. What the hell. If you're going to get shot at, you might as well look as good as you can.

It didn't even occur to him that he would not survive the night. In that moment, his thoughts were consumed by the image of the Pineapple scurrying for safety and begging for his life. If Kurt's own life could somehow be spared in the process, well, that would be pretty damned good, too.

Outside, the gunfire grew louder and closer. He saw tracers speeding past his window with an upward trajectory, only to see it returned like some kind of fiery summer deluge. Jesus, it was really happening.

Outside his door, out in the cellblock, he heard the sound of running feet and raised voices. Someone pounded on the door to the officers' quarters across the hall and yelled, "Sir! Sir! Something is happening!"

"No shit," Kurt mumbled.

The ground fire surprised Jim. He couldn't imagine what would inspire some PDF grunt to such a clearly suicidal act. But their wish was Delta's command.

The Little Birds swooped in low and fast, nose to tail on their approach to the roof of Modelo Prison, laying a blanket of suppressing fire toward the guard towers and the prison yard, yet still some overzealous assholes on the ground felt compelled not to dive for cover. It was a bad night to be carrying a weapon on the streets of the Chorrillo neighborhood. The war hadn't officially started yet, but the grounds of the prison yard and the Comandancia across the street swarmed with targets. As the guy with the big-ass bomb on his back, Sergeant Jim Nelson felt particularly inspired to quench the tracer fire. The reception desks in Heaven and Hell were going to be a little overwhelmed this evening.

The flat, concrete roof of the prison raced up to meet them, and as they closed to within a few feet, Jim unfastened his safety strap and lifted his legs straight out to avoid getting crushed by the skids as they slid to a remarkably smooth halt. The overture was complete, and it was time for the first act to begin.

Before the bird had even stopped, Jim lurched off of his bench and ran to his assigned position next to the access door in the cupola that led to the prison's central stairway. There he shrugged out of the torch tanks and crouched in a defensive position to cover Paul Jones and Parker Sturbridge, the explosives entry team. Within seconds, the entire Delta team was on the roof, swarming like ants to their planned posts, preparing to bring a little piece of Armageddon to this squalid, ugly place.

The entry charge was custom designed for tonight's mission. Carried in four separate pieces and assembled in place on the surface of the metal door to the cupola, the charge resembled a large picture frame when it was finally put together. Paul inserted the initiator and signaled to Parker that it was time to go.

Staff Sergeant Peter Jacobs drove his piton into the roof decking with five hard blows of a hammer. He securely attached the exposed end of his climbing rope to the eyelet, then slung the nylon bag with the rest of the rope over the parapet and into the darkness, where it arced toward the ground. His was the key element of the first moments—one among so many key moments that lay waiting their turn. With his rappelling harness in place, and the figure-eight descender clipped to the caribiner, he was ready to slip over the side to fire the single shot that was his and his alone, to take out Kurt Muse's designated assassin. His job was to be in place with his shot fired before they blew the door to the cupola.

Balancing carefully on the top of the parapet, he leaned backward hesitantly, testing the integrity of his lifeline before committing himself fully to his task. Silhouetted against the gray adobe of the prison wall, he made a perfect target, and he hadn't descended three feet before the first enemy rounds sent shards of shattered concrete into his face. From the air, the prison looked like an asymmetrical L, with the kitchen area serving as the letter's squatty, thick base.

Jacobs pressed the vest-mounted transmit button for his portable radio and spoke rapidly into his throat mike. "Bravo Three taking fire from the kitchen. It's close."

Two seconds later, the roof line erupted with outgoing gunfire as the rest of his troop opened up on the kitchen's windows and red-tiled roof, shredding them in seconds. The suppressive fire calmed things down for Jacobs, but it couldn't extinguish the return fire entirely.

That job fell to a Little Bird gunship, which all but removed the kitchen's roof in a single pass.

Jacobs had practiced this so many times in his head and on the side of the elementary school at Howard Air Force Base that his hands and feet seemed to know on their own what to do. He zipped down to the exact spot, dangling in midair, and brought his CAR-15 to his shoulder, ready to kill a killer. "Bravo Three in position."

But the cell was empty. No killer, no prisoner, no anyone. In the green light of his night vision goggles, Jacobs peered intensely into the darkness, looking for some kind of movement, but there was nothing.

"Shit."

Jim Nelson heard the magic words at the same instant as everyone else. "Bravo Three in position."

An instant later, Paul's voice crackled, "Fire in the hole."

The entry charge blew the cupola door into next month.

On the floor of the bathroom, Kurt tried to make himself as small as possible amid the strobes of muzzle flashes and the rain of hot concrete that blasted in through his window and ricocheted around the walls like BBs in a can.

He couldn't help but wonder whether the brave young corporal had fled his post, or if he was crouching outside the cell door, waiting for Kurt to show his face. Either way, Kurt felt reasonably safe in the bathroom, pretty sure that the guard was in no hurry to bring himself closer to the firing.

The noise of the battle outside was unlike anything Kurt had ever heard. Complete bedlam.

Then came the explosion. It was a horrendous thing, like a direct hit from a bomb, he thought, literally bouncing him off the concrete floor and seemingly moving Carcel Modelo off its foundation.

Seconds later, night turned to day outside as the volume and rhythm of the shooting increased tenfold. This was hell on earth. Explosion after explosion rippled the air, and Gatling guns from God knew how many aircraft created a cacophony of noise that sounded like the fabric of the air itself was being ripped apart by the hands of God.

He had to see for himself. Rising cautiously, first to his knees, and then to his feet, he dared a peek out of the bathroom window. One after another, enormous detonations blasted the Comandancia into nonexistence. Blinding flashes preceded the concussion by a fraction of an instant, before tons of dirt and concrete were launched high into the air.

We've finally done it, Kurt thought. *We've finally grown a set of balls.*

He never did see the camouflaged soldier dangling just a few feet away on the other side of the window.

The detonation of the entry charge was the signal to the two orbiting AC-130 Specter gunships that it was time to unload on the Comandancia. As Jim Nelson led the way into the breached opening, the concussion of the first 105mm Howitzer shell felt like a shove from behind.

Once inside the ruined cupola archway, the world was completely dark, lit only by the lights on the muzzles of their CAR-15s, dancing circles of white light cast on a flat black canvas. Two steps down the first flight of stairs, Jim noticed with a wry chuckle that the concrete walls in the stairway of their mock-up prison were in fact wide open. The narrow field of fire they'd anticipated and practiced for was in fact a wide open kill zone.

They moved down the first flight of stairs like water over rocks, over a dozen men in all, pursuing a mission whose stakes were pure and clear. They were here for one man and one man only. Anyone who stood in their way—anyone, in fact, with a weapon in his hand—would die instantly, but all others were to remain unmolested. That meant a surgical strike in the prison, even as the Comandancia next door was razed to the ground.

Descending to and through the fourth floor, security teams dispersed to hold the stairway and to dispatch any guards or soldiers who might try to engage them.

The rest continued on, led by Jim Nelson, whose job it was to secure the third floor—Muse's floor—and make sure that their precious cargo got home to his family. At the next landing, a second security team was deployed, and as Jim button-hooked around to the left, he found himself face to face with a terrified soldier who would have floated out of his shoes if he raised his hands any higher.

Jim felt his finger tighten on the trigger, but pulled himself back.

This one was sane, doing the right thing. "On the floor!" Jim commanded. "*En el piso! En el piso!* Damn it, I almost shot the son of a bitch!"

The soldier dropped as if his legs dissolved and instantly splayed himself on the concrete floor, in the process saving his own life. The security team would cuff him and hold him. Jim Nelson and his four-man assault team had a more important task to perform. Paul Jones and Parker Sturbridge would secure Moose while Jim and Chris Simone made sure no one shot them in the process.

A dozen steps later, they were there.

52

"On the floor!" Kurt heard. The voice echoed down the concrete hallway, somehow discernable against the battle that raged outside. "*En el piso! En el piso!* Damn it, I almost shot the son of a bitch!"

It was English! They were American soldiers. Kurt could barely believe what he was hearing.

"Cuff him."

His mouth agape, his eyes and throat burning from the acrid smoke and dust, Kurt watched in stunned amazement as fingers of light cut through the darkness and the sound of approaching footsteps grew closer.

"Where's the shooter?" someone asked.

"We got a locked door here," said someone else.

A dark figure appeared in the smoke, indistinguishable as a soldier but for the silhouette of a rifle in his hands. A white light flashed through the bars of the cell door. "Moose," a voice called. "You okay?"

"Yes!" Kurt called. "I'm here! I'm okay!" He approached the door.

"Get down and stay down," the voice said. "We're gonna blow the door."

It was unbelievable. The whole world was being blown up to support his rescue. Kurt scrambled back around the corner into the bathroom and tried again to make himself disappear.

In a hallway this small, there was only one place for their shooter to be hiding, and that had to be behind the door to the officers' quarters.

As Jim took a bead, Chris crouched low and tried the knob. "We got a locked door here," he announced.

They'd have to blow it. Since the door was locked from the inside, someone was clearly barricaded inside, and with four members on the team, they simply did not have the manpower to protect against a wild-ass suicide mission from behind while they executed the rescue.

Almost directly across the hall, Jim heard Parker telling the package to get down. At least Muse was still alive. They still had a good chance to hit a home run.

While Jim covered the door with his weapon high, Chris crouched low to attach a general purpose charge (GPC) to the door knob and lock. If the door opened on its own, the problem would solve itself; if it didn't, the GPC could open any door on the planet. Constructed of a wad of plastic explosive with a dangling tail of detonator cord, a GPC was initiated by two nonelectrical blasting caps embedded in the det cord. With the charge in place, Chris pulled the two safety pins to ignite the ten-second length of old-fashioned fuse.

"Fire in the hole!"

With Muse under cover in the bathroom of his cell, the assault team sought safety on either side of the door. Under most circumstances, the GPC delivers a hell of a whop, but in a narrow concrete hallway, it sounded damn near nuclear as it vaporized the lock on the door to the officers' quarters.

Chris led the way, breaking right while Jim followed a step behind and broke left. Instantly, Jim saw their man. He was trying to hide behind the door to the latrine, appearing to Jim as a half-silhouette. Jim fired two quick shots with his rifle, hitting the target center-of-mass. The wounded man backpedaled out of sight, landing on his ass on the floor of a tiny shower. Jim pivoted around the corner and triple-tapped him, two in the stomach and then a head shot.

"Clear!" he yelled, announcing that his only threat had been neutralized.

Chris echoed, "Clear!"

Across the hall, the concussion of the GPC hadn't finished careening down the corridor before Paul Jones was on his feet with the muzzle of his Mossberg twelve-gauge pressed against the monstrous padlock on Kurt's cell door. Behind him, he heard the CQB gunfire—close quarters battle—but he ignored it. Those guys had their job to do, and he and Parker Sturbridge had a mission of their own. Besides, he couldn't imagine a surer way to die than to point a weapon at Jim Nelson or Chris Simone.

"Keep your head down, Moose!" Parker yelled from over Paul's shoulder. "We're not done yet!" Apparently thinking that the GPC was the main event, Kurt had peeked around the corner. At Parker's command, the prisoner's face retreated quickly.

From the officers' quarters, he heard three more gunshots and voices yell, "Clear!"

Paul pulled the trigger, launching a twelve-gauge slug that fractured the lock, shearing the metal hoop so cleanly that it looked as if it had been dispatched with bolt cutters. Paul slapped the lock away and charged into the cell, where he flung himself atop the prisoner, protecting him from the shrapnel and debris that continued to rain in from the outside.

Kurt thought it was over when he heard the explosion in the hall. In the darkness cut only by the light beams on the rifles, nothing he saw made sense; everything was about noise and smells. He heard shouting and gunshots, and then when the explosion shook the entire floor, he naturally assumed that they'd blown the cell door off the hinges. When he peeked around the corner, even in the smoky night he could see the posture of a soldier aiming a shotgun in his general direction.

"Keep your head down, Moose! We're not done yet!"

Kurt had the odd sense that maybe this was all a very realistic dream. There was an unearthly quality to it all that was at once euphoric and unnerving. After the single report of the shotgun, he heard the slam of metal against concrete, and then suddenly there was a big man on top of him, not hugging him so much as pressing him into the floor.

"Are you all right?" Paul asked. Above and behind him, the other rescuer fumbled with a rucksack, out of which was born a Kevlar vest and helmet.

Just as quickly as he'd been pounced on, he was released again and lifted to a standing position. They wrestled him into the vest and fastened the front for him. Next, they dropped a Kevlar helmet on his head and cinched the chin strap tight.

"This is it, Moose," Parker said. "We're here to take you home."

Two more commandos appeared in his cell. "Hallway's clear," one of them said. "One dead."

Kurt knew that it had to be the corporal. He tried to muster up some sympathy for the son of a bitch, but it just wouldn't come.

A soldier said, "Let's go," and an instant later they were moving, Kurt being driven along by a hand that had grabbed a fistful of trousers at the small of his back, and by hands clenched around both arms at the biceps. The Delta operators formed a human wall around their charge, protecting him with their bodies and their lives from any yahoo with a weapon who decided to take one last shot. He had the feeling that his feet were barely touching the ground as they herded him down the hall and up two levels toward the roof. Before they'd even reached the first flight, someone said, "PC secured. X-Ray ready for exfil. Enroute to your location."

Kurt was vaguely aware of a hog-tied soldier on the floor at the base of the first flight of steps, but before he could take real notice, he was all but airborne, more carried than led up the pitch dark stairs, his head swimming in the emotion of freedom and in the disorientation caused by the bouncing and spinning muzzle lights on his rescuers' rifles. With each new flight, their numbers grew, until finally they numbered twenty-four.

On the final landing, Kurt saw the remains of a mangled steel door all but embedded in the concrete wall. To his left and up, he could see the portal that the door had once guarded, wide open and inviting. Suddenly, the muzzle lights were no longer needed. Beyond the rectangle that was the cupola door, the sky burned like an autumn dawn. As his rescuers whisked him the rest of the way onto the roof and reintroduced him to the fresh night air for the first time in over nine months, he understood where the dawn light was coming from. The Comandancia was completely in flames, great tongues of fire billowing from the windows on all sides and from giant gaping holes in the roof. The night continued to be filled with explosions and the darkness streaked with tracers. Each blast brought a strobe-flash of light. The humid air reeked of acrid smoke and of cordite. It occurred to Kurt there on the roof of Carcel Modelo that there was a certain twisted beauty to the devastation of war. For so many, it would spell death, but for at least one, it spelled a new lease on freedom. He made a conscious effort to savor the moment, soaking in every emotion and image. Precious few people walked the earth who could tell the story he would be able to tell at the end of this night, and he wanted everything to be as vivid as it could possibly be.

Kurt never heard the Little Birds return. One moment the roof had been barren of the machines, and the next, there was a swarm of them, lined up nose to tail rotor.

Pressing on Kurt's head to bend him at the waist, the rescuers rushed him to the first bird in the procession. Kurt didn't know where to look, alternating his gaze from the helicopter to his feet, in the ridiculous fear that he might trip over something. Even if he'd lain out flat, the Delta operators would have continued carrying him. In fact, had it not been for his efforts to keep his feet moving, maybe it all would have progressed faster.

His last thought before being rushed to the chopper and deposited inside was, *Holy shit, there's no way I can fit through that little door.*

As Jim and his assault team rushed the precious cargo toward the helicopter, he couldn't help but wonder if the door would be big enough.

Didn't matter. Kurt Muse was being stuffed into that Little Bird even if it meant leaving his shoulders behind. They ran him across the roof the way that bodyguards all over the world, from the U.S. Secret Service to the thugs of tin-pot dictators in the third world, whisk their charges to safety while under fire. They kept Kurt's head down and his feet moving constantly; no time for second thoughts, no time for the PC to reconsider his situation.

Jim and his team timed it perfectly. The instant the lead bird's skids touched down on the roof deck, Kurt was there. He seemed to pull back a bit when he saw where he was headed, but at this point, Kurt had no more of a vote in what was going down than did the rifle in Jim's hand. They stuffed the big man through the doorless opening and dropped him onto the chopper's bench seat, in the tiny space between the pilots' seats and the aft bulkhead.

With the PC planted, another Delta operator slid into the seat next to Kurt to keep him out of trouble as Jim's assault team boarded the benches for the flight back to the safety of Howard Air Force Base. Even as his ass hit the seat, Jim could feel the weightless sensation that comes with being light on the skids. The pilots of their bird were ready to go, right by-god now. Jim barely had time to tether himself to the bench before they were moving again.

The total elapsed time from touchdown to dust off was six minutes. But the night was about to get a lot longer.

53

The images on television were the most frightening that Annie had ever seen. Alerted by friends—some of them in Panama— that the war had begun, Annie could actually make out the image of Modelo Prison right in the thick of the raging battle.

The first bullet was for Kurt.

Once the phone started ringing, it didn't stop. Everyone Annie knew in Panama was calling her with updates on the invasion. When talking on the phone with Rita Prieto, Annie could actually hear the boom of explosions and the chatter of gunfire. Still, the point of the call was not to deliver news, but to solicit it. Had Annie heard anything? Did she know anything?

People meant well, but as much as she appreciated the gestures of kindness, there are times when talking actually makes things worse.

The television networks were all covering the invasion now, and they were going wall to wall with it, even at this ridiculous hour, and even though they had nothing to report. When they did, they would say nothing of Kurt. It had been nine months already, and none of them were interested in Kurt.

With explosions blooming in the background, sad-faced anchors speculated on developments and spoke to experts who had not been in on the planning, and therefore took five-minute segments to say that they didn't know a thing.

It would be a long night.

She opted to let the children sleep.

Kurt's world was now a swirling nightmare of noise and cordite. In the cramped spaces of the chopper's backseat, he could see virtually nothing of the battle, but there was no missing the *tink, tink* of bullets from the ground piercing the aircraft's skin. The pilots cursed with each impact. "We've got to get going!" the right-seat pilot yelled to whoever might be listening. "We've got to get off of this roof."

Even before the rest of the operators were on board, Kurt could feel the chopper hovering just millimeters off the roof deck. It reminded him of the way he used to hold a hill in his Volvo by hanging on the partially engaged clutch.

Finally, everyone was on board and it was time to go. The pilot twisted in power as he pulled on the collective pitch lever, and suddenly they were airborne. Kurt felt a cheer forming in his throat, but before he could make a sound, a *tink* was followed by a *bang*, and suddenly they were falling like an anvil tossed off a bridge.

If they'd had the element of surprise on their side on the way in, they had none of it now. Every gun in Panama seemed to be trained on this one Delta troop. At this early point in the invasion, there were no good guys on the ground, so if somebody was even thinking about holding a weapon, he was dropped without a moment's thought.

From where Jim Nelson sat, in his same slot on the front seat of the Little Bird's port side, the exfil flight was like the wildest amusement park ride ever created. Three feet past the edge of the roof, the chopper pilot dropped the bird into a nose-down dive that first nearly had them smashing into the prison yard concrete, and then again into the prison yard wall. Honest to God they missed the wall by inches.

"What the hell are you doing?" he yelled over the engine noise, but if the pilots heard, they weren't paying attention.

On the far side of the wall, the chopper landed in the middle of the street, just a block away from the flaming Comandancia. Jim heard something wrong with the engine, and right away knew that things had taken a shitty turn. Before he could say a thing, Chris's voice said in his headset, "Form a perimeter. Give me a status report."

Terrific. Eight guys and a civilian were now going to slug it out on the ground with the entire PDF. This was about to get ugly.

Behind him, Paul and Parker undid their lifelines and fanned out to engage whatever targets they could find. Jim had a hard time with his tether, however, and fell three or four seconds behind his teammates. Before he could recover, Chris's voice returned in his ear.

"Negative! Negative! Back onboard. Everybody back onboard."

Whatever was happening, they were going to make another run at getting airborne. Jim provided covering fire from the bench while his teammates dashed back to their positions on the benches. Someone on the net yelled, "All aboard. Go! Go!"

Seconds later, they were moving again. The aircraft shook violently as the rotors tried to bite into the humidity, but the overloaded bird was too damaged to lift them straight off the ground. When they were barely light on the skids again, the pilot poured on the power and started propelling the aircraft down the streets of the Chorrillo neighborhood. As they gained speed, but no altitude, Jim Nelson cursed under his breath, "Holy shit, we're driving home."

Operation Just Cause wasn't yet ten minutes old, but already the PDF resistance was beginning to show some signs of organization, spurred in part, Jim supposed, by the possibility of shooting down a helicopter that was flying less than two feet off the ground.

The idea was to achieve transitional lift by gaining ground speed, and then use that lift to take the wounded bird off the street and into the sky where it belonged. The problem was the block that ran between the prison and the Comandancia compound: It was too short to get the job done, and an eight-story tenement loomed at the end of the block. The pilot backed off the throttle as he reached the end of the block, causing them to lose whatever momentum they'd gained, and swung a flat turn—a pivot—to face a much longer block.

The bullet-torn engine whined miserably as the pilot poured on the power again and propelled the Little Bird down the tenement-lined street that felt to Jim Nelson to be much like the canyons in the old cowboy movies—the ones from which the Indians always launched devastating ambushes. The presence of dozens of PDF defenders at every compass point only added to the allusion. Overhead, Little Bird gunships did their best to keep the enemy's heads down, but the concern over killing innocents meant that they were far more bark than bite, and the bad guys seemed to understand that.

For Jim's part, the rules of engagement meant less than the steadily diminishing chance of staying alive. There were places in the world where he was willing to die, but this fetid backwater alley was not on the list. Not tonight.

Behind him, Paul struggled to stay on the bench, straddling the wood and locking his ankles to keep from falling off as his hands continued to feed and fire his weapon.

It's hard to judge speed in conditions such as these, but to Jim's eye they were going pretty damn fast and pulling a lot of damn fire as they raced down the long street in search of takeoff velocity. Two-thirds of the way down, about the time that Jim had begun to think it was time to back off the throttle or prepare to eat a tenement building, the ground started to drop away. Suddenly, they were looking down on the first-floor windows instead of looking up at them. This was one hotshot pilot. The second floor windows flashed into view. They were going to make it.

And then somewhere, a Panamanian machine gunner found his aim.

The first burst caught Paul in the chest, piercing his Kevlar vest and knocking him off the bench. Jim Nelson watched in horror as his teammate pivoted sideways and dropped like a stone twenty feet to the grimy roadway below. He slapped the transmit button clipped to his own vest to tell the pilots to stop their climb, but before he could say a word, a 5.56mm bullet slammed through his bench from below and drilled into the back of his left knee. The impact knocked the breath out of his lungs and made him lose his grip on his weapon. But for the sling around his shoulder, his rifle would have dropped, and but for the tether around his waist, he would have followed it. *I'm screwed*, he thought.

He had no idea.

Time slows when you know you're dying. What plays out in fractions of seconds has the clarity and detail of an event that occurs over long minutes.

The Little Bird seemed to hesitate in midair as yet another burst of gunfire raked the engine cowling over Jim's head. In retrospect, it happened in silence, but in real time, it had to have been loud as hell. Chunks of metal and bullet fragments littered the night air and the aircraft jolted as if smacked with a giant hand.

The chopper banked hard to the right, the rotor disk catching the block wall of a tenement, and from there it was all about the laws of physics.

They were falling. Twenty feet, forty feet, no one would say for sure, but there was nothing graceful or dignified about it. No autorotation that the chopper boys praised so loudly whenever they got the chance. This bird might as well have been a rock.

It fell fast and hit hard, bouncing once and then coming to rest upright but listing pitifully, its starboard landing skid snapped free. Parker and Chris went flying on impact, tumbling out onto the street, but the kinetic energy that tried to launch Jim into the night merely threw him to the end of his tether and then yanked him back again. For a second, Jim thought that the safety line had cut him in half. As he rebounded, he skidded hard across the macadam, and as the Little Bird landed for the last time, Jim felt a lightning bolt of pain erupt from his leg. He screamed in agony and tried to roll away, but realized he was trapped. Lying as he was, flat on his back, and looking up at the shooters in the windows lining the street, it took him a moment to realize what had happened.

His left foot, just a few inches south of the joint that had already been ruined by a bullet, had been essentially cut in two. It was with a special horror that he realized that his crushed foot was trapped under the chopper's good landing skid.

A war that he'd helped to ignite was raging all around him, and he was stuck helpless in the middle of the street, pinned under a couple thousand pounds of future scrap metal.

Bullshit.

He was getting out of here. Planting his right foot—his good foot— against the skid for leverage, he started to pull.

All Kurt knew was that they had crashed and that they were in some seriously deep shit. He'd heard the curses from the pilots as their aircraft was shredded by bullets, and he'd heard shouting from the benches that was somehow even louder than the gunfire that found them. An instant later, he felt a brief sensation of weightlessness, and then they hit the ground. The impact rattled his core, bouncing him first off the floor and then off the ceiling, just one more bit of flotsam in a swirling cloud of wreckage.

Finally at rest, the noise was just beginning. The attackers had downed their prize, and now they wanted to make sure that it was dead. Gunfire raged all around, both incoming and outgoing, and while Kurt didn't know what to do next, he knew that staying in the chopper was nowhere on the list. Someone was calling his name. "Moose! Moose! You okay?"

"I'm all right!" Kurt shouted back. He recognized the voice as belonging to his seat mate in the back of the chopper. Much later, he'd come to learn that his name was Brian.

"We're down for good!" Brian yelled. "Get the hell out."

"Let me have a weapon!" Kurt shouted. The entire world was shooting at them right now, and the least he could ask for was a way to shoot back.

Brian hesitated.

"I was in the Army," Kurt assured. "I know this part of the city. I know how to shoot."

"It's not the how I worry about," Brian said. "It's the who." Nonetheless, he pulled a .45 from his thigh holster and handed it over, butt first. "It's cocked," he warned, "and the trigger's got a lighter pull than you're used to."

"I've got it, I've got it."

Brian backed out of the hatch first, then waited for Kurt. "We're gonna find cover and stay there," he advised.

Free of the hatch, Kurt turned, and in that instant he heard a horrible *whop* and saw Brian's head flail violently to the left as his body dropped to a heap on the ground. The momentum of his fall took Kurt to the ground with him. *Shit! Sniper!*

A bead of blood traced down Brian's face from an unseen head wound. "Hey!" Kurt yelled, wishing that he knew this man's name. "Hey! Are you okay? Wake up!"

The man didn't move.

Sure that Brian was dead, and equally sure that the sniper who killed him would soon zero in on Kurt as his next victim, Kurt lay on his belly with his left hand—his shooting hand—propped on Brian's chest for support. If he saw a muzzle flash, he'd do his best to return fire.

The Little Bird was still alive, its fractured rotors turning in a lazy, dying circle. The air reeked of spilled fuel, gunpowder, and blood. Brian's lifeless face was just inches away from Kurt's own. Try as he might not to look, it was impossible. Such a terrible way to—

Brian's eyes snapped open. "Moose! Are you okay?"

Kurt nearly jumped clear of his skin. "Jesus! What happened to you? I thought you were dead."

"Damn rotor blade hit me in the head."

Suddenly, Kurt was keenly aware that he'd lost his own helmet in the crash.

"This is a shitty place to be," Brian said.

They needed cover. As they started to move, though, it was clear that the wiring between Brian's brain and his feet had been damaged by the impact of the rotor blade. Saying nothing, Kurt slung the operator's arm over his shoulder and headed for the side of an apartment building, where the wall looked stout enough to provide some cover. It took a year and a half to stumble across the street, but they made it, collapsing together onto the sidewalk.

In the nighttime, in the middle of a war, Kurt tried to become invisible.

A few seconds later, Kurt heard movement in the street and he looked up to see an operator he recognized from the hallway of the prison. It was Chris, the commander. He recoiled from the sight of Brian's face. "Jesus. Are you okay?"

"Rotor blade," Brian said simply. "Hell of a headache, but I'm functional."

Chris turned to Kurt. "What about you?"

"I'm okay."

"That makes you better than most, then." He turned back to Brian. "You guys can't stay here. It's too exposed." He pointed to something only he could see. "We're sheltered up across the street and have a perimeter established."

Without discussion, they were moving again.

Trying to jog across that street with bullets streaking the sky took Kurt back to the worst kinds of childhood nightmares: needing to run from mortal danger when his legs couldn't possibly pump fast enough. Those twenty-five yards grew to be a hundred and twenty-five.

G Team had taken up a defensive position along the side of the road, on the sidewalk, really, with a brick wall behind them, and parallel parked cars serving as barriers in the front. A jeep Wagoneer was the largest of the barricades and by far the most substantial.

The operators were all a mess. Brian's head continued to bleed, but the one who concerned Kurt the most was the man he already knew as Parker, the first man to appear in the doorway of his cell. A bullet had ripped through Parker's thigh and he was bleeding badly and clearly in unspeakable pain. He was doing his best to do his job, but Kurt could tell that he was flagging quickly.

Of the seven men huddled there in the dark, then, four were critically injured. They had to get a ride out of here and fast. Only Chris, Chief Wolff (the pilot of the Little Bird), and Kurt were whole and largely unhurt.

"Where's Jim?" one of the commandos asked, clearly concerned.

Chris shook his head. "Haven't seen him, and he hasn't answered up on the net."

Jim Nelson was not dying on the street tonight.

Pulling as hard as he could accomplished nothing. He was still as stuck under the weight of the chopper as he'd been since the first moments after the crash. Part of the problem was the awkward angles. He could neither sit nor lay flat. Certainly, standing up was out of the question. And with all the other wounded among them he knew that the team did not have the available manpower to charge out here and pull him away.

If it had been just him and the team, then maybe. Or even if it had been an entirely military crew. As it was, the object of this mission—their precious cargo—was still in harm's way. Until Kurt Muse was safe, he, not Jim Nelson, was the man to protect. It was all about being good soldiers, and Jim was one of the best in the world.

As he started kicking at the skid again with his right foot—his good foot—he couldn't help but think of the stories about how a fox will chew off its own leg to escape a trap. Well, Jim wasn't going to chew, but he wasn't going to die, either. But he was getting ahead of himself. He was still a few options away from drawing his knife.

He slammed his foot over and over again into the steel skid, and on each impact, he could feel the bones in the good foot straining, even as the length of his left leg screamed in agony. It wasn't just the foot. It was the damn bullet in the back of his knee. That was hurting like hell, too.

Wait a second, he thought. How can someone be shot in the back of the knee, yet have the front of his knee remain intact? He didn't care what you were shooting, there's not enough structure in a knee joint to stop much of anything.

Then he got it. The bench. He remembered clearly that the bench reverberated when the bullet struck. Perhaps the wood slowed it down enough to—

In all the concern over his ruined foot, he'd neglected to even check the bullet wound in his leg. Pausing long enough to grope the knee, he could scarcely believe what he found: He could actually *feel* the ass end of the bullet protruding from the crease behind his knee. There wasn't much there—it was buried pretty deeply—but it hadn't turned his knee into the blooming rose that most such injuries resembled. With a little digging through the fabric of his BDUs, he was actually able to remove the round from his flesh. He felt it slide free and then he lost his grip and the dislodged bullet got lost in the folds of cloth.

Maybe it was just the minor victory, or maybe it was the fact that he no longer had a hunk of lead pressing against the structure of his knee, but the relief from pain was immediate.

He took it as a sign that he'd been right all along: he truly was not meant to die tonight.

He started kicking again. Harder and harder, each time leveraging his foot a little farther out of its trap. The pain was exquisite, blinding, as the skid's crushing force advanced from his instep to his toes and beyond. He could actually feel the bones crumbling. He kept kicking.

Finally after twenty, maybe a hundred, maybe a thousand kicks, he finally pulled himself free. And he was the only friendly in sight.

He saw movement ahead and on the left. He rolled to his belly, to a prone position and drew a bead, preparing to fire.

Jim had to smile. Even in the darkness, and even with the Kevlar vest in place, there was no missing that bright green Polo shirt that the PC had decided to wear tonight. It looked like he and two operators—he was pretty sure one was Chris, but it was so hard to tell from this distance—were dashing across the street to some temporary shelter.

He started crawling that way. It was an endless, excruciating trip as he dragged the mangled, shredded foot behind him, inching his way toward the assault team that had turned itself invisible behind its barricades.

He was still fifteen yards out when Chris dashed out of their hiding place to help him to safety.

"We've been worried about you," Chris said, lifting his wounded colleague by his bandoliers and helping him hobble on one leg.

Jim locked his jaw against the pain. "Yeah, well, I've been a little worried about me, too."

Kurt watched, stunned, as Chris dashed out to retrieve his brother in arms.

Back inside the barricade, Jim found a spot on the sidewalk where he could guard his leg even as he brought his weapon back up to his shoulder to cover the team.

Chris spoke a mile a minute into his radio, but in the cacophony of the raging battle, Kurt couldn't make out any words, only the passion that drove them. It was that very passion that inspired Kurt to draw his weapon again.

He watched as Chris dug through his rucksack for something that looked a lot like a flashlight, but without the beam, and held it high over his head. Kurt would learn later that the device was an infrared strobe—a signal device that remained invisible to the naked eye, even as it was impossible to miss for anyone wearing night vision gear.

"Help should be on the way soon," he said.

As if on cue, a giant Blackhawk helicopter made a low pass directly overhead. It pivoted a turn at the end of the block, and then made another pass, this time rocking back and forth in the ancient aviation tradition of acknowledging friendlies by waggling wings.

As the noise of the Blackhawk dopplered away, it was replaced by the relatively higher-pitched buzz of a Little Bird gunship swooping in for an attack run. The birds themselves were invisible in the night, but the fiery flashes erupting from the muzzles of their side-mounted Gatling guns could be seen for miles. Directly across the street from G Team's barricade, a parapet atop the roof of an eight-story apartment building erupted in great chunks of blasted concrete. Another bird followed in its wake, doubling the destruction.

There would be no threat of snipers; at least not from that rooftop. The gunships stuck around, though, no doubt keeping an eye out for any yahoo with an urge to meet his maker.

Paul started to stir, making ugly growling, gurgling noises on the sidewalk. "I'll shoot the son of a bitch," he said.

Chris knelt down next to him. "Paul, you're hurt," he said. "You've been hit. You need to stay down and be quiet."

"I'll shoot him," he said again.

Chris pulled Paul's rifle out of reach and handed it to Chief Wolff. "We'll shoot whoever needs to be shot," Chris assured. "You don't have to worry about any of that. Just stay put."

Paul wanted none of it. Equal parts adrenaline and delirium, his anger was hotter than his skills right now, and his wounds were serious enough that too much movement might well cause him to bleed out.

"Moose," Chris barked. "Take care of Paul. Keep him down. Sit on him if you have to."

On the surface, it seemed like such a simple assignment: just keep a man from hurting himself. But when the man was a trained killer with twice the strength of his caretaker, the equation took on a whole different meaning. But what could Kurt say? Everyone else had a job to do, a flank to cover; all he had to do was stay down and try not to get shot.

He knelt next to Paul and Chris. "Hey, buddy, are you okay?"

"I'm fine," Paul spat.

"No, you're not." Kurt tried hard to keep his voice calm. In the midst of all this madness, he worked hard to quell his growing panic. "You're all broken up inside. You need to take it easy. They've called for help and we'll be out of here soon." *From my lips to God's ear.*

"Hey, Chris, we got something," Brian said, pointing out into the night.

Chris stood, leaving Kurt alone with the wounded soldier.

"It looks like a local," Brian continued. "Out at twelve o'clock. He's bobbing and weaving among the cars."

Kurt stood to see what they were talking about, momentarily abandoning his post with Paul. What he saw froze his breath in his throat. In the wildness of the night, amid the strafing runs and the uninterrupted gunfire, a guy—just a Panamanian guy—was approaching them in the darkness, moving from car to car, popping up to see what he could see and then ducking down again to move one car length closer.

"What the hell does he think he's doing?" Chris asked whomever might care to answer.

"I can take him," Parker said, his voice knotted with pain. "Next time he pops up, I can clean his head from his shoulders."

"No," Kurt said. His voice was emphatic enough to carry weight among the warriors. "He doesn't mean any harm."

"And just how do you know that?" Chris asked.

"He saw the crash, and he's here to see the sights. He's got no weapon."

"You can't see his hands."

"No, but I know these people. He doesn't mean any harm."

The man popped up and disappeared one more time.

"Well, then you'd better let him know that he's being an idiot. Send him home before we fry his ass."

Kurt nodded and stood. "Hey, you!" he yelled in Spanish. "You behind the cars. What are you doing?"

The man popped up again, this time close enough that Kurt leveled the .45 at his chest. The man saw the weapon and disappeared again. "Stop! Are you out of your mind? These are American soldiers. If you take another step—if you don't turn around and run home right now, we're going to shoot you." For a long moment, nothing happened.

"What did you say?" Chris asked.

Kurt gave him the translation. "I think I scared him onto the ground."

"Tell him to show himself one more time, and then to run like hell. Make sure we can see his hands the whole time, or I swear to God I'm going to blow him away."

Kurt translated the command, emphasizing the parts about the shooting and the running. After only a very brief pause, the man rose to his full height from behind the cars and reached his hands as high into the air as they could possibly stretch.

"Okay," Kurt soothed him in his native language. "We see you're not armed. Now, run home."

The man did exactly that, only the word "running" doesn't really give justice to what he did. He sprinted. Dashed. Evaporated. Learned his lesson and lived to see another day.

54

The Little Birds' and the Blackhawks' strafing runs and constant vigilance had kept the war away from G Team's barricade, even as they continued to rain hell on the Comandancia. Perhaps *because* of the unrelenting assault on Noriega's headquarters, the army and police units were too distracted—or their ears were ringing too badly—to pay much attention to this clutch of mangled operators and their precious cargo.

Paul had slipped back into unconsciousness and Parker was close, bleeding so profusely that it was difficult to pinpoint the source. Jim Nelson, likewise, had begun to slip from blood loss and pain, made even worse as the adrenaline began to subside. Despite the pain, however, and the graveness of their injuries, those who were conscious remained vigilantly on station, their weapons played to every visible compass point, waiting to engage any targets who were foolish enough to enter the killing field.

In this lull, Kurt's job was to take care of Paul, to make sure that he kept breathing and to shout out if he stopped. He sat Indian-style on the sidewalk, cradling Paul's head in his lap, absorbing his blood into his clothes, into his skin, into his heart. With the imminent danger gone, Kurt had time to think about the scene around him—*really* think about it. These seven men whom he had never met had willingly risked their lives—continued to risk their lives—for no higher cause than to rescue Kurt Frederick Muse, a nobody. You expected that from the Secret Service on behalf of the president of the United States or others whose lives truly made a difference on a global scale, but never in a million years would he have expected it for himself. As thrilled as he was to be free of Modelo Prison—even if it meant dying here on the street—he found himself struggling to understand the why of it all.

In the distance, he heard the rumbling of what could only be tracked vehicles of some sort. In his mind, he conjured up images of tanks, and in so doing, he felt his spirits soar. The PDF had no such vehicles. The cavalry was on the way.

Two minutes later, he learned that he'd been both right and wrong. It was, indeed, the cavalry coming with tracked vehicles, but where he'd expected to see tanks, he instead saw a parade of two M-113 armored personnel carriers (APCs) crushing a path through the parked cars to come rescue them. Little Birds hovered overhead providing close support as the APCs lumbered to within yards of their location then swung around ass-first to drop the steel personnel doors and invite the assault team inside. A .50 caliber machine gun sat atop each vehicle, manned by a soldier whose head and shoulders were fully exposed through a hatch in the roof.

"Wounded first," Chris said, but everyone seemed to know instinctively what to do.

"Time to move, Paul," Kurt said.

The team members who were well enough to shoot covered those who were not, with the help of the APC gunners and the ever-intimidating Little Birds.

Kurt waited his turn as the pilots of his rescue ship helped to wrestle Parker and Jim Nelson into the first vehicle. When it was time, Chris returned for Kurt and Paul.

"How's he doing?" Chris asked.

"Not so good. In and out." Kurt slid from under the commando's weight and worked with Chris to carry Paul to the open maw of the closest APC.

The M-113's interior was long and narrow. With an advertised capacity for eleven troops plus a driver and gunner, half that number made it feel cramped, with soldiers sitting knee to knee. Jim Nelson was already inside, his mangled leg stretched out on the right-side bench, leaking blood everywhere. They laid Paul on the floor between the parallel benches, all the way to the front of the troop compartment, and seconds later, the remainder of the team—the two pilots—scrambled in and raised the door.

Kurt heard the driver say something into his radio, and then they were moving, a rumbling, jarring trip with all the finesse of a stagecoach on a Shaker table, but it was the most fabulous vehicle Kurt had ever seen. Keep your Cadillacs and Mercedes with their cushy rides and fancy accountrements. This was a vehicle built by and for warriors, and it took people into harm's way in defense of causes larger than any individual occupant. It smelled of oil and fuel, of blood and gunpowder, and of sweat and fear and courage. Illuminated by the light of a single bulb, the simplicity of the design seemed a stark contrast to the complexity of the men it carried, and from the very first moments after the APC was buttoned up, Kurt knew that this was a moment that would forever change his life. It would alter the very foundation of who he was.

"Thank you, guys," he said to the other occupants. "I don't know what to say."

"Don't say anything," Chris said with a scowl. "We're not out of the shit yet."

Kurt understood. He had no idea where they were headed, but he knew where they were, and it was a long ride on a normal day to the nearest military facility. With the world at war, he could only imagine how long it would take, and all of them could only imagine what kind of complications they would face on the way.

The .45 was bothering Kurt, stuck the way it was in the waistband of his trousers, and once they were moving, the discomfort only became worse. He lifted his shirt and removed the weapon, consciously noting for the first time that the thing was still cocked. He vaguely remembered Brian mentioning something about that when he handed him the gun, but now, inside the vehicle, it seemed like an unnecessary risk. Conscious of the slipperiness of his hands, Kurt vigorously wiped his palms on his thighs, removing as much of the blood and sweat as he could, then carefully inserted his thumb between the hammer and the firing pin and pulled the trigger. He felt the click and eased the hammer down.

When he looked up again, he noticed that all eyes were focused on him. "What?"

"There's a safer way to do that," Chris said.

"Don't need to be shot again," Jim added.

Kurt felt himself blush. He was an idiot. He should have dropped the magazine out of the grip and then jacked the seated round out of the chamber. He could almost hear his drill instructor's voice.

He started to apologize when Paul made that odd breathing sound again. It was hard to tell in the yellow light of the troop compartment, but to Kurt's eye, he seemed to be getting worse. He slid down to the floor and grabbed the wounded commando by the bandoliers of shotgun shells slung over his shoulders. "Paul? Paul! Hang in there. Hang in there. We're almost there."

But he wasn't ready to die. Apparently, he'd just forgotten to breathe, and something about the jostling reignited the spark. He made a snoring sound as his lungs expanded again.

Kurt felt the heat of Jim's glare and he turned to assure him. "I think he's okay."

The soldier on the bench nodded. "Paul's tough," he said.

Kurt was done sitting on the bench himself. He'd been given one job to do this night—to see to Paul's well-being—and he wasn't going to blow it now. For the rest of the trip to wherever they were going, he would stay there on the floor, ready to do whatever he could to fulfill his mission.

As they drove through the streets of Panama City, the sounds of the war grew steadily more distant. What had once been sharp, deafening explosions diminished to the sounds of rumbling thunder. Ten, fifteen, twenty minutes into the drive—Kurt had no idea how long—even the thunder seemed to die out, replaced by the sounds of cheering and the clattering of pots and pans.

Turning from Paul to look out through the gunner's hatch, Kurt could see, even in the darkness, that the windows and balconies of the surrounding buildings were packed with Panamanians whooping and cheering the American soldiers, waving the white flags of the opposition. With the outcome of the war never in question, they, too, knew that the world had changed.

Kurt started to point out the obvious to the rest of the occupants, but at first glance realized that he didn't have to. For the first time since this ordeal began, the Delta guys were grinning.

*   *   *

In Burke, Virginia, Annie Muse watched the digital clock jump to 1:30, and she closed her eyes. There still had been no word about Kurt. Just the pictures. The endless images of violence and raging fires. Bad news comes right away, she tried telling herself. Or was it the other way around? No news was good news.

It wasn't true; no news was just that: nothing. Emptiness. More of the same. She didn't know how much more of this she could take.

Plenty more, she decided. Especially if . . .

If it was bad news—and God help her, she was becoming more and more convinced that it was—then she wasn't ready to face it just yet. She'd lived for so long on hope that she didn't know how she could handle grief. It's the one emotion for which she had not prepared herself. Maybe it was the one emotion for which it was impossible to prepare oneself.

It was precisely 1:45 in the morning when she closed her eyes and surrendered herself to fate. "Dear God," she said aloud, "whatever happens is in your hands." For so long, she had tried to control the action—the calls, the questions, the suggestions; all the elements of her soul that she'd focused on bringing Kurt home safely. But she was ready to finally let go. She remembered Tomás telling her that surrendering to God showed true faith. She was ready to take whatever happened, ready to make good, remain faithful, and do what needed to be done.

A sense of peace washed over her in that moment, so profound in its power that it nearly took her breath away.

As the APC pulled to a halt, Kurt heard the driver say into his radio, "Sir, the PC has arrived safely at LZ Juliet. Repeat, the PC has arrived safely at LZ Juliet."

Kurt allowed himself a glimmer of relief. He understood that he himself was the PC—precious cargo—and that he had arrived at a landing zone codenamed Juliet, probably military-speak for the letter J. What he keyed on most intently though, and what brought the smile to his face, was the use of the word, "safely."

He turned to his rescuers, speechless.

"Good work, Moose," Chris said.

And then the personnel door dropped open again. Instantly, the vehicle was awash in activity as medics swarmed in to take custody of the wounded and hustle them off for emergency care. Kurt was the last to step out into the night, and what he saw took his breath away. They were in the Canal Zone, on the road between Balboa Elementary School, where Annie once taught, and Balboa High School, Kurt's alma mater, on whose parade field he had spent countless hours marching and drilling as a junior ROTC candidate.

Now that field and that road were every bit a war zone, with helicopters and Humvees and tents and equipment. The irony of it all was stunning.

He checked his watch as he stepped out onto the grass. It was exactly 1:45 in the morning.

55

They ushered Kurt onto a Blackhawk medevac chopper, onto a corner of a seat next to a gravely wounded young man on a stretcher. Stark naked, the young man with close-cropped blond hair lay perfectly still, face-down. He was impossibly young—twenty, perhaps, but probably closer to high school age—and disturbingly pale. There was no missing the perfectly round hole in the small of his back. Kurt could only pray that the boy was still alive, that he might live on to experience the dreams and ambitions he brought with him to the home of Kurt's youth and his passion.

"Hey, you," someone yelled over the noise of the still-turning rotor blades.

Kurt turned at the sound to see a plastic IV bag being shoved in his direction.

"Hold this," the medic said.

Kurt took the bag and held it in the manner that the medic had, by one finger thrust through the hanging loop in the top of the bag.

"Don't squeeze it or mess with it, okay? Just hold it. It's a short flight." As the medic spoke, he helped a familiar face settle into a spot on the floor near Kurt's feet. It was one of the Delta operators from the roof of Modelo, and he'd been shot through the leg. Someone had splinted the injury, but it was clear from the commando's face that whatever they might have given for the pain wasn't working.

An instant later, the medic was gone, and the operator clearly noted the concern in Kurt's face. "It's nothin'," he said. "Just a scratch."

Kurt didn't belong here. He felt like an interloper, an observer of moments that should belong only to those who had earned the right to bear witness. He pulled the .45 from his waistband for the last time and laid it on the seat next to him.

As the chopper's engine spun up and the blades bit into the thick tropical air, the aircraft lifted majestically off the ground and climbed into the night. It was impossible not to notice the sharp contrast between the grace of this liftoff and that of the doomed Little Bird of just ninety minutes earlier. As the ground started to fall away, Kurt had difficulty comprehending how surroundings that were so familiar, so much a part of his life, could be made to look so foreign in the presence of the people and machinery of warfare.

When they'd risen to treetop level, or maybe a little higher, Kurt was startled to feel a hand grasping the front of his shirt, and then the scruff of his neck as someone pulled him toward the chopper's deck. It was the wounded Delta operator.

"Snipers," the soldier said simply. "Keep your head down."

Finally, when they were high enough, the operator let go of his shirt and pointed out of the open door toward the Canal.

"Well, Moose, congratulations. Looks like you're really going home."

The war had arrived at Howard Air Force Base as well, but the pace of this place was different. They were well within the safe zone here, and the activities were less about taking lives than saving them. Administrative tents and hospital tents had sprung up like mushrooms; dozens of them as far as the eye could see, and all of them bustled with activity.

The instant the Blackhawk's landing gear touched the ground, medics and orderlies disembarked all the wounded, dispatching them in every direction. In less than a minute, Kurt found himself oddly alone, and without instruction. He helped himself out of the chopper and stood in the rear-echelon chaos, trying to figure what his next step might be.

The place seethed with activity. People, trucks, choppers, tracked vehicles, every implement of war. It was impossible not to think back on the images of every war movie he'd ever seen, only to realize that none of them had even come close to touching the reality of this unchoreographed swirl.

He felt invisible standing there, unnoticed and unassigned. But only for a moment.

In the sea of people and dust, in the darkness of the night, Kurt more sensed than saw that one person in the crowd was walking with distinct purpose directly toward him. It was a little startling at first, until the figure closed to within a few yards.

It was Brian, his caretaker from the backseat of the Little Bird. He walked like a zombie, with an emotionless stare that unnerved Kurt. His face was still a mass of crusty blood from the untreated head wound. "Where's my .45?"

Oh, shit, where *was* the .45? Then he remembered. "One second," he said, and he hurried back into the Blackhawk. Thankfully, the weapon lay on the seat, right where he'd left it. He brought it back outside. "Here it is."

Brian's expression hovered somewhere between dismay and disgust as he took back the pistol, gave it a brief examination, and then stuffed it back into its holster before striding back toward the hospital tents. Knowing nothing better to do, Kurt followed him.

He was halfway there when a young noncom with medical insignia approached him, arms outstretched, as if to catch him from falling. "Jesus, sir, are you all right?"

Kurt scowled. "I'm fine."

"Where are you hurt?"

"I'm not."

The noncom cocked his head, confused. Then Kurt understood. He was bloody as hell. "Oh, the blood. This isn't mine. The blood is from other people."

The confusion diminished, but didn't go away. "Are you a civilian, sir?"

"Kurt Muse," he said, offering his hand. "I was—"

"Oh, *you're* Kurt Muse? We've been waiting for you, sir. Glad to see you're all right." He shook hands.

"Me, too."

"You must be beat," the soldier said. "Come with me. We'll find a place for you to sit." He led the way to an empty tent and made a broad gesture with his hand. "Sit anywhere. Sorry we don't have any chairs."

"You've got fresh air. That's plenty for me right now."

The noncom nodded, seemingly comfortable in the knowledge that he'd done his best to make a visitor comfortable. "Like I said, any place at all."

"I'll try to stay out of the way."

Kurt wandered to a corner and stripped off his body armor, realizing for the first time just how soaked he was with sweat. He could not have been wetter if he'd stepped out of a shower. Exhaustion was knocking on the door, too. He put the blood-soaked vest on the ground and sat on it.

"Kurt Muse?"

Kurt jumped, his head whipping around. His mind had wandered off somewhere. A colonel in jungle fatigues had materialized in front of him. As Kurt rose to his feet, the colonel tried to dissuade him.

"No, no, stay put. You've had a long night."

Kurt stood anyway. "It's been an amazing night," he said. He extended his hand and stated the obvious. "Kurt Muse."

The officer returned the gesture. "Colonel Boykin," he said. "Jerry Boykin. I wanted to be the first to welcome you to freedom."

Kurt knew he should be beaming with joy to meet this man, but he found himself managing a jumble of emotions. "Thank you, sir."

"I wanted to know if there's anything I can do for you."

Kurt didn't hesitate. "Well, sir, I'd like to meet my rescuers."

Boykin didn't hesitate either. "I'm afraid that's not possible. Security issues."

"They were hurt," Kurt said. "Some of them were badly hurt."

The colonel nodded thoughtfully. "Not as badly as you might think. Nothing life-threatening. Doctors say they'll all be fine."

Boykin did his best at off-handed delivery, but Kurt saw something deeper in the man's eyes. Hell, he'd seen the injuries himself. He knew better. "If you say so, sir," he said at length. "I just wanted to say thanks. They saved my life."

"Yes they did," Boykin said. "I'll pass your thanks along to them. I'm sure it will mean a lot."

"Words can't do it," Kurt said. "Words can't *touch* it."

Boykin's expression warmed. "You'd be surprised," he said. "I'll tell them you said that, too." He extended his hand again. "Well, Mr. Muse, I've got a long day ahead and a lot of work to do. Try staying out of trouble."

Kurt smiled. "I'll do my best, sir." He didn't realize it at the time, but he had just met the deputy commanding officer of Delta Force.

Ten minutes later, another colonel approached. This time, Kurt saw him coming and rose to greet him.

"You're Kurt Muse," the officer said. "I'm Colonel Greenfield, the unit shrink."

They shook hands. "Pleased to meet you," Kurt said. "You're here to see if I'm damaged goods?"

"Actually, no. Well, yes and no. If you need to talk things through, I'm certainly available for that."

Kurt shook the offer off with a quick gesture of his hand.

"What I really came over for was to welcome you back to the world. I've been following reports about you for months."

"Reports?"

"Doctors Ruffer and Ostrander, mainly. Others, too. We've been keeping an eye on you, waiting for just the right moment. Moose, you are one tough hombre."

Kurt felt himself blush. "I'm not sure that tough's the word," he said. "There were lots of nights when tough was the last word I'd use to describe what I was feeling."

Greenfield made a snorting sound, as if that were the most preposterous thing he'd ever heard. "Those are the moments we call human. There's not a guy out there who doesn't admire the hell out of you. I thought you should know that."

Kurt didn't know what to say. It was all too much. These people—the world's bravest and most skilled warriors—admired *him*? It wasn't possible. It was a nice thing for the doctor to say, but no way in the world was it even remotely possible.

"Anyway," Greenfield said, offering his hand one more time, "like I said, welcome back to the world."

Greenfield had barely walked away when Kurt saw Colonel Boykin approaching again.

"Moose!" He beckoned with an open hand.

Kurt approached, leaving the tent. Somewhere along the line, a young airman had been assigned to accompany Kurt step for step. Kurt assumed it was to keep him from getting into trouble, but the airman seemed to think it was to keep him from causing it.

"Come with me," Boykin said, ignoring Kurt's human shadow. "I think you'll like this."

The colonel led the way to a tent that was like every other tent on the field, except this one was set apart from the others by a few extra yards. The instant Boykin pushed the flap out of the way, Kurt recognized it as a hospital tent, brightly lit by overhead fluorescents powered by the gas generator outside. Half a dozen bloodied men lay in various stages of pain and undress as doctors tended to wounds whose extent could only now be assessed.

"Nice to see your face again, Moose," said the wounded soldier closest to him. Minus all the weapons and gear, he was barely recognizable as Jim Nelson. The others turned at the sound of Jim's greeting and smiled at their visitor.

Stunned, Kurt turned toward Boykin.

"Turns out they wanted to see you, too," the colonel said with a shrug.

What could he say? He had the floor, and he had their attention, but how could he possibly find words to express what he felt? It wasn't just his life they'd saved. It was Annie's life, too, and his children's lives. And in a crazy sense, they'd saved the rest of his extended family and so many of his friends, none of whom would now have to cope with the death of Kurt Muse, and of the dreams and aspirations of those who believed in his cause.

These strangers—these soldiers—had risked everything they were and everything they would ever be just to pluck him—*him*, Kurt Muse, a nobody—from a fate that any one of them might have suffered as a direct result of their selflessness. And here they lay, broken and pierced by bullets, showing only pleasure that their precious cargo had been delivered from harm.

"Thank you," he said, self-conscious of the thickness in his throat. Muse men never show emotion, don't you know. The words sounded as shallow as he had feared, but the wounded warriors seemed to understand. Their smiles broadened.

They looked so young here, so vulnerable and helpless as others took care of them for a change. Kurt took a step closer to Jim Nelson, placed a hand on his shoulder and gave it a gentle squeeze. The commando's muscles felt like marble sculpture under the fabric of the BDUs. "I don't know what else to say."

"Being here like this says everything," Jim said. "We were just doing our job. You made it easy. Now, go and have a good life."

And that's what it was all about, wasn't it? Kurt realized in that moment, in a flash of inspiration, that in many ways these men had the finest job in the world; the greatest calling. It wasn't lives they rescued for a living. It was futures. Save enough of them, and you can alter the course of history.

Kurt felt his emotions breaking; he knew he had to leave. But first, he had to summon one last bout of courage for himself. He had to say what he was thinking. If he didn't get the words out now they would never come, and he would never be able to live with himself.

"I'll never forget you," he said. "Thank you for saving my life. I love you guys."

56

It took a few hours to get things completely organized, but the clock was spinning at an incomprehensible speed. They flew him on an Agency executive jet; very comfortable. They let him have the run of the place, so long as he took care not to step on the window in the floor where they normally mounted a surveillance camera.

In the Miami Airport, as Kurt and his escort, an Agency man named Bob, approached Immigration, Kurt realized for the first time that he didn't have any paperwork to allow him to enter the country. The escort smiled and told him not to worry about it. When they finally arrived at the Immigration cubicle, the INS agent asked Bob if he had anything to declare.

Bob tossed a thumb in Kurt's direction. "Just him," he said, smiling.

In the United States of America now, in the wide open spaces of freedom, the escort asked, "You think maybe we should buy you some new clothes?"

Kurt had become so used to a certain degree of filth that he'd forgotten that he was caked in Paul's blood. Bob and Uncle Sam picked up the tab for a new shirt from the gift store, and Kurt changed in the men's room, taking the opportunity to wash up in the sink. If they'd sold pants he'd have taken a pair of those, too, but airport gift shops are only so accommodating. At least the navy blue fabric camouflaged the stain. He stuffed the bloody shirt in a trash can, but then went back to retrieve it. Considering the price paid to make it so dirty, the shirt couldn't be mingled with paper towels and snot rags. It deserved a loftier status than mere trash.

They had some time to kill in Miami, so the escort took Kurt to an early lunch at a nearby Denny's. He had a hamburger and a beer. Nothing had ever tasted better, and, he suspected, nothing ever would.

When it was time for the last leg, as they walked back through the airport, Kurt couldn't help but notice the throngs of famous journalists crowding the departure lounge for the next flight to Panama.

"You gotta love it," Bob chuckled as they passed three television news guys.

"What's that?"

"One of the biggest stories of the war is passing within inches of them, and they don't even know to ask."

Annie's heart had stopped at the sound of Suzanne Alexander's voice on the other end of the phone. "Annie, we've got him. Kurt is out of prison and in friendly hands."

Annie's mouth fell as her eyes filled. Could it possibly be true? After this much worry, and so much lost time, could he possibly be safe?

"I don't know when we can get him home, but we've got him."

Now it was time to wake up the kids.

The final call took hours to arrive, and it was from Father Frank, with the final details of the impending reunion with her greatest friend. He drove to their house and they followed his car in theirs to the tiny annex building that was a half mile from the main terminal at Dulles.

There really wasn't much to the place. It was the arrival and departure point for executive jets, and as such was reasonably well appointed; but because executives come and go more or less as they please and rarely have to wait for their flights, there was virtually nothing to do. They'd arrived early to avoid being late.

It could have been a wonderful moment—probably should have been—but the fat lady hadn't yet sung in this particular opera, and Annie had suffered too many emotional setbacks to let herself get spun up too early. Kurt would be there when he arrived. Until then, he was still gone.

Father Frank, God bless him, had told her a thousand times to relax, but relaxation simply wasn't possible anymore.

For the sake of the children, who would be positively giddy if she'd only let herself go, she wished that she could just push her doubts to the side for these last moments, but what if the calls from Suzanne, and later from Senator Mack's office had been premature? What if they'd been flat-out wrong, or if the plan crashed on its final approach? Annie wasn't prepared to fall all the way from the stratosphere of jubilation. She simply didn't know that she could ever recover from that.

Christmas miracles do happen. All the time; she'd said so herself, just yesterday. Please, God, let this be one of your finest.

Father Frank said, "He's here." He pointed to the window, through which they could see an unmarked executive jet rolling lazily up to the door. But for the wall and the window they could have reached it in a dozen steps.

Then they saw Kurt.

The kids squealed with delight, dancing in place and pointing and knocking on the glass, but it must have been too loud on the tarmac for Kurt to hear.

He looked so thin, Annie thought, and so horribly pale. He looked positively beautiful.

Finally, the hope arrived; the relief. The dream had finally come true, and in those final seconds as Kurt made the brief walk from the aircraft to the reception lounge, something swelled inside Annie, and she discovered that she was crying. She felt suddenly overwhelmed. It was relief, of course, and joy and love, but there was something more.

She'd been watching the news all day, and she'd been fixated on the word "liberated" as it was used by the droopy-toned caller from Senator Mack's office. She didn't know the details, of course—no one would for years to come—but she knew that countless people had taken unspeakable risks to deliver her Kurt back home. She knew that those kinds of preparations took time and were coordinated by many dozens of people.

That wonderful inflated feeling in her chest was driven in part, she realized, by a feeling of gratitude the likes of which was incomprehensible to anyone who has not had a loved one delivered from the gates of hell. It was a debt that could never be repaid. They'd given her family's life back to them.

In the seconds before the door opened and her world would be set back on its axis, she turned to smile at Father Frank, but he'd already left. His job was done. This was a moment for the Muse family to be alone.

The kids all but tackled Kurt as he entered the lounge, embracing him in a crushing group hug. He bent slightly to receive their arms, and then he lost himself in their love. God, they'd grown so much. Erik had to be nearly a foot taller than last time he'd seen him. Kimberly . . . well, Kimberly had become a woman, and a beautiful one at that. As he pulled her close, it was impossible not to remember his last hug on that awful night so long ago.

And then there was Annie. His beautiful bride. His sweetheart. His best friend. She was enfolded into the hug with the rest, and it was wonderful.

They stood there for a half hour. They hugged, they cried, and no one said a word. They didn't have to. They were a family again.

Fifteen miles away, in Burke, Virginia, there awaited a house that could finally be a home. Snow frosted the roof and a light burned in every window.

A seven-foot tree stood sentry near the fireplace, adorned with unfamiliar ornaments that would from then on be among the family's most precious possessions.

Never again has a tree been so beautiful.

Afterword

by John Gilstrap

The world continues to turn and the calendar moves on. As we write this, seventeen years have expired since the events of this book occurred, and a full telling of the story requires stepping beyond 1989 and taking a look at what has happened to some of the players in the intervening years.

The Delta operator pseudonymously named Jim Nelson lost most of his foot—everything forward of the instep—in the aftermath of Operation Acid Gambit. A few months later, he requalified for Delta Force and served another twelve years.

In fact, of the twenty-three Delta operators who participated in Kurt's rescue and the events that followed, all survived Operation Just Cause and lived on to serve in many missions to come; including one well-documented shootout in the streets of Mogadishu, Somalia, some four years later.

Jim Ruffer and Robert Perry have both retired from military service and are living peaceful and healthy lives. Both would much prefer talking about anyone and anything but themselves. Interviewing them for this project was an honor. Marcos Ostrander lives and practices law in Panama City. He's one of the toughest guys I've ever met, and I mean that as a supreme compliment.

Father Frank—his real name, actually, insofar as anyone in his line of work has a real name—is (or at least claims to be) fully retired these days, living in a location we promised never to disclose. Truth be told, in the spirit of all covert operatives who make our country safe, he contributed virtually nothing during my interview, citing one of the worst memories on the planet. He did keep us from writing one big mistake, however, and for that I will always be grateful.

Tomás Muñoz, the pseudonymous technical genius behind La Voz de la Libertad, lost everything he owned as a result of Noriega's retribution; even his wife lost her U.S. government pension with the Panama Canal Company because her exile kept her from coming to work each day. Of the rest of Kurt's compatriots, most fared pretty well, with several recovering extremely well. For all of them, the future remains bright. To a person, they hold Kurt Muse to be a national hero—no bitterness for what they lost; only pride for what they all tried to accomplish. We don't mention their real names in these pages, but let me attest: they've got tales of incredible courage that have yet to be told.

Charlie and Peggy Muse (Papi and Nana) returned to Panama within weeks of the completion of Operation Just Cause. Intergraphic, the company Charlie had built from nothing to become a prosperous enterprise, was kept running by his employees during his year of exile. Every penny was accounted for, and in one of life's happy coincidences, the shooting war stopped just one block from the business's front door. They live and thrive today in Panama City, both in town and on the Taboga ranch, where Charlie regularly works out with his beloved horses.

Carol and David Skinner likewise returned to Panama, but not before they suffered unspeakable tragedy. While in exile in the United States, their teenage daughter, Joanna (Joey), was killed in an automobile accident. There's a lot of pain and anger associated with that kind of horror, and the wounds heal slowly. Maybe they never really heal. I can't imagine. One of the great privileges ever granted to me came when Carol allowed me to read Joey's diary accounts of the ordeal of their evacuation. I am forever grateful.

The world needs to know one final detail about Kurt Muse: Long before life had righted itself for him, Annie, and the kids, Kurt began a tradition that has become the stuff of legend in the special operations community. With the help of some highly placed assistants, Kurt sat down on the first anniversary of Operation Acid Gambit and called every one of his rescuers to thank them for giving him back his life. For men who are used to toiling under a veil of secrecy that not only excludes thanks but also makes secret their awards for valor, hearing from one of their successes was an utter surprise.

He's made those phone calls seventeen times now, reporting happily on the progress of his and their lives, wives and children, and even on the birth of a few grandkids along the way. December 20 has become one of the special, most-anticipated dates on the calendar.

When Kurt left that hospital tent on his first new day of freedom, he promised that he would never forget the men who liberated him.

He never has. He never will.

Final Thoughts

by Kurt Muse

It is said that "one father is worth more than a hundred schoolmasters." As a boy, I remember listening intently as my father spoke of being honorable, of standing up for what is right, and of not being afraid. When I became a man, I realized the strength of his words. My father is in fact the most honorable and courageous man I know. For better or for worse, his lessons and his living example provided me with the required moral compass and the necessary courage to undertake the daunting task of helping to restore democracy to our beloved Panama.

During my saga of nearly three years, I was blessed to have been involved with and be touched by so many good people—friends, acquaintances, and total strangers alike. Some of you perhaps tried to visit me in prison. You maybe wrote or tried to write me in prison. You may have been a member of St. Mary's Catholic Church in Ancon, where you prayed for me every Sunday. You might have been one of the wonderful souls who kept in phone contact with Anne and the children, comforting them with your caring. Thank you all from the bottom of my heart.

During the evening of my arrest, in the midst of armed and angry PDF soldiers, my friend Tom Ford came to my parents' house to ask my sister, Carol, how he could be of assistance. It took tremendous courage for Tom to expose himself like that to the PDF, but then again, Tom and Julie Ford are truly special friends.

Then there are our special friends, Rita and Alex Sosa. Somehow, on Thanksgiving Day of 1989, Rita was able to convince the guard at Modelo Prison to deliver a traditional turkey dinner to my cell, complete with all the trimmings. You'll never know what comfort such a kindness brings in such a dark time.

Adelaida Robles, or "Lala" as we called her, was our beloved maid of many years. She was family. On the evening of my arrest, Kimberly and Erik were removed from her care forever, yet despite continuous harassment by the PDF, she resolutely continued to watch over our home as if it were her own. We miss this extraordinary lady.

Anne's life after my arrest was an endless journey that would have been ten times more burdensome but for the efforts of her guardian angel, boss, and dear friend, Shirley Makkibin. Her quiet support was keenly felt throughout the ordeal.

On a personal note, there's a name that I want you to remember: Candy Helin. A teacher for the Department of Defense School System and a friend and colleague of Annie's, Candy was in fact the first casualty of Operation Just Cause. Just moments before midnight—H hour—Candy and her husband were driving home in their personal vehicle when a PDF sniper opened fire, killing her. In the tumultuous events of the ensuing hours and days, her sacrifice to her nation and its children went largely unheralded. That's such a shame, because she was a fine lady.

Anne and I were members of St. Luke's Episcopal Church in Panama. Overcoming great obstacles imposed by the bishop, Father Richard Bower managed to visit me in prison for the first few months, until his transfer back to the United States. Thanks so much Richard for taking the time to try to heal my spiritual wounds.

By law, all letters addressed to me in prison had to be translated into Spanish. That responsibility fell to Loyda Sanchez, in Marcos Ostrander's office. Gracias Loyda. *Gracias por todo el cariño mostrado en tus labores.*

Bosco and Belinda Vallarino, after their own harrowing escape from Panama, set up a small in-home recording studio and from there recorded our daily broadcasts for Radio La Voz de la Libertad. Thank you both for your tireless dedication and attention to our details. *Ni un paso atrás,* my friends.

My father-in-law, John Castoro, spent a full and exciting career in the CIA's Directorate of Operations. He was retired by 1989, but he had many friends in Langley with whom he maintained contact during my ordeal. Thanks, John, for everything. I'll never know the details of what strings you might have pulled, but I thank you nonetheless. If only you could have read *Six Minutes to Freedom*. I can see you now with that smile and a wink before you walk away.

Thanks to Roomie, who always knew this story would take its proper place in history.

There may not have been a book, especially a book this well written, had it not been for my friend and fellow Rotarian Pat Barney. He was so impressed with the story I told at one of our Rotary meetings that he told his good friend, John Gilstrap, about it. The rest is, as they say . . . well, you know.

I owe a very special thanks to the men and women of the Department of Defense, the Department of State, and the Central Intelligence Agency. I wish that every citizen could know what I know about your selfless toiling to lend assistance to people who often never even know they are in danger. I was unusually fortunate to have so many of you in my corner. While I cannot and will not mention even the few names I've learned, please know that I know what you did on my behalf and on behalf of my family. I owe my life and the liberty I now enjoy to your hard work and dedication, just as we all owe so much to the civil servants who toil next to you and down the hall.

The Acid Gambit section of this book barely scratches the surface of what transpired on the night of December 19–20, 1989. In a lexicon as vast as the English language, you'd think there would be a bigger word than "thanks." Thanks is for lending that cup of sugar or watching the kids for a few hours. But to express appreciation for risking everything you will ever be and everything you will ever have to bring one man home to his family, words fail. Awe is a good beginning, perhaps.

I bestow special awe on the tactical units involved in my rescue and their supremely talented commanders: The soldiers who liberated me that evening came from the U.S. Army's First Special Forces Operational Detachment-Delta, based in Fort Bragg, North Carolina. A very special thanks to E, Delta's Sabre Squadron commander, and G, the assault troop commander. The helicopters that braved withering ground fire to fly the Delta operators to and from Modelo Prison, and the Little Bird gunships supporting them, came from the U.S. Army's 160th Special Operations Air Regiment, based in Fort Campbell, Kentucky. A special thanks to R, the company commander. The AC-130 Specter gunships that flew overhead, delivering a pinpoint and blistering fire on Noriega's headquarters, came from the U.S. Air Force's Sixteenth Special Operations Squadron, based in Hurlburt Field, Florida. A special thanks to M and J, who captained Air Papa 06 and Air Papa 07 from their specially designed Top Hat formation. God bless you all. Thanks for bringing me home. Our nation, and especially the Muse family, have reason to smile knowing that you are in its service.

During my formative years in Panamanian schools, I remember wondering at the lack of national heroes in a country so rich in colonial history. My seven friends and compatriots in La Voz de la Libertad risked losing their lives, their property, and their livelihood in service of the dream that they would one day be free of the Pineapple's oppression. They are true Panamanian heroes, and I pray that one day their fellow citizens will recognize them as such.

Six Minutes to Freedom is a slice of my family history. I look forward to the day when my grandchildren, Connor Charles, Sydney Anne, and Sean Michael, can read this book on their own. Only then will they begin to understand the true character and the mettle of their mother, back in the day when she was an extraordinary kid named Kimberly, who cared so diligently for their Uncle Erik. By then, of course, they will have been lovingly spoiled by their Nini and Pops, and one day, they can introduce their own children to the story of how their family tried so hard to make a difference.

Authors' Note

Six Minutes to Freedom is equal parts memoir and trib-
ute. It is not, and should not be considered to be, the definitive history
of this slice of time. *SixMin*, as we've come to refer to it among our-
selves, is one man's story; but we chose to tell it in the third person because Kurt's saga affected many people, and we wanted the freedom to
portray their stories as equal to Kurt's own.

For purposes of narrative clarity, some of the characters are in fact
composites of several real people. Examples include the prison guards
and the Delta operators. We feel that as long as we do not play fast
and loose with the factual events, we can streamline the number of
character names we throw at our readers.

Many of the players' names have been changed. Most of the CIA
operatives and all of the Delta Force operators who participated in the
research for this book did so only on the condition that they remain
anonymous. Thus, we took enormous liberties with their identities, in
some cases creating characters from whole cloth to serve the roles of
their anonymous counterparts. We made a point, in fact, to draw these
characters in such a way that they are truly unrecognizable. We felt no
compunction against making short people tall and transforming
women into men and vice versa. It was the least we could do since
some of the players are still actively involved in their ongoing mission
to keep us all safe.

One of the hardest decisions was to change the names of Kurt's coconspirators. It is Kurt's choice to come forward with the details of this chapter in his life—of their lives—and out of respect for his friends and their families, we thought we owed them plausible deniability. While all of them willingly cooperated in the research for *Six Minutes to Freedom*, many still live in Panama among former PDF officers whose take on these patriots' efforts to topple a dictator might be understandably bitter. The last thing we want to do is make their lives more difficult than they've already been.

The final note involves dialogue, which we didn't hesitate to create to serve the dramatic construct of a factual scene. For example, if our research turned up evidence in a diary or in an interview that "Colonel Smith greeted us cordially," we portrayed that moment as a fleshed-out scene in a manner such as this: "Colonel Smith stood as they entered the room and extended his hand. 'Good afternoon,' he said."

Call it dramatic license, if you will. Our intent is not to deceive the reader—again, the facts and tone of the conversations are real—but merely to make the story more enjoyable.